Learning Embedded Systems with MSP430 FRAM Microcontrollers

MSP430FR5994 with Code Composer Studio

Second edition

January 2023

Byul Hur

Preface

This book is the complied materials that I have used in embedded system education over several years. This book is suitable for a textbook or support materials for an embedded system course or microcontroller application course. The target audiences of this book include undergraduate engineering students and readers who already have similar prior knowledge.

This is the second edition published in January 2023. The first edition of this book was published in August 2022. There were prior published books related to MSP432P401R MCUs. This book contains the materials that were reused [1]. The contents of this second edition were revised and customized for MSP430FR59xx MCUs.

This book covers basics including MSP430™, GPIO, timers, display, interrupt, and ADC. Moreover, this book covers topics of software architectures, PWM, motor control, serial communications, TI Driver library, TI-RTOS, Power management, and embedded system security.

An MSP430 IC (Integrated circuit) is a microcontroller unit (MCU) introduced by Texas Instruments™ (TI). The CPU (Central Processing unit) of this MCU is TI's 16-bit RISC (Reduced Instruction Set Computer).

There are several MSP430 IC models available. These MSP430 devices include MSP430FR2xxx and MSP430FR5xxx devices based on FRAM (Ferroelectric Random Access Memory) technology. The FRAM technology applied to MSP430 devices can offer several advantages such as high endurance and fast writing speed.

In this book, we will learn about an MSP430FR5994 MCU. This MSP430FR5994 MCU is one of the MSP430FR59xx devices. After studying this platform, readers can continue to study and use other TI MSP430 microcontrollers.

In order to study this MSP430 model, an MSP430FR5994 LaunchPad™ Development Kit is used in this book, which is an MSP-EXP430FR5994 Launchpad. This MSP-EXP432P401R Launchpad board is a low-cost development platform based on the MSP430FR5994 MCU.

The integrated development environment (IDE) primarily used in this book is Code Composer Studio™. The Code Composer Studio supports TI MCUs including this MSP430FR5994 MCU. As of today, the latest version of the Code Composer Studio is 12. In this version, TI does not charge license fees for Code Composer Studio. Users/Developers can download the set-up file and install the IDE software on their PC, Mac®, or Linux machines.

This book can be used as educational materials for an embedded system course. In order to be effective in teaching embedded systems as an educational course, it is recommended to have hands-on laboratory sessions as well as lecture sessions. This hands-on learning approach can help students understand the materials in this book.

If you have adopted, used, or listed this book as an educational resource, or used as a part of educational activities, please, feel free to contact the author and share your educational experience associated with this book. For the educators who need resources for lectures, you can contact the author by visiting the website. The contact information is posted on the website: *www.rftestgroup.com/books*

If you have any comments or questions, please, do not hesitate to contact the author. I hope this book can be used as a good resource helping you learn about embedded systems.

Acknowledgment

I would like to express my appreciation to many people who have been supporting me in many ways in academia. I have been learning a lot of aspects as I work and teach in a higher educational environment. I am thankful for all those who have shown kindness through the journey in academia.

I am sincerely grateful to all of my family. Particularly, I would like to show my appreciation to Ms. Bongnou Jun, Mrs. Soohee Park, Mrs. Elisa Hur, and Ms. Erin Hur.

I would like to acknowledge current and former teaching assistants and graders. Moreover, I would like to thank my students who have given me insights into engineering education.

Above all, I am deeply grateful to God the Father, God the Son, and God the Holy Spirit. I have dedicated my life to Him. I am thankful for the delicate guidance and care including this book publication journey.

Contents

Chapter 1. Introduction

Embedded systems can be easily found in our modern lives, and there are many applications of embedded systems for home or industrial uses. The core components in these embedded systems are microcontrollers and microprocessors. In Chapter 1, we will learn about the differences between microcontrollers and microprocessors. Next, Texas Instruments™ (TI) microcontrollers including an MSP430FR5994 will be introduced.

For the development of microcontroller applications, an Integrated Development Environment (IDE) is a useful tool. There are several IDEs that can be used in developing an MSP430FR5994 microcontroller application. In this chapter, a TI Code Composer Studio IDE will be introduced.

What is a Microcontroller?

A microcontroller unit (MCU) is typically a small sized integrated circuit (IC) that is used for specific operations in an embedded system. There are several components that are commonly found in a microcontroller unit. Let us examine these components. Typically, a microcontroller unit includes a component of a Central Processing Unit (CPU). This CPU can process digital arithmetic and logical calculations, and the CPU can access the data in registers and memory devices.

Memory devices can be a component of a microcontroller unit. The memory devices can be categorized into Read Only Memory (ROM) or Random Access Memory (RAM). ROM typically contains permanent or semi-permeant data. For instance, a program such as boot firmware can be stored in this ROM memory. RAM is a memory that can read or store data. One of the examples is to use this RAM memory as a part of stack memory. The stack memory is a computer memory that can store various temporary variables created by functions and programs.

One of the useful peripherals in microcontrollers is a General-Purpose Input and Output (GPIO). GPIO is a component that can generate a digital output signal to an external pin or read a digital signal from an external pin. This GPIO is a useful component in microcontroller applications.

Another typical component is a timer. Timers can be used for multiple purposes. The primary application of the timer is a digital counter that is capable of counting up or down. It is also common to find a special timer called watchdog timer. This watchdog timer can trigger a system reset process if a program is in a certain hardware or software failure condition.

In computing, it is typical to find the situation where the execution of a main program is paused, and the system needs to run a different program routine, if there is an internal or external request. This request can be processed by an interrupt controller. This interrupt controller is a common component in microcontrollers.

For input signals, a signal type at the external pin of microcontrollers can be analog instead of digital. These analog signals can be converted to digital signals using an Analog to Digital Converter (ADC). Once the conversion is completed, the CPU can process the digital data or store the data in registers and memory devices.

For output signals, a signal type through an external pin can be analog instead of digital. In this case, a Digital Analog Converter (DAC) can be used. A DAC can generate various voltage levels of analog signals.

The internal data stored in MCUs may need to be exchanged with an external device. In order for this communication, serial communication components can be used in microcontrollers. A serial communication component can be used in exchanging serial digital data between a microcontroller and an external device.

Clock signals in digital circuits are signals oscillating between high and low states. These signals can be used in synchronizing digital components. Clock signals can be provided by an oscillatory circuit component. For MCUs, it is typical to support multiple clock sources through internal and external oscillators.

In general, a typical microcontroller may have these common components mentioned earlier. In addition to these components for some microcontroller models, they have specialized components such as USB/ethernet/wireless communication modules, and precision ADCs.

For application developers, they need to choose a proper microcontroller that meets the needs of their applications. They may need to understand the functions that the microcontroller offers. For an embedded system development, the choice of a microcontroller is an important step, and it involves the understanding of the scope and specification of the given embedded system project. The scope of the embedded systems may vary depending on projects, but, for a simple embedded system project, a decent microcontroller with a few external components could satisfy the needs of the desired project scope and the specification.

Microcontroller/Microprocessor

Microcontrollers have been commonly used in embedded systems. How about microprocessors? Can we implement an embedded system using a microprocessor? The answer is positive. The embedded system can be built using a microprocessor, and it can be considered as a microprocessor application or a microprocessor-based system. In order to understand the differences, block diagrams of a simplified microprocessor-based system and a microcontroller shown in Figure 1.1. The upper portion of Figure 1.1 shows a microprocessor-based system. This is a system with ROM, RAM, I/O port, timer, and ADC. A microprocessor is used, and it can be found on the upper left side. In order to make this system function properly, it is typically to use additional external components. For instance, the system may need an external RAM memory IC and an external ADC IC. This microprocessor and the external components are connected using data bus and address bus lines. These components can be mounted on a PCB (Printed Circuit Board). For instance, an assembled PCB with a microprocessor and the external components such as memory ICs can be considered as a microprocessor-based system, and it can be used as a part of an embedded system.

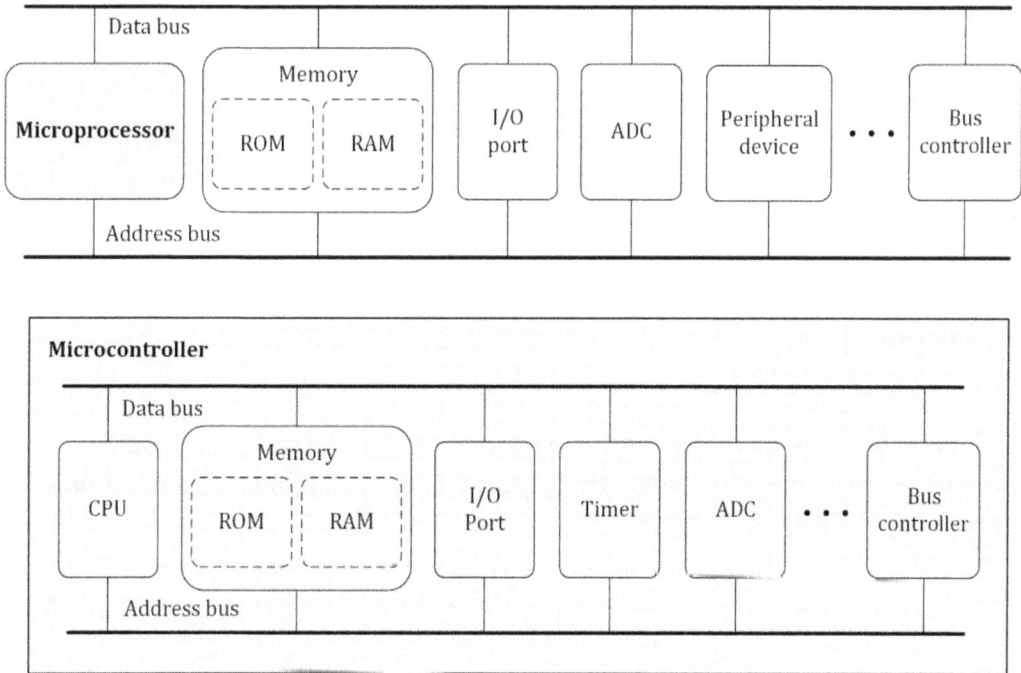

Figure 1.1. Microprocessor-based system and Microcontroller.

On the other hand, the lower portion of Figure 1.1 shows a microcontroller with similar components that we previously described in a microprocessor-based system. The difference is that all of the components shown in the grayed box are integrated on a single chip. This one chip contains various components, and it can provide multiple functions. It can be a part of an embedded system. By using a microcontroller, a developer may need less effort and needs a smaller number of external components in creating an application of embedded systems. Moreover, it can make the size of an embedded system compact. This is a benefit of choosing a microcontroller.

However, in general, microcontrollers may not be suitable for a system that requires fast and highly complex computations. This is partially because a microcontroller typically has a limited small memory space, and it might not be suitable to handle tasks that need a large memory space and fast computing speed. If a developer needs to build a system that requires processing highly complex tasks, a microprocessor-based system might be a reasonable choice.

16-bit/32-bit Microcontrollers

For some applications of embedded systems, a reasonable choice of microcontroller models can be 16-bit microcontrollers and 32-bit microcontrollers. Depending on the application, developers can choose high-end microprocessors such as 64-bit microprocessors or low-end microcontrollers such as 8-bit microcontrollers. In this chapter, let us examine and compare 16-bit and 32-bit microcontrollers.

The number of bits is associated with the primary instruction length of a CPU. Typically, a 32-bit instruction may represent a bigger integer number than a 16-bit instruction. Moreover, the number of the bits is also related to the widths of data bus, address bus, and registers. However, for some architectures, this number of bits does not necessarily match with the widths of data bus, address bus, or registers. For instance, there can be an architecture that uses more bits for address bus than the number of bits of registers or data bus.

In general, a 32-bit microcontroller can process a bigger integer number per instruction cycle than a 16-bit microcontroller. And a 32-bit microcontroller has more widths of data bus, address bus, and registers than a 16-bit microcontroller. For a wide range of low-cost embedded systems, 16-bit microcontrollers are suitable. For better performance or for complex systems, 32-bit microcontrollers can be used in applications of embedded systems.

There are many IC manufacturers providing various 16-bit and 32-bit microcontroller models. For instance, Microchip® (https://www.microchip.com) provides 16-bit and 32-bit microcontroller units (MCUs). For 16-bit MCUs, there are 16-bit PIC® MCUs. For 32-bit MCUs, there are Arm® Cortex® and MIPS based MCUs. Moreover, NXP® semiconductors (https://www.nxp.com) provides Arm processor based MCUs.

Texas Instruments™ (TI) provides 16-bit and 32 MCUs. Some of the MCU models are shown in Table 1.1. For 16-bit TI MCUs, there are many MSP430™ MCU models. These MSP430 MCUs are low power MCUs, and they are suitable for many applications of embedded systems. The CPU architecture is simple to understand, and these MCUs are based on a TI proprietary architecture. Although the CPU architecture is not fully disclosed, the manufacturer provides technical documentations to assist developers to understand how the microcontroller functions.

	MSP430™ MCUs	Arm®-based MCUs	C2000™ MCUs	Wireless connectivity MCUs
Features	TI proprietary 16-bit MCUs Ultra-low power	Arm-based 32-bit MCUs	TI proprietary 32-bit MCUs or Arm-based 32-bit MCUs	Wireless Arm-based or TI proprietary MCUs
Models	MSP430x2xxx MSP430x4xxx MSP430x5xxx MSP430x6xxx	TM4Cxxx MSP432Pxxx MSP432Exxx	TMS320xxxx	CC1xxx CC2xxx CC3xxx RF430xxxxx

Table 1.1. TI microcontrollers.

For 32-bit MCUs, TI has MCUs that are based on Arm Cortex-M cores and TI peripherals. For instance, TM4C123x and TM4C129x microcontrollers are based on Arm® Cortex-M4F cores. Moreover, there are TI's 32-bit MCUs that are digital signal processors (DSPs) optimized for real-time control applications. They are C2000™ MUCs, and they can be used in automotive and industrial applications.

Developers can add wireless communication capability to their embedded system projects. For the wireless connectivity, there are several low-power wireless microcontrollers. The wireless technologies include Bluetooth®, WiFi®, Zigbee®, and Near-field communication (NFC).

Developers can switch the MCU as it is desired. A portion of the program or entire program developed for a specific MCU model can be reused in other MCU models. However, this complexity of the conversion process may vary depending on the combination of the MCU models, as it can be simple and straightforward, or it can be highly complex or even impossible to implement certain functions to the other MCU models.

Low-power Microcontrollers

Some applications of embedded systems are battery operated. The operating time of these systems is relevant to the use of energy. In order to increase the operating time, there can be several efforts, and they include the choice of a low-power microcontroller and the use of low-power modes efficiently. Moreover, even for some applications of embedded systems that are not battery operated, there can be a need to reduce energy consumption.

MSP430 MCUs support low-power management techniques, and the MCUs offer several lower power modes. For example, two specific MSP430 MCU models are selected to show the active and low power modes of operation. One of them is

MSP430FR5994 and the other one is MSP430F5529. The information related to power consumption is shown in Table 1.2.

	MSP430FR5994 (MSP43FR59xx)	MSP430F5529 (MSP430F55xx)
Core	TI proprietary 16-bit core	TI proprietary 16-bit core
Active Mode Current	[1]225 µA at 1 MHz (3.0 V) ([1]Unified memory, FRAM memory execution)	[2]360 µA at 1 MHz (3.0 V) ([2]PMMCOREV0, Flash memory execution)
Low-power Mode 4 (LPM4) Current	[3]0.6 µA (3.0 V) ([3]Including SVS, 25 °C)	[4]1.4 µA (3.0 V) ([4]PMMCOREV0, 25 °C)

Table 1.2. Power comparison between selected MSP430 MCUs [2][3].

In active mode, both MCUs have already shown relatively low current consumption. To further reduce the power consumption, these MCUs can be controlled to be in low mode. The table shows the current consumptions when they are in active or low power modes. In a lower-power mode 4, both of the MSP430 MCUs have shown that the power consumption is very low.

Developers may need to understand and measure the power consumption of their embedded systems. If the system is a battery application, it is more important because it is related to the system life expectancy. Using the MSP430FR5994 Launchpad board and the Code Composer Studio, developers can measure the MCU current consumption easterly using EnergyTrace Technology.

Integrated Development Environment (IDE)

In order to test and debug a microcontroller, various development software packages need to be installed and used. The manual installation and configuration of several necessary software packages can be complicated. In this reason, an integrated development environment (IDE) can be used to make the system development easy. An IDE may contain headers, library files, program templates, and plug-in files that are needed to build microcontroller and microprocessor applications. Moreover, an IDE typically provides a user-friendly GUI (Graphical User Interface).

There are several IDEs that can be used for the development of MSP430 applications. The summary of the IDEs is shown in Table 1.3. Texas Instruments provides an IDE called Code Composer Studio. This Code Composer Studio (CCS) supports a wide range of TI's MCUs. It is optimized with C/C++ compilers. As of January 2023, the latest version is 12. In this book, the CCS version 12 is used.

Code Composer Studio provides large amounts of resources and libraries without a charge. However, if the developers want to create a commercial product, it is recommended to carefully examine the license agreement of Code Composer Studio and libraries that are used in their programs.

	Texas Instruments	IAR Systems
Program	Code Composer Studio	IAR Embedded Workbench
License	Full function No license fee	32 kB code size limit Upgradable
Compiler	TI C/C++	IAR C/C++

Table 1.3. Software Development Packages for MSP430.

IAR systems® (https://www.iar.com) provides an IDE that supports TI MCUs and processors. This IDE is called IAR embedded workbench®. It also supports MSP430 MCUs. IAR systems provides a fully functional license for a limited time, or a code size-limited kick start license without the time limit.

For many simple educational or small-scale embedded systems projects, code size limited IDEs may work well. When the developers need to unlock the code size limit for complex projects, the license can be purchased later for full functionality.

For programs in this book, they were created and tested based on the Code Composer Studio IDE. These programs do not necessarily work under other IDE environments.

Chapter 2. Development Tools

To provide technical support and resources, MCU manufacturers often provide evaluation modules, boards, and kits for their MCUs, and developers can build their functional prototypes using these kits. These hardware boards are also called development boards (or dev. boards). The cost of these development boards depends on many factors, and the cost may vary depending on the MCU models. In many cases, it is necessary to purchase an additional JTAG programming tool to load and debug programs.

Texas Instruments (TI) has introduced Launchpad™ boards, and they are affordable development kits based on selected TI MCUs. Launchpad boards have BoosterPack™ headers. There are various pre-assembled BoosterPack plug-in modules. Users can easily expand the functions of their systems by adding stackable BoosterPack plug-in modules to their Launchpad boards.

MSP430 ICs are microcontroller units (MCUs) introduced by Texas Instruments, and there is a wide selection of MSP430 MCU models. One of the MSP430 MCU groups is an MSP430 FRAM family. In this chapter, several MSP430FR2xxx and MSP430FR5xxx MCUs will be introduced. In addition, we will look into Code Composer Studio IDE and run a test program using an MSP430FR5994 Launchpad.

FRAM MCUs

FRAM stands for Ferroelectric Random-Access. It is a non-volatile memory. MSP430 FRAM MCUs are integrated with technologies of MSP430 and FRAM. These MSP430 FRAM MCUs may have several advantages over Flash memory based MSP430 MCUs.

For Speed, FRAM write speed can be faster compared to the write speed of Flash or EEPROM memory. Moreover, for Power consumption, FRAM cells can be operated in a low voltage, and they may need low current in changing the data. Furthermore, for Data reliability, FRAM memory can endure a higher number of read and write cycles.

MSP430 FRAM MCUs can be used in many applications, and they are particularly useful, for instance, in the data logging, remote sensing, and low-power battery applications where they need to endure a large number of read and write operations and need to make the energy consumption very low.

MSP430FR2311 Launchpad Overview

There is a group of MSP430FR23xx MCUs. An MSP430FR2311 MCU is one of these MSP430FR23xx MCUs. In addition to the advantages of FRAM technology, a transimpedance amplifier (TIA) is integrated with this MCU. This analog module can provide a current-to-voltage conversion and good current response. A Launchpad board based on this MSP430FR23xx MCU model is shown in Figure. 2.1. Specifically, this is an MSP430FR2311 Launchpad board.

This MSP430FR2311 Launchpad board has 20-pin booster pack header pins. This header configuration is defined by Texas Instruments. There are various functional plug-in modules that are available and compatible with this header configuration.

This Launchpad board can be powered through the microUSB located at the top of Figure 2.1. There is an isolation jumper block. They can be used to isolate the connections between the on-board eZ-FET debug probe and the MSP430FR2311 MCU.

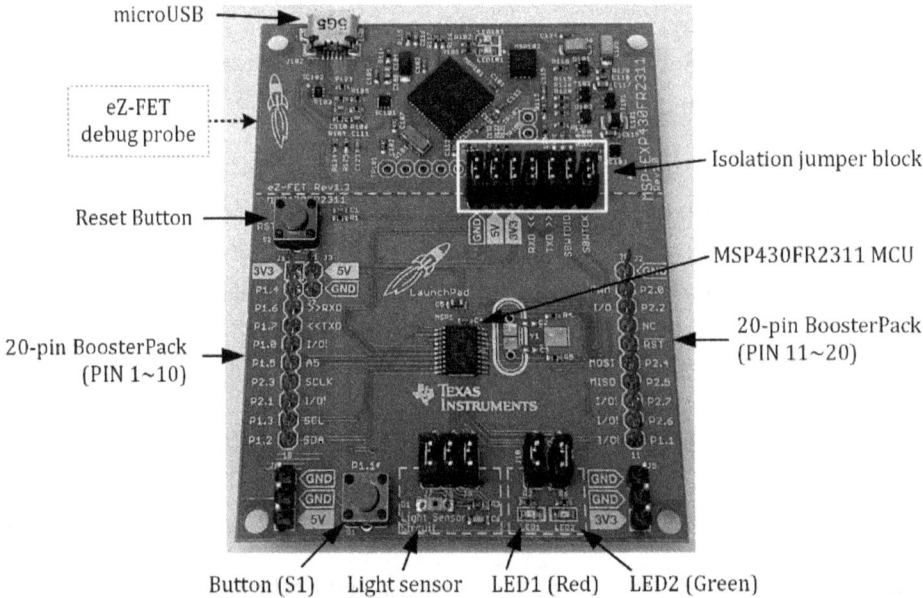

Figure 2.1. MSP430FR2311 Launchpad board (MSP-EXP430FR2311) [4].

There are two push buttons (S1 and S2) on the bottom side. Moreover, there is one red LED (Light-emitting diode) (LED1) and one green LED (LED2). Furthermore, a light sensor is placed on this Launchpad board.

MSP430FR2355 Launchpad Overview

An MSP430FR2355 MCU is also one of these MSP430FR23xx MCUs. This MCU includes SAC modules. SAC stands for Smart Analog Combo, and an SAC module includes integrated operational amplifier, programmable gain amplifier (PGA), and DAC (Digital-Analog Converter) units. On this specific MCU, there are four SAC modules. A picture of an MSP430FR2355 Launchpad board is shown in Figure 2.2.

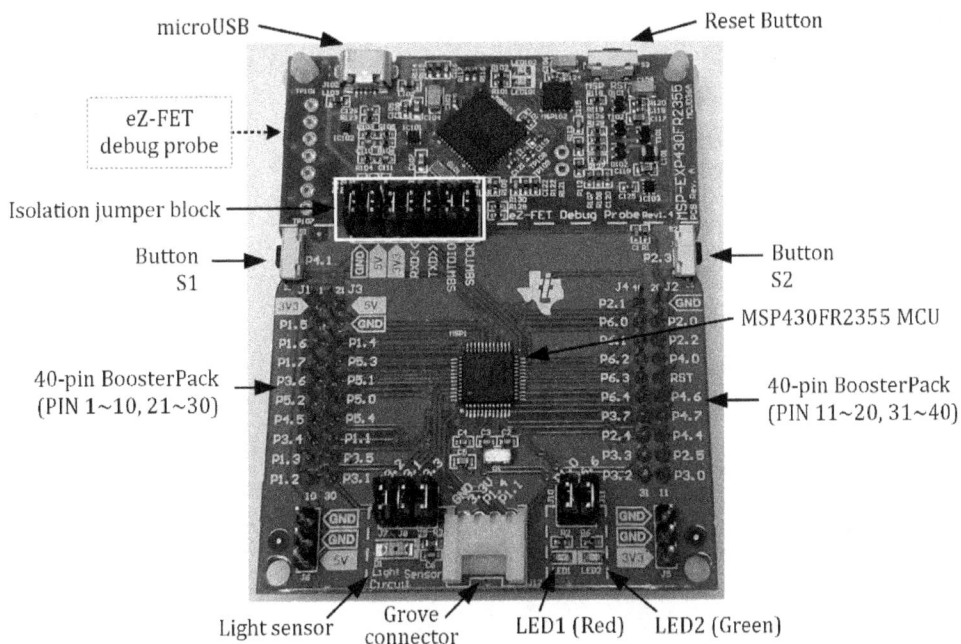

Figure 2.2. MSP430FR2355 Launchpad board (MSP-EXP430FR2355) [5].

This Launchpad board has 40-pin booster pack header pins. This header configuration is also defined by Texas Instruments. There are various functional plug-in modules available and compatible with this header configuration.

The power can be provided through the microUSB located at the top of Figure 2.2. There is an isolation jumper block between the eZ-FET debug probe and the MSP430FR2355 MCU.

There are two push buttons (S1 and S2) on the right and left sides. Moreover, on this board, there are two LEDs and two buttons. Moreover, a Grove connector is placed on this Launchpad board. This is a four-pin header that can be used to connect to a Grove system. A grove system includes base units and various Grove sensor modules by Seeed Studio®.

MSP430FR5969 Launchpad Overview

There is a group of MSP430FR59xx MCUs. An MSP430FR5969 MCU is one of these MSP430FR59xx MCUs. While an MSP430FR2355 MCU includes a 32kB FRAM memory space, this MSP430FR5969 MCU provides a bigger FRAM memory space of 64kB. A Launchpad board using this specific MCU is shown in Figure 2.3. The part number of this Launchpad board is MSP-EXP430FR5969.

This Launchpad board has 20-pin booster pack header pins. It also has two buttons and two LEDs. Moreover, a super capacitor is placed on the board, which can be used to demonstrate very low power capabilities. The super capacitor can be used to keep providing power to the Launchpad board, and the board can be operated for a limited time, when an external power supply source is removed or disconnected.

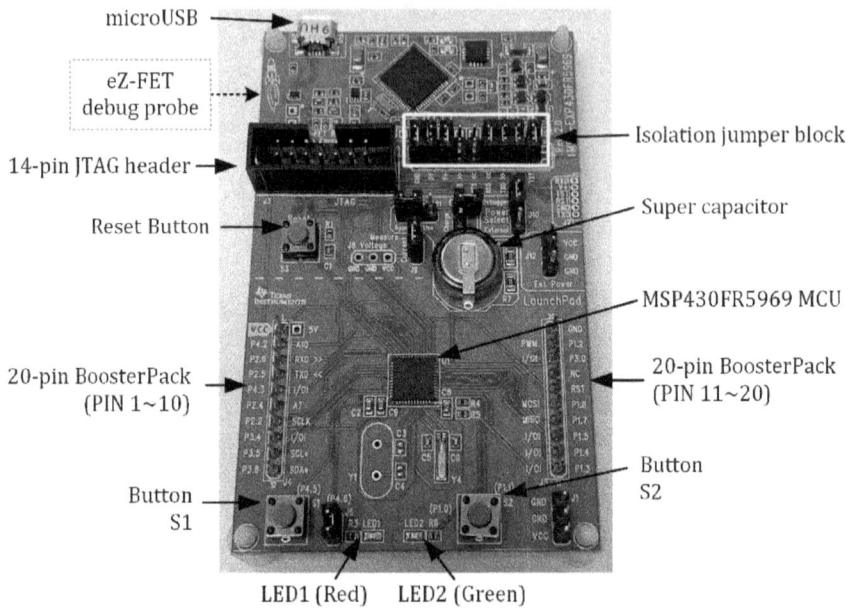

Figure 2.3. MSP430FR5969 Launchpad board (MSP-EXP430FR5969) [6].

MSP430FR5994 Launchpad Overview

An MSP430FR5994 MCU is one of these MSP430FR59xx MCUs. An MSP430FR5994 Launchpad development board is based on this MSP430FR5994 MCU. The part number of this Launchpad board is MSP-EXP4305994. A picture of this MSP430FR5994 Launchpad board is shown in Figure 2.4.

In this book, we will learn about an MSP430FR5994 MCU using this model of the MSP430FR5994 Launchpad board. In this book, this Launchpad board can be referred to as an MSP430FR5994 Launchpad board or simply an MSP430 Launchpad.

This Launchpad board has 40-pin booster pack header pins. As mentioned, there are various functional plug-in modules that are compatible with this header configuration.

A user can plug in a USB cable through the microUSB located at the top of Figure 2.4. This micoUSB connection can provide power to the MSP430FR5994 MCU and the on-board eZ-FET debug probe that is located at the top portion of the board. There is an isolation jumper block that can be used to isolate the power between the MSP430FR5994 MCU and the on-board eZ-FET debug probe.

This is a low-cost development board, and a user can debug this board without an extra JTAG programming tool because this development board has an on-board eZ-FET debug probe.

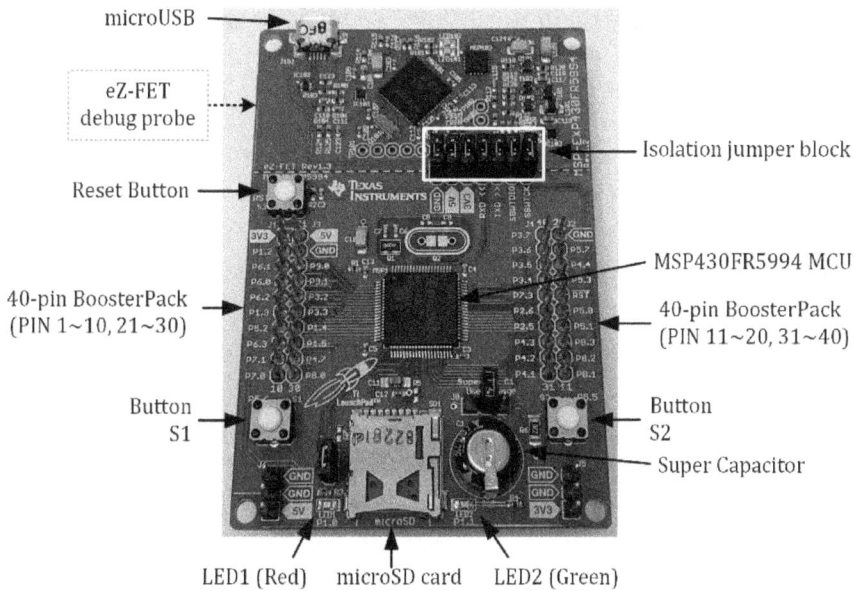

Figure 2.4. MSP430FR5994 Launchpad board (MSP-EXP430FR5994) [7].

There are two push buttons (S1 and S2) on the bottom side, and there are two LEDs, one red LED (LED1) and one green LED (LED2). Moreover, there is a microSD card connector. On this Launchpad board, a super capacitor is placed on the board, and this super capacitor can be used to provide power to the board to operate it for a limited time without an external power supply.

For more details about this Launchpad board, readers can obtain relevant resources visiting the TI's web page:

https://www.ti.com/tool/MSP-EXP430FR5994

In this web page, readers may be able to access an MS430FR5994 Launchpad Development Kit User's Guide file [2]. This document contains relevant information regarding this Launchpad board.

Code Composer Studio (CCS)

Code Composer studio is an IDE for TI microcontrollers and microprocessors, which supports various TI MCU models. Code Composer Studio was built based on an Eclipse open-source software framework. Users can take advantage of the latest improvements of Eclipse, and TI provides useful resources, libraries, and examples for the users through Code Composer Studio IDE. This IDE can run under Windows, Mac®, and Linux machines.

CCS Download and Installation

The installation file of Code Compose Studio can be downloaded via the web link:

https://www.ti.com/tool/download/CCSTUDIO

There are off-line installer and web (on-demand) installer files. Users can choose either of them. During the installation process, you may be prompted to select components as shown in Figure 2.5. It is up to the users to choose any of these options. But, in order to support MSP430 MCUs, users need to select the MSP430 component as shown in Figure 2.5. Additionally, users can select any other components. You can review the list of the selected components. Then, you can click the next button to continue the installation process.

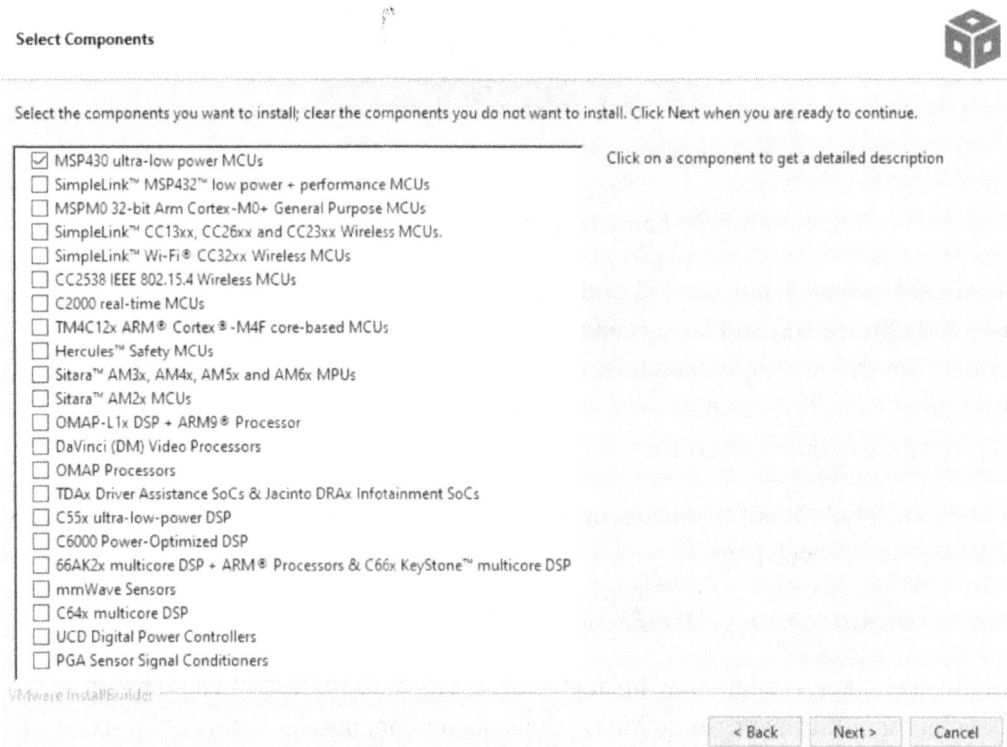

Select Components

Select the components you want to install; clear the components you do not want to install. Click Next when you are ready to continue.

Click on a component to get a detailed description

- ☑ MSP430 ultra-low power MCUs
- ☐ SimpleLink™ MSP432™ low power + performance MCUs
- ☐ MSPM0 32-bit Arm Cortex-M0+ General Purpose MCUs
- ☐ SimpleLink™ CC13xx, CC26xx and CC23xx Wireless MCUs.
- ☐ SimpleLink™ Wi-Fi® CC32xx Wireless MCUs
- ☐ CC2538 IEEE 802.15.4 Wireless MCUs
- ☐ C2000 real-time MCUs
- ☐ TM4C12x ARM® Cortex®-M4F core-based MCUs
- ☐ Hercules™ Safety MCUs
- ☐ Sitara™ AM3x, AM4x, AM5x and AM6x MPUs
- ☐ Sitara™ AM2x MCUs
- ☐ OMAP-L1x DSP + ARM9® Processor
- ☐ DaVinci (DM) Video Processors
- ☐ OMAP Processors
- ☐ TDAx Driver Assistance SoCs & Jacinto DRAx Infotainment SoCs
- ☐ C55x ultra-low-power DSP
- ☐ C6000 Power-Optimized DSP
- ☐ 66AK2x multicore DSP + ARM® Processors & C66x KeyStone™ multicore DSP
- ☐ mmWave Sensors
- ☐ C64x multicore DSP
- ☐ UCD Digital Power Controllers
- ☐ PGA Sensor Signal Conditioners

VMware InstallBuilder

[< Back] [Next >] [Cancel]

Figure 2.5. Component selection for MSP430 MCUs.

Now, we will create a project and write a simple blink program for an MSP430FR5994 MCU. After successfully installation, you can run Code Composer Studio. As shown in Figure 2.6, you can create a new CCS project.

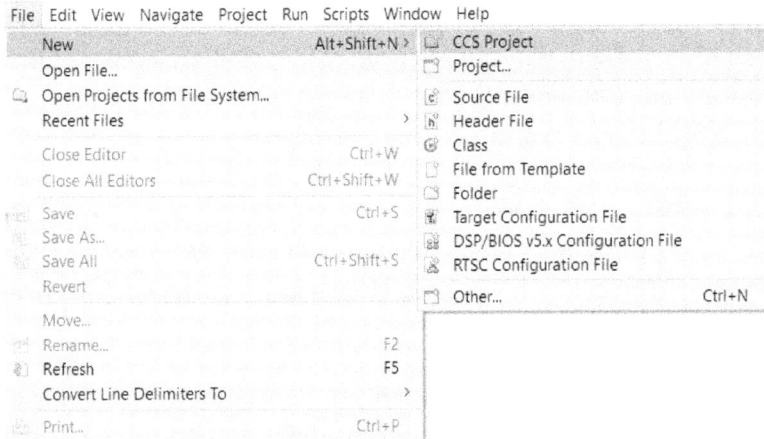

Figure 2.6. Creating a New Project.

Next, you can see the screen as shown in Figure 2.7. You can select a proper MCU model that is "MSP430FR5994". For the project name, "blink" is typed. But, users can enter any other favorite project name instead.

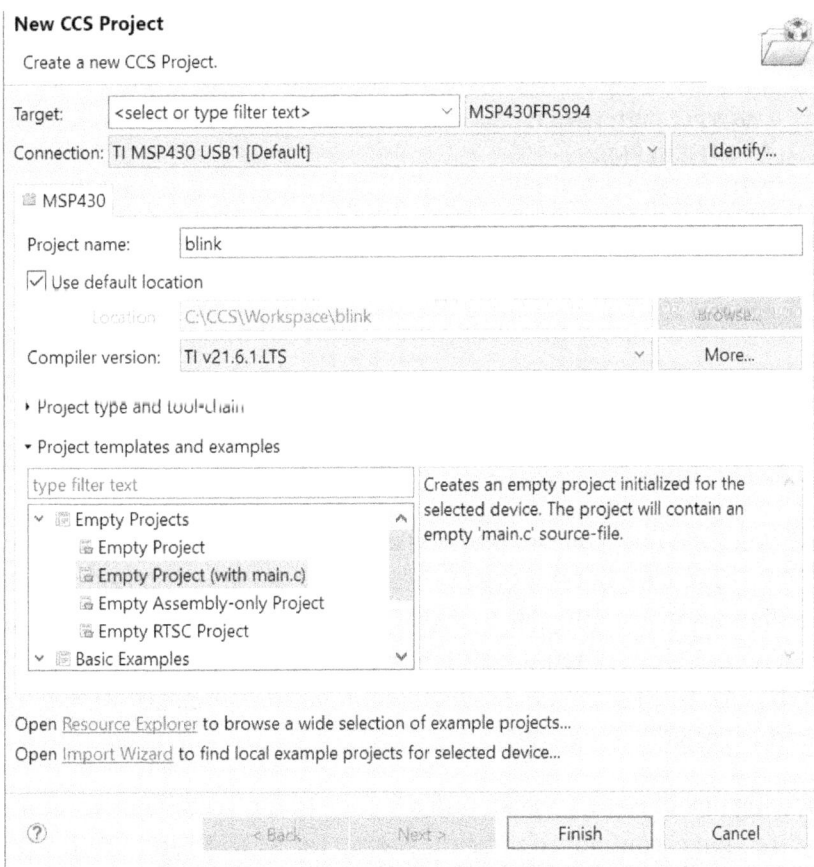

Figure 2.7. New CCS Project setup.

There are two project templates. You can choose "Empty Project (with main.c)." You can click "Finish" icon. Next, you can see project files that are created on the left side of the window of Code Composer Studio. You can double click "main.c," and you can edit this source file to write your own code.

LED Blink Program in C/C++

You can write your program by modifying the *main.c* file as it was described in the earlier sub-section. You can type the code shown in Program 2.1. This program is a simple LED blink program.

In this program, the first line inside of *main()* is associated with configuring a watchdog timer. The watchdog timer is purposefully configured to be on hold. This is simply for an educational purpose to make it easier for students to write programs easier to avoid protection behaviors by the watchdog. In this book, the example programs were created assuming that the watchdog timer is on hold. However, it would be typical and desired to enable a watchdog timer for commercial products and professional programming in order to manage basic fault conditions of hardware or software.

```c
#include <msp430.h>
int main(void) {
    WDTCTL = WDTPW | WDTHOLD;  // hold the watchdog timer
    PM5CTL0 &= ~LOCKLPM5; // clear LOCKLPM5 bit
    P1DIR |= 0x01; // set the direction (P1.0)
    P1OUT |= 0x01; // set the output value (P1.0)
    while (1){
        P1OUT ^= 0x01; // toggle (P1.0)
        _delay_cycles(250000); // delay
    }
    return 0;
}
```

Program 2.1. LED Blink Test Program.

In the following code line, you can find this code as follows: PM5CTL0 &= ~LOCKLPM5. This code can clear the LOCKLPM5 bit in PM5CTL0 register. This register configuration is applicable to specific MSP430 FRAM MCU models such as an MSP430FR5994 MCU. When the MCU is started up, I/O pins may remain locked. In order to be effective for the port register configuration, this LOCKLPM5 bit needs to be cleared in PM5CTL0 register.

In the following line of code, you can find the code that can configure a GPIO port. The GPIO direction is configured to be the output for P1.0. A red LED (LED1) is internally connected to the P1.0. Next, the logical output of this port is configured to be high.

Next, it shows a code block that is a "while" loop. In this while loop, the value of this P1.0 gets toggled. Also, the system gets delayed for a certain period of time. Thus, it will blink the red LED (LED1) with a reasonable rate. If the program is running successfully, you can see a flashing red LED.

If the LED is not flashing, you can check whether the shunt jumper (J7) for LED1 is placed properly or not. The shunt jumper for LED1 is supposed to be placed properly, and it is located close to the LED1. In Chapter 5, we will learn more details about digital IOs.

BH EDU Board Kit

In order to build and learn about embedded systems, learners would choose to obtain additional parts and kits to form a system for their own experiments. In this book, we will learn about selected electronics parts and how to use them such as an LCD module, an Accelerometer IC, and a motor driver IC.

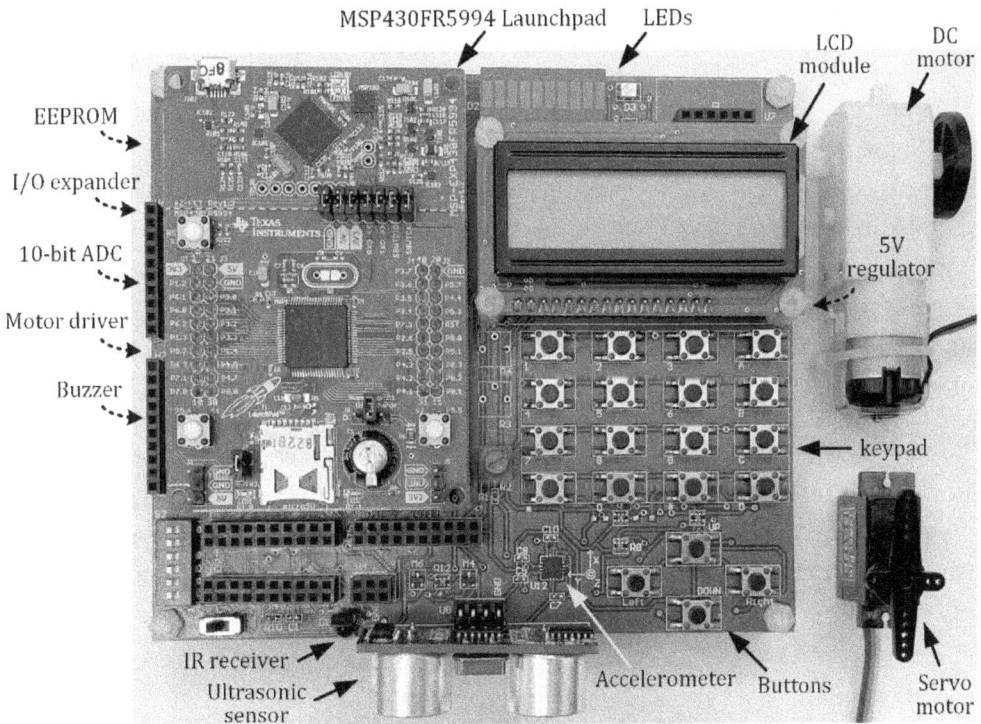

Figure 2.5. BH EDU board kit with an MSP430FR5994 (Version 2.1.x) [8].

In order to support embedded system educations, BH EDU boards were developed. With additional parts, BH EDU kits were formed. These kits can be used for lectures and laboratory sessions for users to conduct experiments. A picture of a BH EDU board with an MSP430FR5994 Launchpad board is shown in Figure 2.5. The details of this BH EDU board and TI BH EDU kit [8] can be found in the web link:

https://github.com/bh-projects/TI-BH-EDU-board-kit

TI BH EDU kits can assist students' experiential learning via hands-on laboratory sessions. Learners can use these kits to build their own educational embedded systems. For embedded system developers, it is important to have a decent level of knowledge of analog/digital circuits and systems. It is assumed that the users/readers already have prior knowledge of circuits and systems. Basic digital logic circuits are introduced in Appendix A.

Readers can learn about MSP430 microcontrollers without this kit. It is not essential to obtain this kit to study the materials described in this book, since the circuit diagram and the generalized connection diagrams are given in this book. Therefore, readers can obtain their own proper parts to perform their relevant experiments as needed. However, readers may need to use the same electronics parts or the electronics parts that are functionally equivalent components.

For instance, a specific model of an LCD component was selected and used in this book. Some level of the knowledge can be common and generic; however, any of the hardware connections and software programming portions are not necessarily reusable in other LCD modules. If readers would choose to different hardware components or connections, they would be conducting experiments at their own risk and they would need to study and examine documentations from the manufacturer carefully. Also, they would need to consult with the manufacturer for further technical support.

While the author has prepared this book with his best effort, it makes no representation or warranty of any kind with regard to the contents of this book including hardware connection diagrams, schematics, and programs. It is worth noting that the author shall not be liable in any event for incidental or consequential damage in connection with the use of the contents of this book.

Chapter 3. MSP430FR5994 architecture

An MSP430FR5994 MCU is based on a 16-bit RISC (Reduced Instruction Set Computer) architecture. The clock frequency can go up to 16 MHz. For the MCU, it is acceptable to choose the supply voltage from 1.8 V to 3.6 V. In this book, we choose to use the supply voltage is 3.3 V, and, in general, it is assumed that the supply voltage to the MCU is 3.3V.

Pin Diagram of MSP430FR5994IPZ

Several package options are available for an MSP430FR5994 MCU model. The part number of the MCU IC on the Launchpad board is MSP430FR5994IPN. The package is an 80-pin Low-profile quad flat package (LQFP). The pin diagram of this MSP430FR5994IPN IC is shown in Figure 3.1.

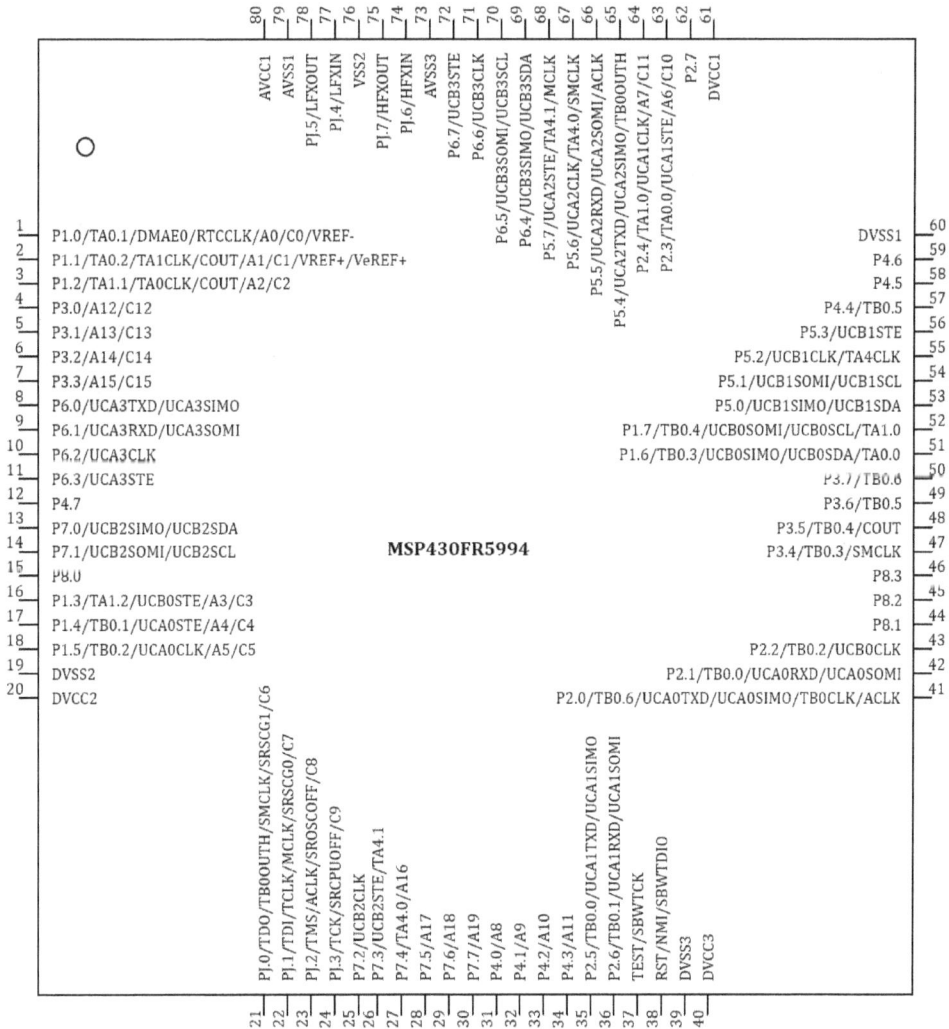

Figure 3.1. MSP430FR5994IPN Pin Diagram [2].

The naming conventions are similar to typical MSP430 MCUs. The ports and pins are named Px.y. For instance, for the pin number of 4 in Figure 3.1, this pin is associated with P3.0. This is a general-purpose input/output function, and this pin refers to the first bit (or bit 0) of Port 3. Moreover, this pin can function as an analog input (A12), or it can function as a comparator input (C12) after a proper port configuration. This means the multiple functions are shared through this pin. Many other pins of this IC provide multiple functions.

The technical details of this MCU can be found in various documents provided by the manufacturer. For instance, readers can download and access the datasheet of an MSP430FR5994 MCU [1]. As of January 2023, the revision D of the datasheet released in 2021 is available to download from the Texas Instruments' web page. The manufacturer may release newer revisions, if needed. The datasheet and technical documents can be found in the web link:

https://www.ti.com/product/MSP430FR5994

Functional Block Diagram

An MSP430FR5994 MCU has an internal 256 kB FRAM memory and 8 kB SRAM memory space. The simplified functional block diagram is shown Figure 3.2.

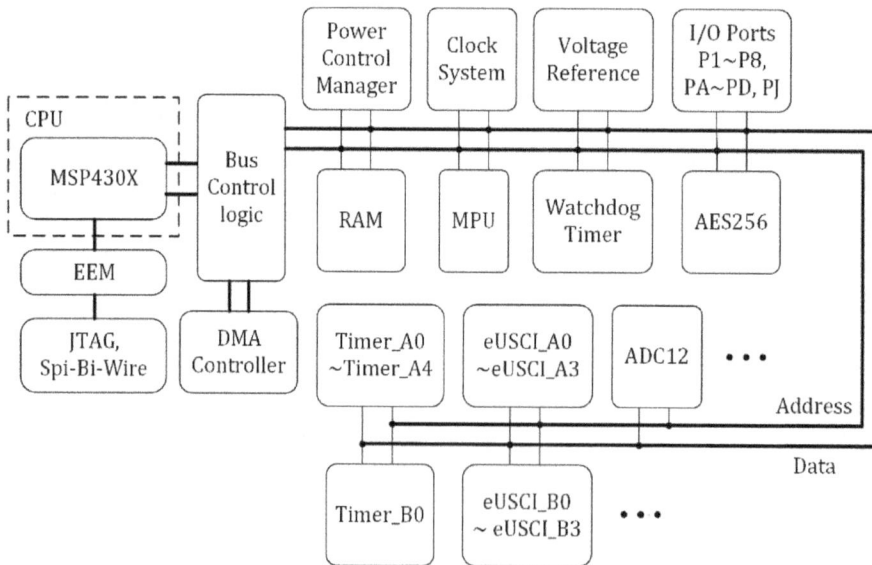

Figure 3.2. Simplified MSP430FR5994 Functional Block Diagram [2].

A RAM block that includes FRAM and SRAM memory is connected to address and data lines. Several peripheral module blocks are connected to these address and data bus lines. For instance, a 12-bit ADC block is connected to the address and data bus lines. eUSCI_Ax and e_USCI_Bx blocks are connected to these bus lines.

Moreover, Timer_Ax and Timer_B0 general-purpose timer blocks are connected, and clock system, watchdog timer, and voltage reference blocks are also connected. There are several peripheral device blocks connected to these bus lines. There is a bus control logic, and it is assumed that it can make the peripheral blocks and the CPU (Central Processing Unit) work together properly. For the CPU, an MSP430X CPU is used as shown on the left side in Figure 3.2. Let us examine an MSP430X CPU in the following sections.

MSP430X CPU Overview

The CPU that was implemented in an MSP430FR5994 MCU is a TI proprietary 16-bit RISC processor. Specifically, it is an MSP430X CPU, which can be simply referred to as CPUX. This MSP430X CPU is compatible with an MSP430 CPU. An MSP430X CPU is a 16-bit processor, and it supports a 20-bit address bus.

An MSP430X CPU supports several methods to access the memory address range that is higher than 64 KB. The MSP430X CPU provides extended MSP430X instructions. They can give access to its 20-bit address space. These extended MSP430X instructions can be used, when the capability of 16-bit address or data length is limited or exceeded.

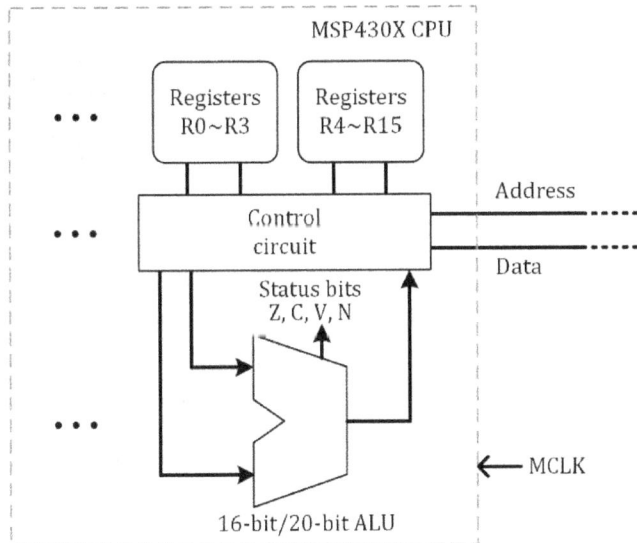

Figure 3.3. Simplified block diagram of a portion of an MSP430X CPU [9].

A simplified block diagram of a portion of an MSP430X CPU is shown in Figure 3.3. The CPUX includes 16 registers R0 to R15, and they are connected to an ALU (Arithmetic-Logic Unit) through a control circuit. The control logic represents a generalized circuit block. The ALU can perform relevant operations and it can generate status bits including Z, C, V, and N. This ALU unit can process 16-bit data, and it can process 20-bit data via extended MSP430X instructions.

For more information about the MSP430X CPU architecture, users can examine various documents and resources including technical documents provided by the manufacturer [9].

MSP430X Registers

There are 16 registers that are implemented in an MSP430X CPU. Figure 3.4 shows these MSP430X registers. The registers R4 to R15 are general-purpose registers. These 12 registers can be used in storing and processing 8-bit, 16-bit, or 20-bit data, and they can be used for general use. These general-purpose registers support several formats including byte, word, and 20-bit data formats.

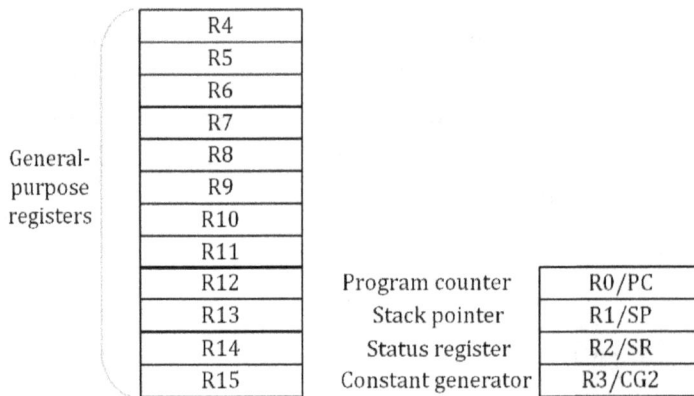

General-purpose registers				
	R4			
	R5			
	R6			
	R7			
	R8			
	R9			
	R10			
	R11			
	R12	Program counter		R0/PC
	R13	Stack pointer		R1/SP
	R14	Status register		R2/SR
	R15	Constant generator		R3/CG2

Figure 3.4. MSP430X registers [9].

The registers R0 to R3 are special registers that are used for dedicated functions. The register R0 serves as a program counter (PC). This is a 20-bit program counter, and the value of the register may indicate the next instruction to be fetched. For instance, during a reset sequence, the MCU can load the value stored in the address of the reset vector and store it in the PC.

The registers R1 serves as a stack pointer (SP). This is a 20-bit stack pointer, and it can be used to point to a proper stack memory address to store return addresses when a subroutine or an interrupt is called.

The register R2 serves as a status register (SR). A detailed description of the status register will be followed in the next sub-section. This status register is a 16-bit register, and the remaining combinations are related to a CG1 constant generator register. The register serves as a CG2 constant generator register. An MSP430X CPU supports several commonly used constants using the CG1 and CG2 constant generator registers.

Status Register

The register R2 serves a dedicated function as a 16-bit status register (SR). The status register (SR) contains important information including the result status of an operation. Users should not write 20-bit values to the status register as it could cause an unpredictable operation [9].

The status register (SR) bits are shown in Figure 3.5. The first bit from the right is a Carry bit (C). This bit can be set when the result of an operation generates a carry. The second bit from the right is a Zero bit (Z). This bit can be set when the result of an operation is zero. The third bit from the right is a Negative bit (N). This bit can be set when the result of an operation is negative. The nineth bit from the right is an overflow bit (V). This bit can be set when the result of an arithmetic operation causes an overflow. These C, Z, N, and V status bits can be used in conditional jump instructions.

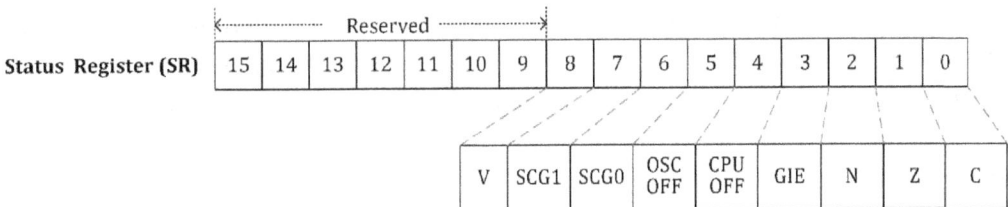

Status Register (SR)	15	14	13	12	11	10	9	8	7	6	5	4	3	2	1	0
	Reserved						V	SCG1	SCG0	OSC OFF	CPU OFF	GIE	N	Z	C

Figure 3.5. Status register bits [9].

The fourth bit from the right is the bit that can enable or disable *general interrupt*. When this bit is set, the *general interrupt* is enabled.

There are bits related to *CPU OFF* and *OSC OFF* functions. These bits can be used in turning on or off oscillators and CPU. Moreover, there are bits related to *SCG0* and *SCG1*. These bits can control clock generators in the clock system. The combination of these bits is related to the low-power modes.

Memory Map

Table 3.1 shows the memory map for an MSP430FR5994 MCU. The address range from 0x04000 to 0x43FFF is to access the 256kB FRAM. This is the memory space where the user's program can be stored. Moreover, in this FRAM address range, interrupt vector information can be stored. Specifically, interrupt vector and signature information are stored in 0x0FF80 to 0x0FFFF.

The address range from 0x01C00 to 0x3BFFF is used to access the 8kB RAM. The device descriptor (TLV) information is stored in the address range from 0x01A00 to 0x01AFF. TLV information includes ADC and REF calibration data.

The address range from 0x00020 to 0x00FFF is used to access peripherals. This address range is assigned for the access of peripheral devices including Port 1~ Port 8, Timers, eUSCI_Ax, and eUSCI_Bx.

Address Range	Memory Space	Description
0x00000 ~ 0x00009	Reserved	
0x0000A ~ 0x0001F	Tiny RAM	
0x00020 ~ 0x00FFF	Peripherals	
0x01000 ~ 0x017FF	ROM	Bootloader (BSL) memory
0x01800 ~ 0x019FF	FRAM	Information memory
0x01A00 ~ 0x01AFF	FRAM	Device descriptor (TLV)
0x01C00 ~ 0x02BFF	RAM	
0x02C00 ~ 0x03BFF	RAM	Shared with low-energy accelerator
0x04000 ~ 0x43FFF	FRAM	Code memory, Interrupt vectors and signature

Table 3.1. Memory map (MSP430FR5994) [2].

The peripheral device can be accessed via the assigned address range. The method of accessing peripheral devices is related to the memory-mapped I/O. For reference, a general description of memory-mapped I/O techniques is presented in Appendix C. Appendix C includes a control block that was designed using a Verilog Hardware Description Language (HDL). A basic description of the Verilog HDL is presented in Appendix B.

Chapter 4. Assembly Language

An executable object file can be created, and the executable object file can be converted to a hex file. A linker can create the executable object file from object files, and the object files can be created by an assembler from assembly code. An executable hex file can be created from an assembly language program, and this executable hex file can be processed to store an executable program in an MSP430FR5994. As described, an assembly code is one of the methods to generate an executable program for an MSP430FR5994 MCU. In this chapter, MSP430X instructions and assembly programs based on a TI compiler and Code Composer Studio IDE (Integrated Development Environment) for an MSP430FR5994 MCU will be introduced.

MSP430X Instructions and Assembly code

An MSP430FR5994 MCU has an MSP430X CPU that is a 16-bit processor. This CPU supports a 20-bit address bus. An MSP430X CPU is compatible with an MSP430 CPU. A brief introduction of MSP430X instructions and assembly program examples are presented in this chapter. In an assembly source program, there are several section definitions including ".text", ".data", and ".bss".

For ".text" section, it contains executable code. For ".data" section, it contains initialized data. For ".bss" section, it contains uninitialized variables. The executable instructions will be stored in the ".text" section.

An operation code (opcode) is an instruction such as **add**. An operand is a value or an argument. A double operand instruction example is shown as follows:

Instruction   source, destination

An instruction can be chosen, and two operands can be followed. In this double operand instruction, users may need to be familiar with the order of the source operand and destination operand.

An assembly instruction example, shown in Assembly 4.1, can add the values stored in two registers of R10 and R11. In this example, the result of adding R11 and R10 is to be written back to the register R10.

Assembly 4.1. add.w R11, R10

An MSP430X CPU supports 8-bit and 16-bit operations. In addition, it supports 20-bit operations. 8-bit data or byte handing operations can be indicated using **.b** suffixes. 16-bit data or word handling operations can be indicated using **.w** suffixes. For instance, the **.w** suffix is added to the **add** instruction. If a 8-bit data operation is desired, **.b** suffixes can be used instead. An 8-bit add instruction is **add.b**. If a suffix is omitted in an assembly instruction, predefined/default bit operation per assembly instruction would be selected and processed. The default bit modes for assembly instructions can be found in the technical documentation [9].

It is worth mentioning that users may need to be aware of unused bits when the operations are mixed. For instance, let us say that the values stored in R10 and R11 are 0x01234 and 0x00001, respectively. For the word handling operation such as the case shown in Assembly 4.1, the result is the value of 0x01235 in R10. However, if a byte handing is used instead such as **add.b**. The result is the value of 0x00035 because higher bits are cleared. Users may need to understand the behaviors of unused bits and instructions. In this book, to make the operations clear, proper suffixes are used where applicable.

An MSP430X CPU supports MSP430X extended instructions for 20-bit operations. In the following sections, we will study byte or word instructions that are compatible with an MSP430 CPU. For 20-bit operations, a brief introduction of MSP430X extended instructions can be found in the latter portion of this chapter.

In the previous example, the values stored in two registers were added. An immediate value can be used instead. An assembly instruction example that can perform add operation of an immediate value of 12 and the value in R10 is shown in Assembly 4.2. The result is to be stored back in R10.

>   *Assembly 4.2.* add .w #12, R10

Moreover, there are single operand instructions. As an example, a *push* instruction is selected, and the example is Assembly 4.3. In this example, the value of R10 will be pushed and the value is to be stored in a stack memory space.

>   *Assembly 4.3.* push.w R10

Selected arithmetic instructions are shown in Table 4.1. The table includes add, subtract, increment, decrement, and arithmetic shift operations. In addition to the MSP430X core instructions, emulated instructions are available to make the code easier. Emulated instructions in the table are indicated by the asterisk (*) symbol. Table 4.1 includes the instructions that can process addition or subtraction operations. It also includes add and subtraction operations with a carry bit.

In addition to the binary computations, an MSP430X provides a **dadd** instruction that can perform a decimal addition operation. This is a base 10 addition. In some applications, BCD (Binary-Coded Decimal) format can be useful. For instance, the BCD data format can be effective in handling data for 7 segment displays or LCD (Liquid Crystal Display) displays.

There are instructions for increment or decrement operations such as **inc, incd, dec,** and **decd**. As mentioned, these instructions are indicated by the asterisk symbol, and this means that they are emulated instructions. For instance, if the following instruction: "inc.w R10" is used, the internal conversion by the assembler or compiler can be "add.w #1, R10".

Moreover, Table 4.1 includes the arithmetic shirt right or left. For the shift right, the method of processing MSB (Most Significant Bit) and Carry bit can differentiate between arithmetic and logical shift right operations. For the shift left, this is an emulated instruction, and it doubles the value in the register using an **add** instruction.

Instruction	Execution	Description
add R11, R10	R10 ← R10 + R11	Add
addc R11, R10	R10 ← R10 + R11 + C	Add with carry bit
sub R11, R10	R10 ← R10 – R11	Subtract
subc R11, R10	R10 ← R10 – R11–((NOT)C)	Subtract with carry bit
dadd R11, R10	R10 ← R10 + R11 + C (Decimally)	BCD addition
* inc R10	R10 ← R10 + 1	Increment by 1
* incd R10	R10 ← R10 + 2	Increment by 2
* dec R10	R10 ← R10 – 1	Decrement by 1
* decd R10	R10 ← R10 – 2	Decrement by 2
rra R10	MSB -> MSB ->.... LSB -> C	Shift right (Arithmetically)
* rla R10	ADD R10, R10	Shift left (Arithmetically)

Table 4.1. Selected arithmetic MSP430X instructions (*Emulated instructions) [9].

Selected logical instructions are shown in Table 4.2. Bitwise logical AND, OR, XOR, and NOT operations can be performed using **and, bis, orr,** and **inv** instructions, respectively. Moreover, the operation that can selectively clear bits is useful. An MSP430X CPU provides a **bic** instruction to clear bits selectively. Moreover, logical shift right or left operations can be performed using **rrc** or **rlc**. The carry bit is used in both cases of operations.

Instruction	Execution	Description
and R11, R10	R10 ← R10 (AND) R11	Bitwise AND
bis R11, R10	R10 ← R10 (OR) R11	Bitwise OR
xor R11, R10	R10 ← R10 (XOR) R11	Bitwise XOR
* inv R10	R10 ← (NOT) R10	Invert; Bitwise NOT
bic R11, R10	R10 ← R10 (AND) ((NOT) R11)	Clear bits
rrc R10	C -> MSB ->.... LSB -> C	Shift right (Logical)
* rlc R10	ADDC R10, R10	Shift left (Logical through Carry)

Table 4.2. Selected logical MSP430X instructions (*Emulated instructions) [9].

Selected compare and branch instructions are shown in Table 4.3. There are several instructions to perform compare operations. A **cmp** instruction can be used to compare the values stored in two registers. The status flags are to be updated on the result of the subtract operation of two values. A **tst** instruction can be used to compare the value stored in a register with zero.

A **bit** instruction can be used to compare the bitwise logical values of two registers. The values of the condition flags are to be updated on the result of the bitwise AND operation of two values.

Instruction	Execution	Description
cmp R11, R10	Status flags on R10 – R11	Compare
tst R10	Status flags on R10 – 0	Test
bit R11, R10	Status flags on R10 (AND) R11	Test bits
jmp *label*	PC ← address in *label*	Unconditional branch
* br *label*	PC ← address in *label*	Unconditional branch
call *label*	SP ← SP-2; @SP ← PC ; PC ← address in *label*	Call subroutine
* ret	PC ← @SP (16bit); SP ← SP+2	Return from subroutine
reti	PC ← @SP (20bit); SP ← SP+2	Return from interrupt

Table 4.3. Selected compare/branch MSP430X instructions (*Emulated instructions) [9].

A simple unconditional branch operation can be performed using the **jmp** or **br** instruction. For a subroutine call, a **call** instruction is used. To exit the subroutine and return, a **ret** instruction can be used. A main program can be interrupted and can process an interrupt service routine (ISR). A **reti** instruction can be used instead to return from an ISR.

MSP430X CPU provides conditional jump instructions. Table 4.4 shows the selected conditional jump instructions. There are various conditions including equal, not equal, carry, no carry, greater or equal, or less. These conditions are determined by status bits including zero (Z), carry (C), negative (N) and overflow (V) bits.

Instruction	Condition	Description
jeq *label*	equal	branch to *label* if Z bit is Set
jne *label*	not equal	branch to *label* if Z bit is Reset
jz *label*	zero	branch to *label* if Z bit is Set
jnz *label*	not zero	branch to *label* if Z bit is Reset
jc *label*	carry	branch to *label* if C bit is Set
jnc *label*	no carry	branch to *label* if C bit is Reset
jge *label*	greater or equal	branch to *label* if N and V bits are the same
jl *label*	less	branch to *label* if N and V bits are not the same

Table 4.4. Selected conditional jump MSP430X instructions [9].

A "move" instruction in an MSP430X CPU supports various formats of operations. Selected move instructions are shown in Table 4.5. A **mov** instructions can be used in register and memory operations.

Instruction	Execution	Description
mov R11, R10	R10 ← R11	Register operation
mov #*imm*, R10	R10 ← immediate value (imm)	Immediate mode operation
mov 0(R11), R10	R10 ← @R11	Load (Indexed)
mov @R11, R10	R10 ← @R11	Load (Indirect register)
mov *label*, R10	R10 ← address in *label*	Load (Symbolic)
mov &*label*, R10	R10 ← address in *label*	Load (Absolute)
mov R11, 0(R10)	@R10 ← R11	Store (Indexed)
mov R10, *label*	@(address in *label*) ← R10	Store (Symbolic)
mov R10, &*label*	@(address in *label*) ← R10	Store (Absolute)

Table 4.5. Selected move MSP430X instructions [9].

The value of one register can be moved to another register using a **mov** instruction. Moreover, an immediate value can be written to a register using a **mov** instruction. For the immediate data, a number sign "#" is used in front of the number.

A **mov** instruction can be used in accessing data stored in a memory space such as load and store operations. An MSP430X CPU provides several addressing modes including indexed, indirect register, symbolic, and absolute modes.

As it was introduced, a certain memory space is associated with physical I/O devices. Performing load/store operations using this specific memory space may access physical I/O devices. This is related to the topic of a memory-mapped I/O. This topic has been introduced in Appendix C.

Selected several instructions such as address, **push/pop**, and **nop** instructions are shown in Table 4.6. The address of a memory space can be stored using a **mov** instruction. For the 16-bit address that is located in the lower 64 KB address range, a **mov** instruction (**mov.w** to be specific) can perform the task of storing the address.

An MSP430X CPU supports address instructions to access a 20-bit address. For the 20-bit address, a **mova** instruction can perform the task of accessing and storing the 20-bit address. This is a part of MSP430X extended instructions.

Instruction	Execution	Description
mov #*label*, R10	R10 ← address in *label* (16 bit)	Address of *label* to R10 (16 bits)
mova #*label*, R10	R10 ← address in *label* (20bit)	Address of *label* to R10 (20 bits)
push R10	SP ← SP-2; @SP ← R10	Push operation to the stack
* pop R10	R10 ← @SP; SP ← SP+2	Pop operation from stack
* nop	mov R3, R3	No operation

Table 4.6. Selected address/push/pop/nop MSP430X instructions (*Emulated instruction) [9].

Some operations may need to access data in a stack memory space. This operation can be performed using **push** and **pop** instructions. A value can be stored in a stack memory space using a **push** instruction. A value stored in a stack memory can be loaded using a **pop** instruction.

In general, a *no operation* instruction can take an instruction space, but it does not affect the context or status of the CPU. *No operation* instructions can be useful as they can introduce short delays that could be needed for the CPU or program routines. MSP430X CPU includes a **nop** (no operation) instruction. This is an emulated instruction, and the actual implementation of this instruction is "mov R3, R3".

A brief introduction to selected assembly instructions was presented in this chapter. For readers who wish to learn more about MSP430X CPU assembly language programming, they can examine other educational resources or documents provided by the manufacturer [9][10].

Assembly Language Test Environment

In general, Assembly language programming in MSP430 CPUs can be effective if it is efficiently coded by an experienced programmer. Moreover, studying Assembly language programming can be useful in deepening the knowledge about the MSP430X CPU architecture. However, for a fairly complicated system, it may not be practical to write an entire code in Assembly language, and we will study C/C++ programming in the following chapters.

Texas Instruments provides a TI compiler that is integrated with Code Composer Studio. We will follow the TI assembler convention and use TI compiler and Code Composer Studio for Assembly programming. For more details of the TI assembler convention, readers can examine MSP430 Assembly Language Tools document [10].

Assembly Language Project

As described in Chapter 2, users can create a simple test project. Specifically, this was a C/C++ project. Users can perform a similar task to create a new assembly language project.

Using Code Composer Studio, users can choose the following selections to open a "New CCS Project" window.

> *File -> New -> CCS Project*

Users can see a *New CCS Project* window as shown in Figure 4.1. For the assembly test project, users can choose an "Empty Assembly-only Project". The proper MCU name that is "MSP430FR5994" needs to be selected. In this example, the project name was entered as "asm_test". However, users can choose any preferred project name.

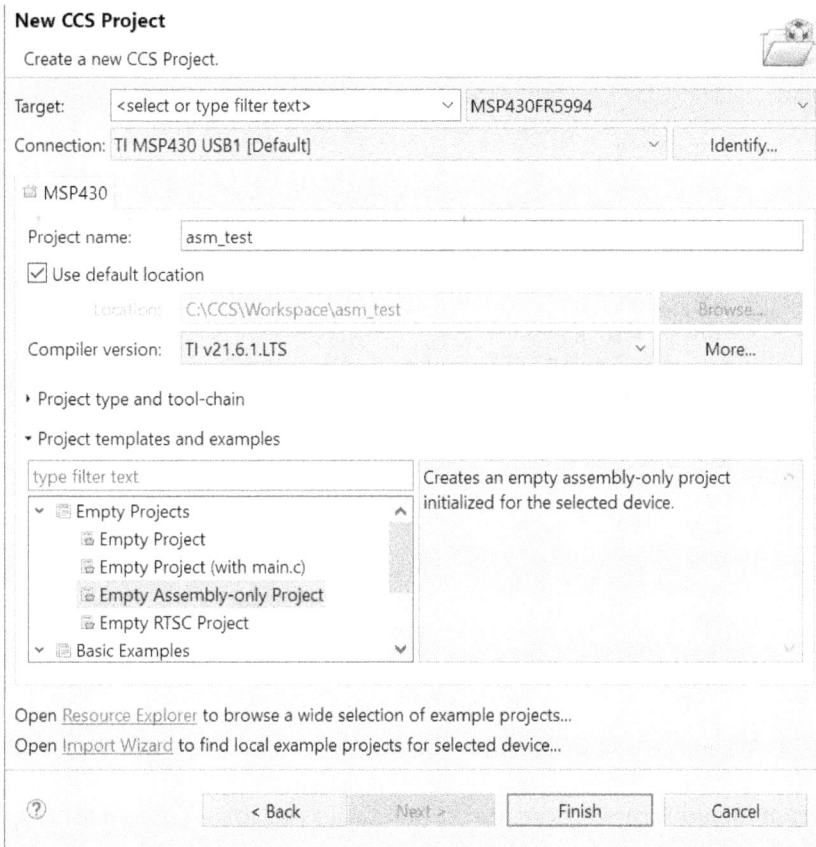

Figure 4.1. New Assembly CCS project.

Once the project is created, users can find an assembly program on the left side of the program window. In this case, the file name is "main.asm" as shown in Figure 4.2

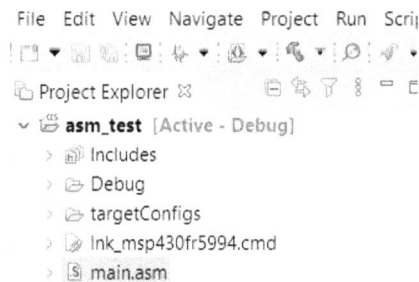

Figure 4.2. Assembly source file.

Users can open the file. It is a pre-filled text file. Users can edit the file to enter an assembly code. As an example, an assembly test program is shown in Program 4.1, users can enter this assembly test program.

```
        .cdecls C,LIST,"msp430.h"
        .def   RESET
        .text
        .retain
        .retainrefs
RESET:
        mov.w #__STACK_END, SP  ; stack init.
        mov.w #WDTPW|WDTHOLD, &WDTCTL  ; hold the watchdog timer
        bic.w  #LOCKLPM5, &PM5CTL0  ; clear LOCKLPM5 bit
        mov.w #12, R10  ; R10<-12
        mov.w #10, R11  ; R11<-10
        mov.w R10, R12  ; R12<-R10
        add.w  R11, R12  ; R12<-R12+R11
        mov.w R10, R13  ; R13<-R10
        sub.w  R11, R13  ; R13<-R13-R11
_loop:
        jmp _loop  ; branch
        nop
        .global __STACK_END
        .sect  .stack
        .sect  ".reset"
        .short  RESET
```

Program 4.1. Assembly test program.

This program includes move, add, and subtract instructions. When users type and enter an assembly code, it would be helpful to know that proper indentations or tabs need to be kept. Once users can make this test code work, they can modify this test program to create their own assembly program to perform a complicated task.

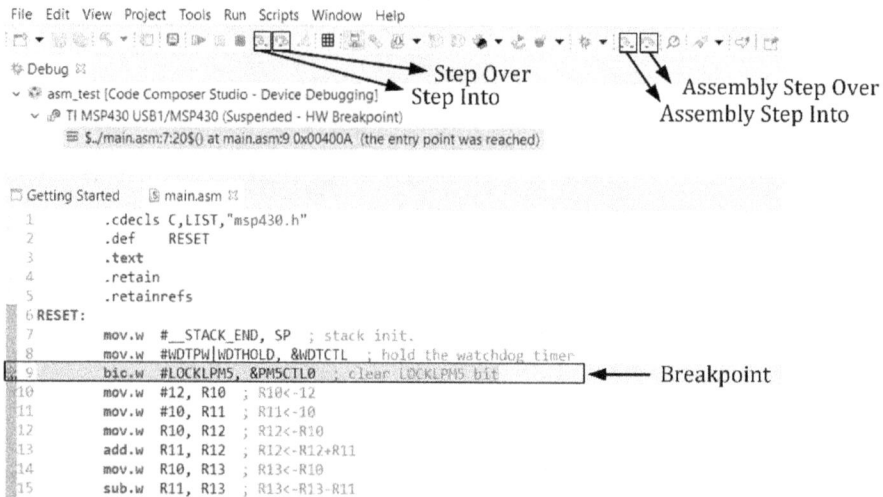

Figure 4.3. Debugging environment for Assembly language.

For debugging purposes, users can access "step into" or "step over" to step through the program. These "step into" and "step over" icons are shown in Figure 4.3. They are useful in debugging a program in C/C++ language. Users can access "assembly step into" or "assembly step over" instead. Users can set a breakpoint as shown in Figure 4.2. Breakpoints are useful in debugging a program. Once the program gets started in debug mode, the program will suspend at the line where users set the breakpoint. Next, users can step through the assembly code.

Now, let us examine a functional assembly program. A simple LED blink example in Assembly language will be presented in the following sub-section,

LED Blink Program in Assembly Language

A test program that can blink an LED in C language was presented previously in Chapter 2. In this section, an Assembly program that can blink an LED is presented. This Assembly LED blink program is shown in Program 4.2.

```
                .cdecls C,LIST,"msp430.h"
                .def   RESET
                .text
                .retain
                .retainrefs
RESET:
                mov.w  #__STACK_END, SP  ; stack init.
                mov.w  #WDTPW|WDTHOLD, &WDTCTL  ; hold the watchdog timer
                bic.b  #LOCKLPM5, &PM5CTL0  ; clear LOCKLPM5 bit
                bis.b  #0x01, &P1DIR  ; P1DIR (P1.0)
                bis.b  #0x01, &P1OUT  ; P1OUT (P1.0)
_loop:
                xor.b  #0x01, &P1OUT  ; XOR
                mov.w  #0xF400, R10  ; R10<-0xF400
_lp1:
                dec.w  R10  ; decrement
                cmp.w  #0x00, R10  ; compare
                jne  _lp1  ; conditional branch
                jmp  _loop  ; branch
                nop
                .global __STACK_END
                .sect  .stack
                .sect  ".reset"
                .short  RESET
```

Program 4.2. Assembly LED blink program.

This program sets the first bit of P1 direction register (P1DIR) using the "*bis.b #0x01, &P1DIR*" instruction. And, the program sets the first bit of P1 output register (P1OUT) using the "*bis.b #0x01, &P1OUT*" instruction. On an MSP430FR5994 Launchpad board, a red LED is physically connected to the pin related to P1.0. Based on this hardware configuration, the LED can be controlled to be turned on or off by the value of the first bit of Port 1.

In the main assembly loop (_loop), a bitwise XOR operation using an **xor** instruction is used to toggle the first bit in the P1OUT register. This program executes the code block labeled as "_lp1". This is a code block for a delay function. In this _lp1 block, the value of the register R10 gets decreased. Using a **cmp** compare instruction, the status flags can be updated. Depending on the results, the "jne _lp1" instruction can be executed. When the R10 becomes zero, the program can branch to _loop and will keep repeating the "_loop" code block. Thus, when the program is running successfully, users can see that a red LED (LED1) on an MSP430FR5994 Launchpad board is blinking.

We have briefly mentioned the P1 direction register and P1 output register. These registers are related to General-purpose I/Os. In the following chapter, we will study more detail about General-purpose I/Os in an MSP430FR5994 MCU.

MSP430X extended instructions

An MSP430X CPU is a 16-bit CPU, and it supports MSP430X extended instructions to handle 20-bit operations. To give an explanation, an example assembly program that handles 20-bit data is shown in Program 4.3.

```
            .cdecls C,LIST,"msp430.h"
            .def   RESET
            .text
            .retain
            .retainrefs
RESET:
            mov.w  #__STACK_END, SP ; stack init.
            mov.w  #WDTPW|WDTHOLD, &WDTCTL  ; hold the watchdog timer
            bic.w  #LOCKLPM5, &PM5CTL0  ; clear LOCKLPM5 bit
            movx.a #0x22000, R10 ; R10<-0x22000
            movx.a #0x11000, R11 ; R11<-0x11000
            movx.a R10, R12 ; R12<-R10
            addx.a R11, R12 ; R12<-R12+R11
            movx.a R10, R13 ; R13<-R10
            subx.a R11, R13 ; R13<-R13-R11
_loop:
            jmp _loop ; branch
            nop
            .global __STACK_END
            .sect  .stack
            .sect  ".reset"
            .short RESET
```

Program 4.3. MSP430X extended instruction test program.

In this program, the registers R10 and R11 can store the values of 0x22000 and 0x11000, respectively. The result of the addition of these two values is to be stored in R12. The result of the subtraction is to be stored in R13.

MSP430X extended instructions can be used when the capability of the 16-bit address or data length is limited or exceeded. MSP430X extended instructions can handle the 20-bit address range. In an MSP430FR5994 MCU, a portion of FRAM can be accessed using 16-bit address instructions, and the rest of the FRAM located at the address range that is higher than 64 KB can be accused using MSP430X extended instructions.

Chapter 5. General-Purpose I/O

A general-purpose input/output (GPIO) module in a microcontroller typically includes circuits that can be used in reading digital input signals or generating digital output signals through external I/O pins. A peripheral in microcontroller is typically a device, module, or a part of circuits other than a CPU and a memory device that can be used for interfacing with systems outside of the microcontroller. In this aspect, a GPIO module is a peripheral that can be used for interfacing external circuits and devices. GPIO modules are useful for various applications.

Functional GPIO Block Diagram

An MSP430FR5994IPZ IC model has 80 pins. Some of the pins are connected to internal GPIO circuit blocks. For each pin, there are similarities in GPIO configurations, but they are slightly different from each other because each pin may have been designed to provide different functions.

An MSP430FR5994 IC has multiple digital I/O ports such as P1~P8, PA~PD, and PJ. There are internal GPIO registers associated with these names of ports. While some ports have less, one port can be found that there are eight associated I/O pins. For instance, for P1.0, Port 1 is the relevant port. In this port, there are several registers such as P1DIR and P1OUT using this port name of P1. In these registers, the first least significant bit (LSB) is the relevant bit for P1.0. And this bit is associated with a specific physical pin. In this book, for ease of explanation, this physical pin can be simply referred to as P1.0.

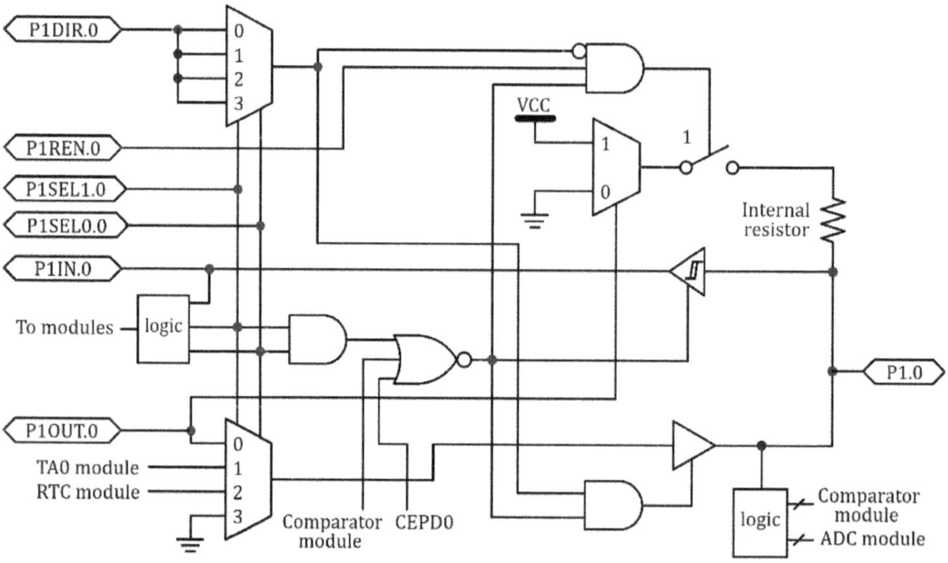

Figure 5.1. Simplified functional block diagram for P1.0 [2].

In this chapter, Port 1 (P1) is selected as an example to explain the functions of a GPIO module. Other ports have similar configurations; however, there are clear differences because each port may provide different functions. For more details, readers can examine the documents provided by the manufacturer [2].

Port 1 (P1) is associated with specific I/O pins including eight pins. These eight pins are related to P1.0~P1.7. To simplify the explanations, let us choose P1.0 as an example. Figure 5.1 shows a simplified functional block diagram for P1.0.

This functional block diagram shown in the figure does not necessarily represent the physical circuit implementation on a chip; however, it can be used to help readers understand the functional behavior. There are various registers related to Port 1. Let us examine the functional behavior based on each of these registers.

Direction Register (P1DIR)

The direction register of P1 is named P1DIR. Each bit in P1DIR register can select the direction of the associated I/O pin. If the first least significant bit (LSB) of the P1DIR is 0, the direction of P1.0 is *input*. If the first LSB of the P1DIR is 1, the direction of P1.0 is *output*. For instance, if the P1DIR is 1, the direction of P1.0 is *output*.

If the direction of a pin is supposed to be input, however, if it would be accidentally configured as output instead, in the unfortunate case, it might cause a hardware problem. Users need to be cautious in configuring output directions if they are debugging a system with a potential hardware issue.

Output Register (P1OUT)

When the direction is configured as *output*, each bit in P1OUT register can determine the output signal of the corresponding I/O pin. First, the direction of the pin needs to be configured as *output*. Then, the logical level of the output can be low, if the associated bit of the P1OUT register is cleared. Or, the logical level of the output can be high, if the associated bit of the P1OUT register is set.

For instance, for P1.0, the direction of the pin can be configured as *output* by setting the first LSB of the P1DIR. Then, if P1OUT is 0, the logical level of the associated pin of P1.0 can be low. Or, if P1OUT is 1, the logical level of the associated pin of P1.0 can be high.

Pull-up or Pull-down Resister Enable Register (P1REN)

A GPIO module has internal resistors as shown in Figure 5.1. Internal resistors can be enabled by setting P1REN register. Next, the corresponding pins need to be properly configured as input in order to enable these internal resistors. Then, they can be configured either pull-up or pull-down depending on the values of P1OUT as shown in Table 5.1.

According to the datasheet [2], this typical value of the internal resistor is 35 kΩ. This is not a high precision resistor, and it may have a wide process variation.

P1REN.y	P1DIR.y	P1OUT.y	I/O configuration
0	0	0	Input
0	0	1	Input
0	1	0	Output
0	1	1	Output
1	0	0	Input / internal pull-down resistor
1	0	1	Input / internal pull-up resistor
1	1	0	Output
1	1	1	Output

Table 5.1. I/O port configuration [9].

Users can configure GPIO registers in order to use this internal resistor as a pull-up or pull-down resistor without the need to place an external resistor. This technique can be useful and effective depending on circuits of the system and applications.

Input Registers (P1IN)

When the direction is configured as *input* by clearing bits in P1DIR register, the associated pins would function as *input*. In this state, the logical level of each bit of P1IN register will follow the same logical level of the corresponding I/O pin.

For instance, for P1.0, the direction can be configured as *input* by clearing the first LSB of the P1DIR. Then, the value of the first LSB of P1IN gets updated to be the digital value depending on the input signal of P1.0.

As shown in Figure 5.1, the first LSB of input register P1IN can read the logical level of P1.0 through a Schmitt trigger. The analog voltage level at the pin of P1.0 can be converted to a digital value through the Schmitt trigger.

From the diagram, it can be seen that there is status that the values of P1IN can get updated even the direction is configured as output. Readers can examine this behavior by generating a logical level for a certain pin and checking the value of input register relevant to the pin.

Function Select Registers (P1SEL1, P1SEL0)

Most of pins in an MSP430FR5994 MCU are internally multiplexed with other relevant peripheral modules. This means that they can provide many functions. For instance, P1SEL1 and P1SEL0 registers are used to select the function of P1.

There are possible I/O functions based on PSEL1 and PSEL0 registers as shown in Table 5.2. When both bits of P1SEL1 and P1SEL0 are cleared, the function of the associated pin is a GPIO function. Other than this case of the configuration, there are three alternate functions. The function assignments may vary depending on the pin. For more information, users can refer to the datasheet [2].

For instance, a physical pin number 1 can function as a typical GPIO for P1.0. Or, it is possible to make it generate digital signals using Timer_A0 instead depending on the value of P1SEL1 and P1SEL0 registers. By selecting an alternate function, this pin may not function simply as a GPIO function.

P1SEL1.y	P1SEL0.y	I/O function
0	0	GPIO
0	1	Alternate function / Primary module
1	0	Alternate function / Secondary module
1	1	Alternate function / Tertiary module

Table 5.2. I/O function selection [9].

In some ports, when one of the alternate functions is selected, PxDIR register may not necessarily control the pin direction. It may vary depending on the pin. Developers may refer to the datasheet [2] to gain the understanding of the behavior of the relevant available functions.

Port Interrupts

For the interrupt capability of Port1, P1 Interrupt Enable Register (P1IE) needs to be enabled. P1 interrupt flags are associated with P1IFG bits. Each bit of P1IFG can be set when the selected signal edge occurs at the corresponding pin. The interrupt edge can be configured. Interrupt Edge Select Registers (P1IES) make pins responsive to either low-to-high or high-to-low transitions. Ports interrupt configuration may vary depending on the ports. For more information, users can refer to the datasheet [2].

LEDs and Buttons on MSP430FR5994 Launchpad

An MSP430FR5994 Launchpad board has two LEDs (LED1 and LED2) and two push buttons (S1 and S2) as shown in Figure 5.2. The LED1 is connected to P1.0, and it is a red LED. Shunt jumper JP7 can free up P1.0 because it disconnects from the LED1. The LED2 is a green LED, and it is connected to P1.1.

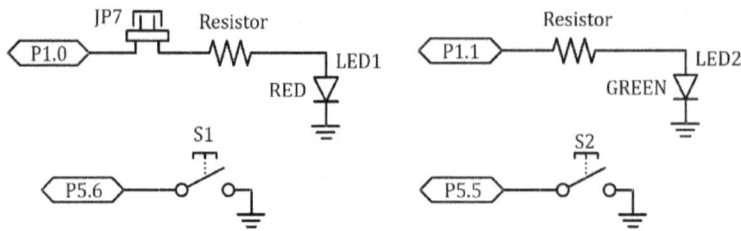

Figure 5.2. LEDs and push buttons on MSP430FR5994 Launchpad board [2][7].

Two push buttons (S1 and S2) are mounted on the board. P5.6 and P5.5 are connected to S1 and S2, respectively. For S1, if the push button is pressed, P5.6 can be 0. However, if the push button is not pressed, P5.6 could be at a high impedance state, and the BIT6 of P5IN may not be relevant to the physical push button state. Therefore, in this case, a pull-up resistor can be placed at the pin of P5.6.

The pull-up resistor can be an additional external resistor placed between the pin and the push button. If the performance of the push button is not a primary concern, an internal pull-up resistor can be used. The pull-up register can be configured using P1REN register as we studied previously.

Assuming the pull-up resistor is configured properly, let us revisit the behavior of this switch. If the push button is not pressed, P5.6 can read 1 properly due to the pull-up resistor connection. If the push button is pressed, P5.6 can read 0. In order to understand this behavior, we can write a simple code to test the S1 button and the red LED.

Button Test Program

The button test program is shown in Program 5.1. In this program, the S1 button and the red LED (LED1) will be used. In this code, an internal pull-up resistor is configured for P5.6. In the while loop, it checks whether the associated bit of input register of P5.6 is set or not. In the parentheses, it performs a masking operation. This technique is to obtain a relevant bit only from the P5IN register. Therefore, when a user presses the button, the first bit of output register P1 will be set and the red LED will be turned on.

```
#include <msp430.h>
int main(void) {
  WDTCTL = WDTPW | WDTHOLD;  // hold the watchdog timer
  PM5CTL0 &= ~LOCKLPM5;  // clear LOCKLPM5 bit
  P1DIR |= 0x01;  // output direction (P1.0)
  P1OUT &= ~0x01;  // clear the output (P1.0)
  P5DIR &= ~0x40;  // input direction (P5.6)
  P5REN |= 0x40;  // enable internal resistor (P5.6)
  P5OUT |= 0x40;  // pull-up resistor (P5.6)
  while (1){
```

```
    if ((P5IN & 0x40)!=0)  // read P5IN and perform masking
      P1OUT &= ~0x01;  // clear (P1.0)
    else
      P1OUT |= 0x01;  // set (P1.0)
  }
  return 0;
}
```

Program 5.1. Button test program in C/C++.

Debouncing Switches

We studied the behavior and the test program for a push button switch. We will study more about the push button switch behavior and switch applications. Push buttons are electrical components commonly used in electronics applications. The input signals from push buttons can be asynchronous, and, practically, the signals may not be electronically clean. This means that the transition is not clean between 0 and 1 when a button is pressed or released.

This behavior is described in Figure 5.3. This figure shows the signal from a switch circuit as the button is pressed or released. Roughly, the logic value was changing from 1 to 0, and it also was changing back to 1. However, you can see the noise fluctuating during the transitions. This random behavior is related to switch bounce. In order to avoid unexpected results, developers may make an effort to process and handle this non-ideal behavior. This is related to debouncing switches. The methods of resolving this issue include hardware and/or software approaches.

Figure 5.3. Switch bounce.

Hardware Approaches (Debouncing Switches)

Figure 5.4 shows simple hardware switch debouncers. The circuit on the left has one RC filter and one inverter logic gate. This is simple, but this can be effective if the parameters of the RC filter are designed properly. In this configuration, the charging time may not be balanced. In order to control the charge time, a diode can be used as shown on the right side.

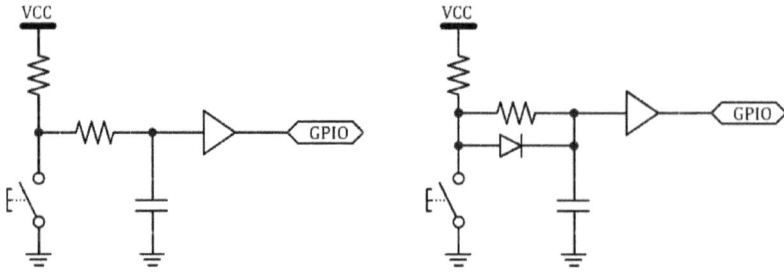

Figure 5.4. A simple switch debouncer.

A better hardware approach is to use two cross-coupled NAND gates to form a simple Set-Reset (SR) latch, and it also needs to use a double-throw switch as shown in Figure 5.5. Two pull-up resistors may pass a logical high level, while the switch may pass a logical low level. This approach can be effective, but it comes with non-trivial extra cost of hardware components.

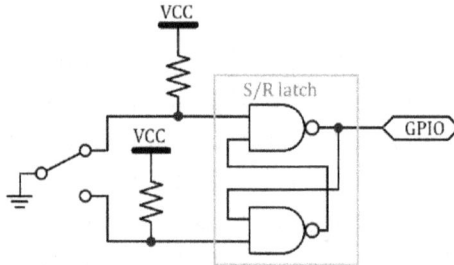

Figure 5.5. Switch debouncer using SR Latch.

Software Approaches (Debouncing Switches)

Software debounce approaches includes simple to complex algorithms. The software routines could become more complex depending on the number of buttons. Using software approaches, developers may resolve this non-ideal behavior at some level even without completely understanding the characteristics of unwanted noise. However, it is a good idea to perform testing to obtain the behavior of the noise as it may vary depending on a system. One of the simple software approaches is to delay the reading or processing the next button input status using a proper time delay obtained by measurements and testing. Generally, the slow read rate can ignore some of the noise and may seem to resolve most of the problems. However, one downside is a slow response. Developers may need to make an effort to determine an optimum delay for their specific embedded system.

Keypad Matrix

It is common to find electronics applications with many switches. For instance, for a computer keyboard, it may have more than 100 switches. For the applications with many switches, instead of using each GPIO pin per switch, the connection of the switches can be formed as an array or matrix. Therefore, the input status of many switches can be read and processed using a smaller number of GPIO pins.

As an example, let us consider a 16-keypad module. There are many 16 keypad modules including a 16-keypad module from Vellman® [11]. Figure 5.6 shows a generic 16-key keypad component, and each key includes one switch. 16 keys are connected in array or matrix.

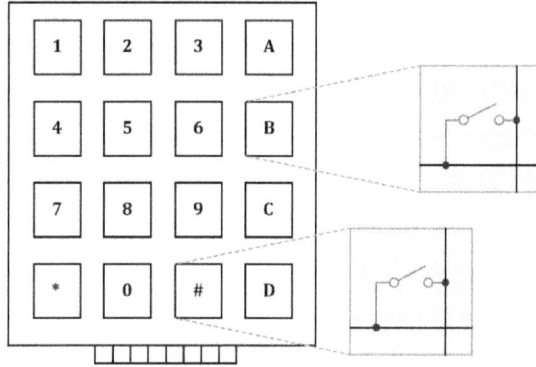

Figure 5.6. Keypad matrix.

A keypad component drawn as an abstract block diagram is shown Figure 5.7. The pin arrangement is also described in the figure. For a 16-keypad module, there can be 4 rows and 4 columns. Until one of the switches is pressed, none of the lines has been connected to each other. For instance, if key 5 is pressed, ROW2 and COL2 lines become connected to each other.

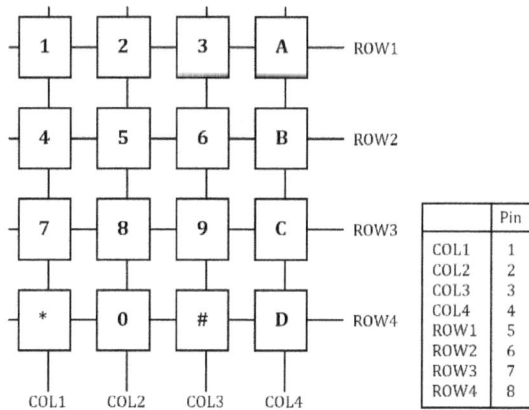

	Pin
COL1	1
COL2	2
COL3	3
COL4	4
ROW1	5
ROW2	6
ROW3	7
ROW4	8

Figure 5.7. Keypad matrix connection [11].

Now, a keypad component is connected to an MSP430FR5994 Launchpad board as shown in Figure 5.8.

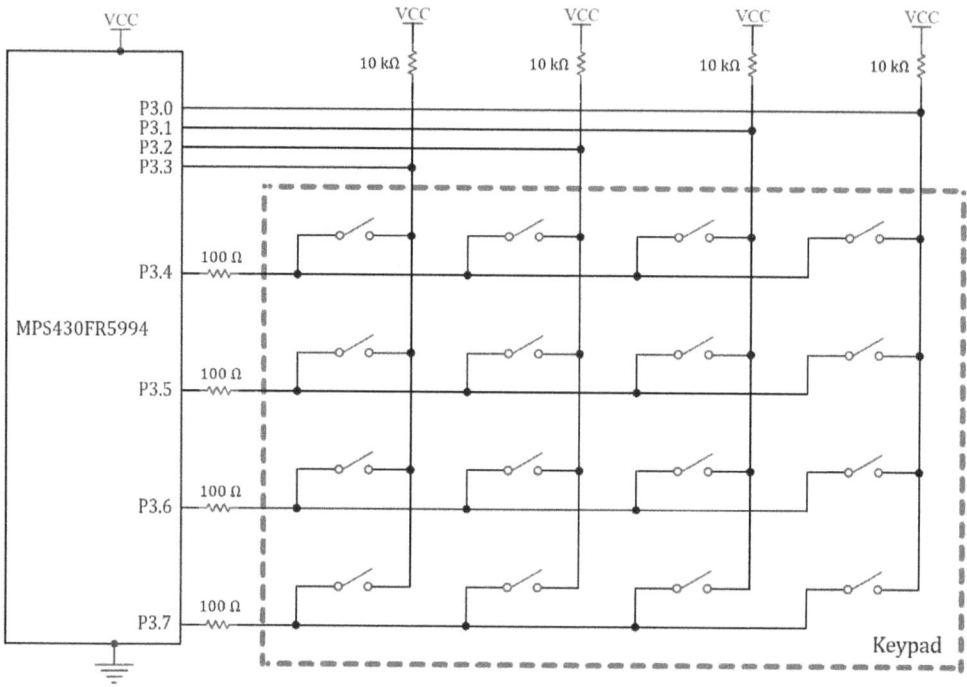

Figure 5.8. Keypad matrix example.

Eight pins are connected to P3.0 ~ P3.7. External pull-up resistors at P3.0 ~ P3.3 are placed. Four resistors were connected at P3.4, P3.5, P3.6, and P3.7. These resistors were added for protection.

For a control program, a proper port configuration is essential. The port directions for P3.0 ~ P3.3 need to be configured as input, and the port directions for P3.4 ~ P3.7 need to be configured as output.

The push button status can be determined by scanning process. First, let us control P3.4 is to be a logical low level, and the rest pins of P3.5, P3.6, and P3.7 are to be logical high levels. In this state, the button state of ROW1 can be read through P3.0 ~ P3.3. For instance, in this state, one button on the far right in this row is pressed. Then, P3.0 can read a logical low level and the rest of them can read logical high levels.

For the next step, P3.5 is controlled to be a logical low level and the rest ports of P3.4, P3.6, and P3.7 are controlled to be logical high levels. In this state, the button state of ROW2 can be read. After taking two more similar steps for the rest of ROW3 and ROW4, it will complete a scanning cycle, and the position of the button that was pressed can be determined.

This scanning process can detect not only the response of one button but also multiple keypad responses. However, the detection of multiple keys pressed in the same column might cause shorting power to the ground. Some keypad models have internal resistance. For these keypad models, it may not result in a critical issue. However, if the matrix keypad connections are made using individual switches without protection resistors, it may cause a critical condition that causes shorting power to ground. In this reason, as shown in Figure 5.8, extra resistors for protections were added to avoid potential excessive current conditions.

On a BH EDU board, this protection scheme was applied. Moreover, external pull up resistors were placed. Users need jumper wires to connect the proper headers for the keypad and their Launchpad board headers.

Chapter 6. Register level C/C++ programming

MCUs can execute machine code that consists of digital numbers written for the machine. For low level programming, users can write a program in Assembly language. An assembler can convert assembly code to machine code. Assembly language is more human friendly than machine code. Assembly Language can effectively describe the low-level behavior of an MCU. However, if a user would choose to describe a complex behavior of a microcontroller application in Assembly language only, it might have taken an excessive amount of effort in development. In this reason, a higher-level abstraction can help in writing a program for a complex system. C or C++ can be a reasonable choice for some microcontroller applications. C/C++ language is a higher level of abstraction than Assembly language.

There are several styles of C/C++ programming in the development of microcontroller applications. One of the low-level approaches is register level C programming. In this approach, the level of abstraction is not very high. This method is related to controlling registers directly to gain access to an MCU. This method helps developers understand low-level hardware and software aspects of their microcontroller application in development. And it can help in learning fundamental concepts and behavior of a microcontroller.

In this book, for C/C++ language programming, it begins with learning about an MSP430FR5994 MCU using this register level C/C++ programming. Later in this book, we will learn about higher-level abstraction styles of C/C++ programming using TI driver library and real-time operating system.

Conventions

For MSP430FR5994 C/C++ language programming, there are several conventions that users can use. For instance, if users want to generate a logical high level for P1.0, they can write a code line in C/C++ as follows:

```
P1OUT = 1;
```

In order to make this code line work as intended, the direction needs to be configured properly. It is assumed that the direction was configured to be *output*. In this example, the decimal number of 1 is used. A hexadecimal number is useful in describing a digital system. A hexadecimal number can be used instead, and the following code lines are equivalent.

```
P1OUT = 0x01;
```

```
P1OUT = 01h;
```

Moreover, there are predefined names such as for common numbers in the MSP430 header. They are BIT0 ~ BIT7. For instance, BIT0 is the same as 0x01, BIT1 is the same as 0x02, and so forth. This can be a convenient way of describing the one bit of a register. Using the predefined names, the following line is equivalent.

    P1OUT = BIT0;

A number can be expressed using a shift operator. For instance, 1 << 1 means 0x02 because it performs one left bit shift using 1. This can result in the same number as BIT1. For instance, 1 << 2 means 0x04, and it is the same as BIT2. Therefore, the following line is an equivalent expression.

    P1OUT = 1 << 0;

The shift operations in C/C++ language can be processed by the compiler. An equivalent expression in this chapter does not mean it would result in the same assembly code or machine code.

Each developer may prefer different styles when they write a program. The choice is also dependent on the functions that the microcontroller can provide. This means that readers may find the use of these conventions in source code written by others. So, it would be useful to understand these common conventions.

Bit Access

Let us revisit the code line of P1OUT=0x01. This code line can set the first least significant bit (LSB). This is the desired behavior. However, this code line clears other bits. For instance, if a device is connected to P1.1, this code may also clear the output of P1.1. This means that there is a chance that unwanted bits could be accidentally affected. This is the reason that it is important to access and update relevant bits only. Let us consider the following code line.

    P1OUT |= 0x01;

This is one of the ways to set the first bit only while it can leave other bits unchanged. To understand the behavior, let us expand it, and it is P1OUT = P1OUT | 0x01. The behavior can be understood better in this expanded form. However, it is not common to write a code line like this expanded form because this might not generate an efficient code for the compiler.

Now, let us consider a method that can clear the first LSB only and can leave other bits unchanged, we can write the code line as follows.

    P1OUT &= ~0x01;

To understand the behavior, let us expand it. It is P1OUT = P1OUT & ~0x01. Although the behavior can be understood better in this expanded form, for the same reason, it is not common to write a code line like this expanded form.

Hardware connections of microcontroller applications may vary. Embedded system developers may need to be careful in configuration and accessing GPIO pins to avoid the access of unwanted GPIO pins that are connected to external devices. In this reason, it is recommended to access the relevant bits only in a port such as using the described selectively set or clear conventions when applicable and possible.

Chapter 7. Timer basics

Timers are versatile and useful peripherals for microcontroller applications. An MSP430FR5994 MCU has a watchdog timer as well as general-purpose 16-bit timers. In this book, we will learn about a Timer_A module, which is a 16-bit timer,

Clock Sources

One of key parameters in a timer is the selection of a clock source. First, let us study a clock system in an MSP430FR5994 MCU. Several clock sources and system clock signals are available to use in an MSP430FR5994 MCU.

External oscillators can be used in providing clock signals for an MSP430FR5994 MCU. A low-frequency oscillator (LFXT) such as a 32.768 kHz crystal or a high frequency oscillator (HFXT) such as a 4 MHz crystal can be placed and connected to the MCU.

An MSP430FR5994 MCU can be operated without any external oscillators. It has an internal digitally controlled oscillator (DCO) with selectable frequencies. There are several calibrated DCO frequency settings.

Moreover, an MSP430FR5994 MCU has an internal Very-Low-Power Low-Frequency Oscillator (VLO). It also has MODCLK that is an internal oscillator.

Clock Signals

An MSP430FR5994 supports several clock signals in the clock module. Clock signals include Auxiliary clock (ACLK), Master clock (MCLK), and Subsystem master clock (SMCLK)

Auxiliary clock (ACLK) is selectable as LFXTCLK, VLOCLK, or LFMODCLK. ACLK can be divided by up to 32, and it can be used by peripheral modules.

Master clock (MCLK) is selectable as LFXTCLK, VLOCLK, LFMODCLK, DCOCLK, MODCLK, or HFXTCLK. MCLK can be divided by up to 32, and it can be used by CPU, and peripheral modules.

Subsystem master clock (SMCLK) is selectable as LFXTCLK, VLOCLK, LFMODCLK, DCOCLK, MODCLK, HFXTCLK. SMCLK can be divided by up to 32, and it can be used by peripheral modules.

In Chapter 2, we created a new CCS project by selecting "Empty Project (with main)", and we studied a program that can blink an LED. In this project setting, a master clock (MCLK) is configured to use a 1 MHz DCO clock.

In this project setting, SMCLK is also configured to use the 1 MHz DCO clock. Using this configuration, the waveform of SMCLK at 1 MHz is shown in Figure 7.1.

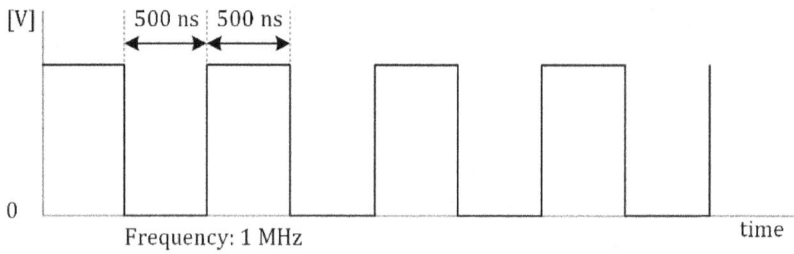

Figure 7.1. SMCLK waveform at 1 MHz.

In this book, we will provide program examples based on this clock source setting. However, as needed, users can change the frequency settings to use a higher clock frequency.

Timer_A

An MPS430FR5994 MCU has six 16-bit general-purpose timers. A Timer_A module includes a 16-bit timer and counter. A Timer_A module can provide up to multiple capture and compare register blocks, and the selected pins are connected to capture and compare register blocks. Timer_A modules can be used to generate PWM output signals. A simplified functional block diagram of Timer_A1 is shown in Figure 7.2.

An MSP430FR5994 MCU includes multiple Timer_A modules such as Timer_A0 to Timer_A4. There are similarities among the Timer_A modules. To simplify explanations, Timer_A1 module is selected in this chapter.

A clock source is selectable for Timer A1. TASSEL bits are associated with the selection of a clock source. The frequency of the selected clock source can be divided by two divider blocks. The divider settings can be configured by ID and TAIDEX bits. Then, at the rising edge of this clock signal, the timer TA1R value will be increased or decreased. There are capture and compare blocks, and specifically, they include TA1CCR0 capture and compare block to TA1CCR2 capture and compare block. And they are simply called TA1CCR0 block to TA1CCR2 block in this book.

The Timer_A1 module can be used to generate PWM signals, or it can be used as a capture function of digital signal. These functions are grayed out, and they can be found in the dotted boxes named OUTPUT MODE and CAPTURE MODE. In this chapter, we will focus on basic timer and compare functions. Later, in this book we will revisit this timer block to learn about these OUTPUT MODE and CAPTURE MODE functions.

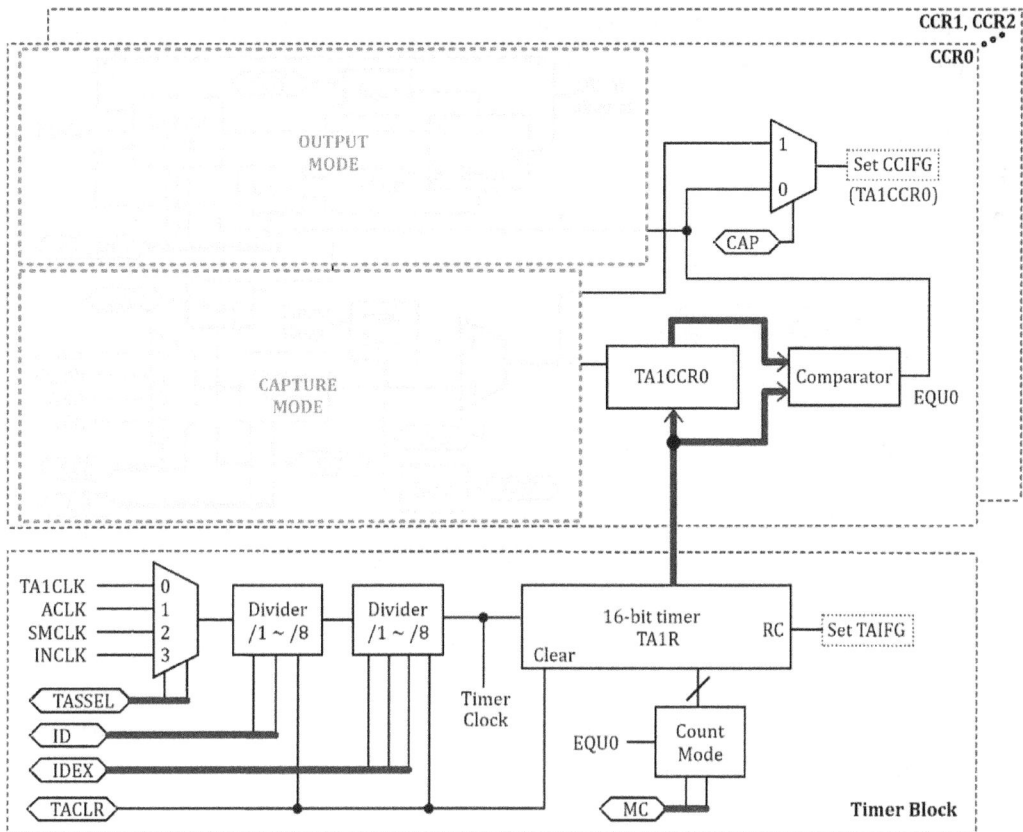

Figure 7.2. Simplified functional block diagram of Timer_A1 [9].

16-Bit Timer Counter

The timer register TA1R holds the value, and the value of the register can be increased or decreased. MC bits control this timer mode behavior. TACLR bit can clear the value of the TA1R register. Moreover, there is a TAIFG, which is an interrupt flag. It can be set when the value of the counter overflows and it rolls off to zero. Timer can be halted when MC bits are cleared.

As described, the clock source for Timer_A1 module is selectable. The choice depends on the functional requirements of the applications. In general, you can choose ACLK, if it is preferred to use a counter that is running slow for your application. If you need a counter that is running fast, you can choose SMCLK. The clock speed of the SMLCK is programmable.

As mentioned, the clock frequency of SMCLK is 1 MHz in the default project setting introduced in this book. If needed, this SMCLK clock can be slowed down using two dividers connected in series. ID bits can configure the divider up to 8, and the further division can be done up to 8 by setting TAIDEX bits.

For Timer _A1 module, a TA1CCR0 register in TA1CCR0 block can be found, and this register can be used to set the upper bound of the counter in certain timer modes.

Timer Modes

Timer modes are listed in Table 7.1. As described, if MC bits are cleared, the timer can be halted. Other than this MC bit state, the timer keeps counting up or down. If the MC bits are configured to 1, the operation of the timer is in Up mode.

Mode	MC bits	Description
Stop	0	Timer is halted.
Up	1	Timer counts up to TA1CCR0 value, then, rolls off to zero (Repeatedly)
Continuous	2	Timer counts up to 0xFFFF, then, rolls off to zero (Repeatedly)
Up/Down	3	The timer counts up to the TA1CCR0 value and counts down to zero (Repeatedly)

Table 7.1. Timer Modes [9].

In Up mode, the counter reaches the value of TA1CCR0; then it rolls off to zero. This is the pattern of operation, and it will keep repeating. This count pattern for Up mode is shown in Figure7.3. The value of TA1R keeps increasing, but it resets the counter when it reaches TA1CCR0.

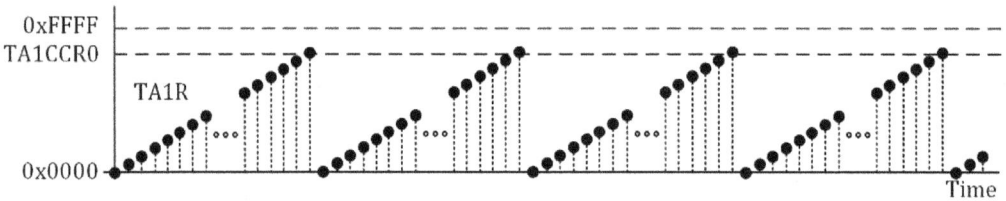

Figure 7.3. Count pattern for Up mode [9].

Let us examine the interrupt flag behaviors in up mode. The flag setting in Up mode is shown in Figure 7.4.

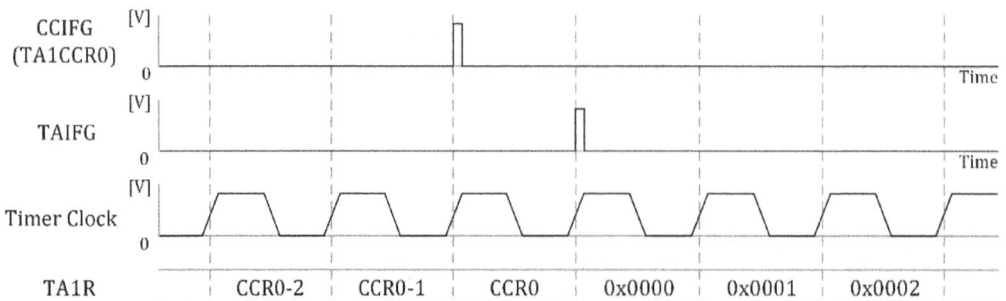

Figure 7.4. Counter and Flag behavior in Up mode [9].

There are two important interrupt flags associated with Timer_A1. They are CCIFG and TAIFG. The CCIFG is a part of TA1CCR0, and the TAIFG is a part of TA1CTL. There is one TAIFG in TA1. However, there are multiple CCIFGs in TA1. For instance, a CCIFG bit is in TA1CCR0 block. And there is another CCIFG bit in TA1CCR1 block.

In this Up mode, the counter behavior is dependent on CCIFG in TA1CCR0 block. As the counter reaches the value stored in TA1CCR0 register, a CCIFG interrupt flag is to be triggered. Then, as the counter is rolled off to zero, a TAIFG interrupt flag is going to be triggered.

Next, if MC bits are configured to 2, this operation of the timer is in Continuous mode. In this mode, the counter reaches 0xFFFF; then, it rolls off to zero. This count pattern in Continuous mode is shown in Figure7.5. This figure shows that the value of TA1R keeps increasing until 0xFFFF; then, it rolls off to zero.

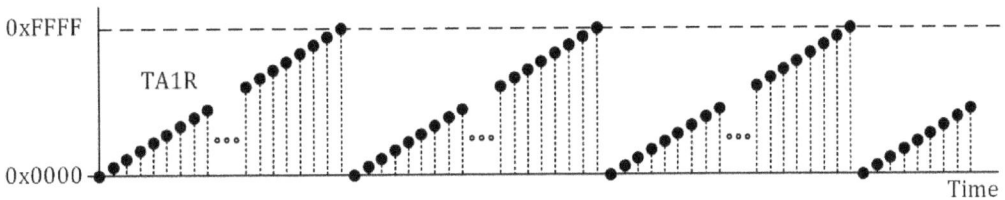

Figure 7.5. Count pattern for Continuous mode [9].

Let us examine an interrupt flag behavior as shown in Figure 7.6. Since this is in Continuous mode, a CCIFG is not necessarily relevant, but the behavior of TAIFG interrupt flag can be important. As the value of TA1R rolls off to zero, a TAIFG interrupt flag is to be triggered.

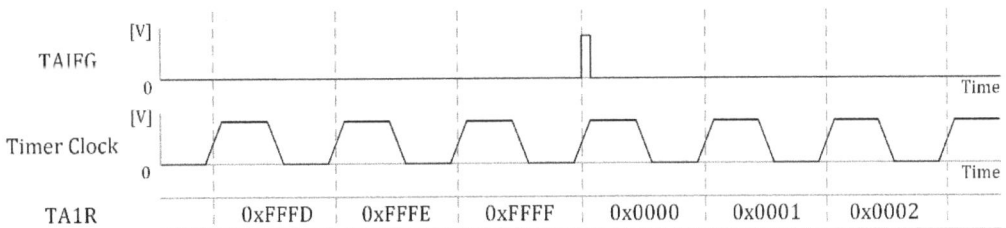

Figure 7.6. Counter and Flag behavior in Continuous mode [9].

A pulse generation program example is shown in Program 7.1. This code is based on the use of a CCIFG flag, and it is also based on a polling method. In this example, P8.0 is chosen to generate relevant output signal. The TA1CCR0 register is also simply called TA1CCR0 in this book. TA1CCR0 is initialized as 2000. TA1CTL is configured to use SMCLK as a clock source, and it is configured in Up mode. In the while loop, it keeps checking whether the CCIFG flag is set or not. If it is set, it toggles an output value of P8.0, and clears the CCIFG flag.

This program can generate a relevant digital signal through the pin of P8.0. It is recommended to use an oscilloscope to check this waveform. If successful, a square wave clock can be seen, and the frequency of the digital signal can be about 250 Hz.

```
#include <msp430.h>
int main(void) {
  WDTCTL = WDTPW | WDTHOLD;  // hold the watchdog timer
  PM5CTL0 &= ~LOCKLPM5; // clear LOCKLPM5 bit
  P8DIR |= BIT0; // output direction (P8.0)
  TA1CCR0 = 2000; // TA1CCR0 value
  TA1CTL = TASSEL_2 | MC_1 | TACLR; // TA1CTL setup
  while(1) {
    if ((TA1CCTL0 & CCIFG)!=0) { // check whether CCIFG is set
      P8OUT ^= BIT0; // toggle (P8.0)
      TA1CCTL0 &= ~CCIFG; // clear CCIFG flag
    }
  }
  return 0;
}
```

Program 7.1. Pulse generation program using CCIFG flag (Polling based).

Another pulse generation program example is shown in Program 7.2. This code is different because it is based on the use of a TAIFG flag instead. However, this program is also based on a polling method. There can be examples using interrupts. Interrupt-based program examples will be introduced in the next chapter,

In Program 7.2, P8.0 is the same choice to generate an output signal as shown in Program 7.1. TA1CCR0 is initialized as 2000, and TA1CTL configuration is the same as the one in Program 7.1. However, in Program 7.2, it is based on TAIFG flag instead. In the while loop, it keeps checking whether the TAIFG is set or not. If it is set, it will toggle an output value of P8.0, and it will clear the TAIFG flag. If successful, similar to the result of Program 7.1, a square wave clock can be seen, and the frequency of the digital signal can be about 250 Hz at P8.0.

```
#include <msp430.h>
int main(void) {
  WDTCTL = WDTPW | WDTHOLD;  // hold the watchdog timer
  PM5CTL0 &= ~LOCKLPM5; // clear LOCKLPM5 bit
  P8DIR |= BIT0; // output direction (P8.0)
  TA1CCR0 = 2000; // TA1CCR0 value
  TA1CTL = TASSEL_2 | MC_1 | TACLR; // TA1CTL setup
  while(1) {
    if ((TA1CTL & TAIFG)!=0) { // check whether TAIFG is set
      P8OUT ^= BIT0; // toggle (P8.0)
```

```
        TA1CTL &= ~TAIFG; // clear TAIFG flag
    }
  }
  return 0;
}
```

Program 7.2. Pulse generation program using TAIFG flag (Polling based).

Piezo buzzer

We studied program examples that can generate square wave clock signals. The clock frequency was within an audible frequency range. This could mean that an audible can be generated if we can use a proper component such as a piezo buzzer.

piezoelectric
disk element

piezo buzzer

Figure 7.7. Piezoelectric disk element and piezo buzzer.

A piezo buzzer has a piezoelectric disk element as shown in Figure 7.7. The word, Piezo, is from the Greek root, peizein, which means "to press." This is a transducer component. A transducer means that it can convert energy from one form to another form. In this case, piezoelectric disk element can convert the electrical energy to mechanical energy and vice versa. A piezo buzzer is a component with the piezoelectric disk element in a plastic package, which can be used as a small and low-cost speaker.

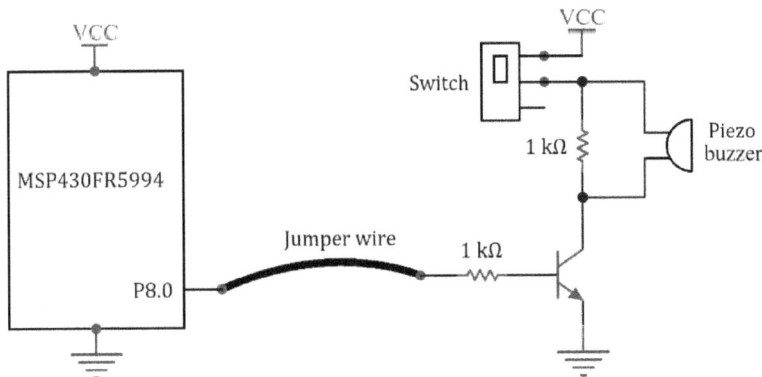

Figure 7.8. Piezo buzzer application.

A connection diagram for a piezo buzzer application is shown in Figure 7.8. It shows a piezo buzzer component, and it can be a small sized generic piezo buzzer. On a BH EDU board, TDK piezo buzzer model, PS1740P02E, is used [12].

A transistor and two resistors are used in this buzzer application. In addition, there is a switch (SW). This switch is not essential; however, it would be useful because it can cut off the sound immediately by isolating the power. The reason for adding this cut-off switch is to provide a method of turning off the buzzer, while users are developing an application. Otherwise, it could become uncomfortable as they have to hear the buzzer sound for a while. This switch can be simply replaced with a jumper.

If a developer needs to pursue a simpler circuit configuration, there is an alternative connection scheme. Instead of directly connecting a piezo buzzer and the pin of P8.0, it is recommended to add a resistor such as a 1kΩ resistor in series between the piezo buzzer and the pin of P8.0. The other node of the piezo buzzer pin needs to be connected to the ground.

Note	Freq. (Hz)	Note	Freq. (Hz)	Note	Freq. (Hz)
C4	261.626	C5	523.251	C6	1046.502
C#4	277.183	C#5	554.365	C#6	1108.731
D4	293.665	D5	587.330	D6	1174.659
D#4	311.127	D#5	622.254	D#6	1244.508
E4	329.628	E5	659.255	E6	1318.510
F4	349.228	F5	698.457	F6	1396.913
F#4	369.994	F#5	739.989	F#6	1479.978
G4	391.995	G5	783.991	G6	1567.982
G#4	415.305	G#5	830.609	G#6	1661.219
A4	440.000	A5	880.000	A6	1760.000
A#4	466.164	A#5	932.328	A#6	1864.656
B4	493.883	B5	987.767	B6	1975.533

Table 7.2. Selected frequencies of musical notes.

In case, users want to create a program that can generate a musical tone. As a reference, selected frequencies of musical notes are shown in Table 7.2. C4 is the middle C in a piano keyboard. The frequency is 261.626 Hz. The frequency you could hear using either Program 7.1 or Program 7.2 is about 250 Hz. It is the frequency between C4 and B3 musical notes. For an experiment, users can generate different frequencies to play a music scale. Different frequencies can be generated by changing the value of TA1CCR0 register. Next, users can create their own simple buzzer music song using these basic musical notes.

Chapter 8. Interrupt

A typical microcontroller has the capability to suspend what it is doing and process an interrupt service routine (ISR) upon the request of an interrupt service. This *interrupt* service can improve Response time, and it also can provide a capability that can process and run multiple tasks concurrently. However, there could be some problems if an *interrupt* request is not properly handled.

When an *interrupt* service is requested, its full context including registers, processor status, and some of the relevant data may need to be saved properly. When returned, the context may need to be restored properly. If there are shared data and they are not managed properly, the system may suffer from a shared data problem between concurrent tasks.

There can be non-maskable interrupt services, which cannot be disabled by a program routine or a user. Developers may need to understand the details of non-maskable interrupt services that may vary depending on different MCU models. Priorities of interrupt services were typically already defined in a hardware level. This could mean there can be a case where some interrupt services that the developer would use can be low priority interrupt services. In this case, the low priority services may suffer from latency. In this reason, for developers, it is recommended to understand the interrupt priority and handle the interrupt requests properly in their programs.

Interrupts in an MSP430FR5994 MCU

An MSP430FR5994 MCU can handle interrupt requests. First, registers related to an *interrupt enable* for a specific peripheral module and a *general interrupt enable* need to be properly configured to be enabled. Then, when there is an interrupt request from the specific peripheral, the MCU can execute a relevant interrupt service routine.

There are several interrupt types including System reset, Non-maskable, and Maskable. There can be several conditions that can trigger a system reset, which includes a power-on reset. For *Non-maskable interrupts* (NMIs), there are system NMI and user NMI. For NMIs, in general, the *general interrupt enable* (GIE) bit may not simply disable them. For maskable interrupts, the *general interrupt enable* (GIE) bit or individual *interrupt enable* bit can disable makable interrupts.

Interrupt priorities were already defined in a hardware level. The interrupt priorities can be used in determining an interrupt to be executed first if there are more than one pending interrupts.

Interrupt sources and interrupt vector addresses are shown in Table 8.1. From this table, interrupt priority information can be obtained. For instance, a watchdog timer interrupt request has a higher priority than a Port 1 interrupt request.

Interrupt Source	Address	Interrupt Source	Address
System Reset	0xFFFE	P2	0xFFD8
System NMI	0xFFFC	TA3	0xFFD6
User NMI	0xFFFA	TA3	0xFFD4
Comparator_E	0xFFF8	P3	0xFFD2
TB0	0xFFF6	P4	0xFFD0
TB0	0xFFF4	RTC_C	0xFFCE
Watchdog timer	0xFFF2	AES	0xFFCC
eUSCI_A0	0xFFF0	TA4	0xFFC8
eUSCI_B0	0xFFEE	TA4	0xFFCA
ADC12_B	0xFFEC	P5	0xFFC6
TA0	0xFFEA	P6	0xFFC4
TA0	0xFFE8	eUSCI_A2	0xFFC2
eUSCI_A1	0xFFE6	eUSCI_A3	0xFFC0
DMA	0xFFE4	eUSCI_B1	0xFFBE
TA1	0xFFE2	eUSCI_B2	0xFFBC
TA1	0xFFE0	eUSCI_B3	0xFFBA
P1	0xFFDE		
TA2	0xFFDC		
TA2	0xFFDA		

Table 8.1. Interrupt sources and interrupt vector addresses [2].

Memory addresses of the interrupt handlers are stored in the memory locations of the vector addresses. When an interrupt is accepted and processed, a relevant interrupt vector address can be accessed, and it can be used to branch and execute a relevant interrupt service routine (ISR).

I/O Port ISR

Program 8.1 shows an Interrupt based button and LED example. The function of this program is similar to the one shown in Program 5.1. In this code, P5IE register is used. Configuring this register, the interrupt for P5.6 is enabled. P5IES register is used to configure to be responsive to high-to-low transition. A general interrupt enable was configured properly to take an effect on processing interrupts.

In the program, there is a "Port5_ISR_handler" subroutine. This interrupt service routine (ISR) can be executed if a relevant Port 5 interrupt service is requested and processed. First, it checks whether the interrupt flag for BIT6 of Port 5 is set or not. If the flag is set, it will toggle the value of the output of P1.0. Since P1.0 is connected to a red LED, it will toggle the red LED. The program has a code line for a time delay. This function of this time delay is also for debouncing switch. Next, it clears the interrupt flag, and exits the interrupt service routine.

In the while loop, there is a code line of __no_operation(). As is, there is no particular task to be executed. Users can add their own task in this while loop as needed. Then, it can process this task in the while loop and the button process task concurrently.

This example program is functional; however, this program contains a bad coding practice that is not typically recommended in writing an ISR code. A good practice is to write an ISR code short as possible. This means it is a good idea to spend a short amount of time in an ISR routine and manage the program to spend most of CPU time in the main routine. However, in this ISR routine, an extra time delay was intentionally added. This was needed for the switch debounce. For this reason, this code may need to be revised. One of the possible solutions is to use a shared variable and process this variable in the main while loop to execute a short delay. Making an ISR short is very important and a recommended practice. This topic is related to software architectures that we will study in Chapter 12.

```c
#include <msp430.h>
int main(void) {
    WDTCTL = WDTPW | WDTHOLD;  // hold the watchdog timer
    PM5CTL0 &= ~LOCKLPM5; // clear LOCKLPM5 bit
    P1DIR |= BIT0; // output direction (P1.0)
    P5DIR &= ~BIT6; // input direction (P5.6)
    P5REN |= BIT6; // enable internal resistor
    P5OUT |= BIT6; // pull-up resistor
    P5IES |= BIT6; // interrupt on high-to-low transition
    P5IFG &= ~BIT6; // clear interrupt flag
    P5IE |= BIT6; // enable interrupt (P5.6)
    _enable_interrupt(); // enable general interrupt
    while(1) {
        no operation(); // no operation
    }
    return 0;
}


#pragma vector=PORT5_VECTOR
_interrupt void Port5_ISR_handler(void) {
    if(P5IFG & BIT6) {
        P1OUT ^= BIT0; // toggle (P1.0)
    }
    _delay_cycles(500); // debounce
    P5IFG &= ~BIT6; // clear interrupt flag
}
```

Program 8.1. Interrupt based button and LED program.

Timer_A1 ISR

In the previous chapter, we studied the timer_A1 and the two different programming examples. Both programs were based on a polling method. In this section, Interrupt based programs will be presented. Program 8.2 shows the Interrupt based pulse generation program using CCIFG.

In this code, CCIFG interrupt for TA1CCR0 block is enabled. This was achieved by the code line as follows: "TA1CCTL0 = CCIE;" As it was described previously, a general interrupt enable needs to be configured properly using the following code line: "_enable_interrupt();"

In the while loop, it toggles the pin of P1.0. In this program, the name of the ISR subroutine is "Timer1_A0_ISR". In the ISR, it can toggle the pin of P8.0. A CCIFG flag in TA1CCR0 block can be automatically reset when the Timer1_A0_ISR is served. In this reason, a code line that clears the CCIFG was not included. Therefore, this program can blink the red LED and it can generate digital clock signal concurrently.

A user can hear buzzer tone if a piezo buzzer is connected to the pin of P8.0. In the previous Chapter, it was suggested to write a simple piezo buzzer music as an experiment. Using this interrupt-based code, the simple piezo buzzer music program can be written easier and more efficiently.

This program is also a flexible clock generation method. A clock signal can be generated using a preferred GPIO pin. Users can modify the code to choose their own GPIO pin instead of the pin of P8.0.

```
#include <msp430.h>
int main(void) {
  WDTCTL = WDTPW | WDTHOLD;  // hold the watchdog timer
  PM5CTL0 &= ~LOCKLPM5; // clear LOCKLPM5 bit
  P1DIR |= BIT0; // output direction (P1.0)
  P8DIR |= BIT0; // output direction (P8.0)
  TA1CCR0 = 2000; // TA1CCR0 value
  TA1CTL = TASSEL_2 | MC_1 | TACLR; // TA1CTL setup
  TA1CCTL0 = CCIE; // enable CCIE
  _enable_interrupt(); // enable general interrupt
  while(1) {
    P1OUT ^= BIT0; // toggle (P1.0)
    _delay_cycles(250000); // delay
  }
  return 0;
}

#pragma vector = TIMER1_A0_VECTOR
_interrupt void Timer1_A0_ISR(void) {
  P8OUT ^= BIT0; // toggle (P8.0)
}
```

Program 8.2. Pulse generation program using CCIFG flag (Interrupt).

Now, pulse generation code using TAIFG flag is shown in program 8.3. In comparison with the code using CCIFG flag, this code based on TAIFG flag has a different interrupt configuration. For instance, in order to configure a TAIFG interrupt flag, TAIE bit was set in TA1CTL register.

```c
#include <msp430.h>
int main(void) {
    WDTCTL = WDTPW | WDTHOLD;  // hold the watchdog timer
    PM5CTL0 &= ~LOCKLPM5; // clear LOCKLPM5 bit
    P1DIR |= BIT0; // output direction (P1.0)
    P8DIR |= BIT0; // output direction (P8.0)
    TA1CCR0 = 2000; // TA1CCR0 value
    TA1CTL = TASSEL_2 | MC_1 | TAIE | TACLR; // TA1CTL setup
    _enable_interrupt(); // enable general interrupt
    while(1) {
        P1OUT ^= BIT0; // toggle (P1.0)
        _delay_cycles(500000); // delay
    }
    return 0;
}

#pragma vector = TIMER1_A1_VECTOR
_interrupt void Timer1_A1_ISR(void) {
    if((TA1CTL & TAIFG)!=0) { // check whether TAIFG is set
        P8OUT ^= BIT0; // toggle (P8.0)
        TA1CTL &= ~TAIFG; // clear TAIFG flag
    }
}
```

Program 8.3. Pulse generation program using TAIFG flag (Interrupt).

The name of the ISR subroutine in this program is "Timer_A1_ISR". This is a different one from the one used previously in the previous CCIFG based case. In this ISR, it checks whether TAIFG is set or not. If it is set, it can toggle the pin of P8.0. Then, it clears the TAIFG flag. Similar to the previous case, this code also can blink a red LED, and it can generate the clock signal concurrently. Apparently both Program 8.2 and Program 8.3 can perform similar behaviors for the ones we have seen in Chapter 7, however, the internal operations and programming routines are different.

Chapter 9. Display

In many embedded systems, it is common to use a small or large display module. The requirement for a product may vary, and there is a wide selection of the display modules. The display modules can be categorized in several ways. First, we can categorize it whether it is a monochrome or color display. It is common to see color displays in embedded systems. If a product does not require a color display, the implementation would become easier as a monochrome display can be selected instead. Next, we can categorize it as a graphic or a character display. A graphic display is common because the format of displaying data can be flexible and it is typically user friendly. One of the problems is that the development may take longer than a character display. If the requirement of the product is simply to display the numeric or character data, a character display may be a reasonable choice as it can reduce the developmental effort significantly. In this chapter, we will study and learn how to control a monochrome character liquid-crystal display (LCD) module.

Liquid Crystal Display (LCD)

A liquid-crystal display (LCD) is an electronically modulated optical device. It uses light modulating properties and polarizers. LCD does not emit light directly. It is used with a backlight display or a reflective part.

LCDs can be either positive or negative. This is dependent on the polarizer arrangement. For instance, a character on a positive LCD can be a black letter on a backlight color background. On the other hand, a character on a negative LCD can be a white color letter on a color backlight background.

A typical LCD module includes an LCD controller and an LCD glass. There are many small units in two polarizers between two electrodes on an LCD glass. An LCD controller can generate alternating voltages across the two electrodes. LCD segments glow when both of their back and front planes are enabled.

For an MSP430FR5994 MCU, in this book, we use the supply voltage of 3.3 V, and we will use an LCD module that can be operated in the voltage of 3.3 V, as it can minimize the circuit design effort for some of the examples in this book. However, it can be found easier to find an LCD module that can be operated in the supply voltage of 5 V. If readers choose to use a 5-V LCD module, they need to check the datasheet and the documents provided by the LCD manufacturer.

LCD module

As described, a 3.3-V LCD module is selected to make it work with an MSP430FR5994 MCU. The part number of the selected LCD is NHD-0216HZ-FSW-FBW-33V3C. There are many generic LCD modules with a similar programming method; however, this LCD model is the one mounted on a BH EDU board. For the reader who owns a generic LCD module, the theory and the programming method in this chapter can be applied since there are similarities. But, they may need to refer to the datasheet and documents from the LCD manufacturer carefully.

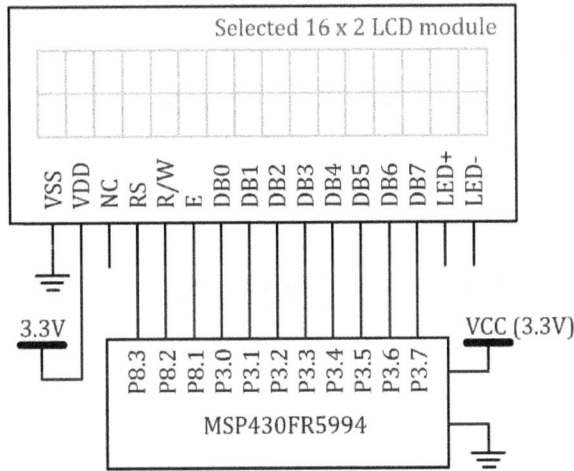

Figure 9.1. Connection diagram for the selected LCD module (NHD-0216HZ-FSW-FBW-33V3C).

The connection diagram using this specific 3.3-V LCD module (NHD-0216HZ-FSW-FBW-33V3C) is shown in Figure 9.1. The third pin from the left is N/C (no connect) for this module. This may be the difference compared to a generic LCD module. This pin is, typically, "contrast adjust" in a generic LCD module. It can change the contrast of an LCD screen by applying a different voltage level to this pin. This voltage level provided through this pin is important to display the characters correctly. However, in this specific 3.3-V LCD module, this pin is not used.

Symbol	Pin	Description
VSS	1	Ground
VDD	2	Supply Voltage (+3.3V)
NC	3	No Connect
RS	4	Register Select signal. RS=0: Command, RS=1: Data
R/W	5	Read/Write select signal. R/W=1: Read, R/W=0: Write
E	6	Enable signal (Falling edge triggered)
DB0 ~ DB7	7~14	Data bus lines.
LED+	15	Backlight LED Anode (+3.0V)
LED-	16	Backlight LED Cathode (Ground)

Table 9.1. Pin description [13].

The pin descriptions are shown in Table 9.1. In this chapter, an 8-bit operation will be used, which means we use DB0 ~DB7. However, it is possible to use it in a 4-bit operation instead. In that case, users need to use only DB4 ~ DB7 among the data bus lines. On a BH EDU board, the connections to the backlight LED (pin 15 and pin 16) were intentionally removed. If needed, users can create circuit connections to use the backlight LED. For reference, the normal voltage for this backlight LED from the datasheet is 3.0 V and the max voltage is 3.2 V.

Instruction

There are two control pins, *RS* and *R/W*. Moreover, in order for communication, the edge signal of *E* with a proper time delay needs to be generated manually. It is worth mentioning that this pin of *E* is falling edge sensitive. The operations according to *RS* and *R/W* bits are shown in Table 9.2.

RS	R/W	Operation
0	0	Write command
0	1	Read Busy flag (DB7) and address counter (DB0 ~ DB6)
1	0	Write data
1	1	Read data

Table 9.2. Operations according to RS and R/W bits [13].

If *RS* pin is low, this means that it is related to "command". If *RS* pin is high, this means it is related to "data" operations. *R/W* pin is used to choose either *read* or *write* operation. In some of designs of the LCD applications, it can be found that this pin of *R/W* is simply connected to ground. In that case, data can be written to the LCD module; but the data cannot be read from the LCD module. This LCD configuration is functional, but it may not be an efficient method in some cases. For optimal control of an LCD module, the busy flag can be checked before sending the next data. In this case, it may be necessary to configure R/W properly to be able to read from an LCD module.

Busy Flag (BF)

As mentioned, a busy flag can be checked before sending the data. If *RS* is low and *R/W* is high, busy flag can be read through DB7 as shown in Table 9.2. If *BF* is high, it indicates that the internal operation is still in processing.

Address Counter (AC)

Address Counter (AC) can be used for the Display Data RAM (DDRAM) address or Character Generator ROM (CGROM) address. After read or write operation, the AC can be automatically increased (or decreased) by 1

Display Data RAM (DDRAM)

Display data RAM (DDRAM) can store display data in 8-bit character codes. Predefined area in DDRAM is allocated to show corresponding characters according to character codes on an LCD display. For the selected LCD module, it can display 16 characters per line on an LCD display, and the number of lines can be up to two. In this reason, this selected LCD module is also simply called the selected 16 x 2 LCD module in this book. The DDRAM address allocation for the selected 16 x 2 LCD module is shown in Figure 9.2.

LCD position	1	2	3	4	5	6	7	8	9	10	11	12	13	14	15	16
DDRAM address	00h	01h	02h	03h	04h	05h	06h	07h	08h	09h	0Ah	0Bh	0Ch	0Dh	0Eh	0Fh
	40h	41h	42h	43h	44h	45h	46h	47h	48h	49h	4Ah	4Bh	4Ch	4Dh	4Eh	4Fh

Figure 9.2. DDRAM address allocation the selected 16 x 2 LCD module [13][14].

The first line address starts from 0x00 and it ends at 0x0F. The second line address starts from 0x40 and it ends at 0x4F. As can be seen, there is a noticeable address gap in-between the first line and the second line.

Character Generator ROM (CGROM)
Character Generator ROM (CGROM) can provide 5 x 8 dot or 5 x 11 dot character patterns associated with 8-bit character codes. In other words, the CGROM has predefined/built-in character information. For instance, if the value of 0x41 is stored in a specific DDRAM address, the character pattern from CGROM associated with 0x41 can be provided to display a character on an LCD module. In this case, 0x41 is a character 'A' defined in ASCII table. Therefore, the character 'A' can be displayed on an LCD module at the LCD position relevant to the DDRAM address if a proper DDRAM address is used.

Predefined built-in font table can be found in the datasheet and documents provided by the manufacturer [13][14]. Mapping of the characters in lower addresses of the built-in font table is somewhat similar to the one in an ASCII code table. Users can use some symbols, numbers and alphabets defined in the ASCII code table. However, mapping of the characters in the built-in font table is not the same as the one in the ASCII code table. More character patterns including Japanese characters can be found in the upper addresses of the built-in font table.

Character Generator RAM (CGRAM)
Character Generator RAM (CGRAM) can be used to create user defined character patterns. For 5 x 8 dots, users can create eight-character patterns. For 5 x 11 dots, users can create four-character patterns. User-defined character patterns can be stored and accessed using specific addresses of the built-in font table. For example, for this selected LCD module, the addresses of 0x00 to 0x07 in the table are associated with the eight user-defined characters.

Instruction Table

A selected instruction table for the selected LCD module is shown Table 9.3. For *"Clear Display"*, both *RS* and *R/W* need to be low, and the value of the command is 0x01. It may take about more than 1.5 ms to process this instruction. It is recommended to do it during the initialization of the LCD module. However, it would not be a good idea to use this instruction frequently during the normal operation.

Moreover, users can set the LCD position. For instance, if they want to write characters in the 2nd line of the LCD display. They can choose an LCD instruction related to *"set DDRAM address"* from the instruction table. There is a parameter associated with an address counter. They can choose 0x40 for the parameter. Then, it will result in a "command" instruction of 0xC0. As described, the command instruction is related to the low levels of *RS* and *R/W* pins.

RS	R/W	DB7	DB6	DB5	DB4	DB3	DB2	DB1	DB0	Description
0	0	0	0	0	0	0	0	0	1	Clear display
0	0	0	0	0	0	0	0	1	-	Return home
0	0	0	0	0	0	0	1	I/D	SH	Entry mode set
0	0	0	0	0	0	1	D	C	B	Display ON/OFF
0	0	0	0	0	1	S/C	R/L	-	-	Cursor/Display shift
0	0	0	0	1	DL	N	F	-	-	Function set
0	0	0	1	AC5	AC4	AC3	AC2	AC1	AC0	Set CGRAM addr.
0	0	1	AC6	AC5	AC4	AC3	AC2	AC1	AC0	Set DDRAM addr.
0	1	BF	AC6	AC5	AC4	AC3	AC2	AC1	AC0	Read Busy flag & address counter
1	0	D7	D6	D5	D4	D3	D2	D1	D0	Write data
1	1	D7	D6	D5	D4	D3	D2	D1	D0	Read data

Table 9.3. Selected instruction table [13][14].

LCD test program

An LCD test program example is shown in Program 9.1. This is an example program created for an MSP430FR5994 using a pseudo code given by the manufacturer. This code was written to be *functional* for a breadboard prototype environment. This means that extra time delays were added, and this code is not written for a good performance.

```
#include <msp430.h>
void LCD_command(unsigned char);
void LCD_write(unsigned char);
void LCD_init(void);
int main(void) {
    WDTCTL = WDTPW | WDTHOLD;  // hold watchdog timer
    PM5CTL0 &= ~LOCKLPM5; // clear LOCKLPM5 bit
    P3DIR |= 0xFF; // output direction (P3)
```

```
   P3OUT &= ~0xFF;
   P8DIR |= 0x0E;  // output direction (P8)
   P8OUT &= ~0x0E;
   LCD_init();  // LCD init.
   LCD_write('T');  // write a character
   LCD_write('e');
   LCD_write('s');
   LCD_write('t');
   while(1) {
      _no_operation();
   }
   return 0;
}

void LCD_command(unsigned char in) {
   P3OUT = in;
   P8OUT &= ~BIT3;  // clear RS
   P8OUT &= ~BIT2;  // clear R/W
   P8OUT |= BIT1;  // set E
   _delay_cycles(200);
   P8OUT &= ~BIT1;  // clear E
}

void LCD_write(unsigned char in) {
   P3OUT = in;
   P8OUT |= BIT3;  // set RS
   P8OUT &= ~BIT2;  // clear R/W
   P8OUT |= BIT1;  // set E
   _delay_cycles(200);
   P8OUT &= ~BIT1;  // clear E
}

void LCD_init() {
   P8OUT &= ~BIT1;  // clear E
   _delay_cycles(15000);
   LCD_command(0x30);  // wake up
   _delay_cycles(300);
   LCD_command(0x30);
   _delay_cycles(300);
   LCD_command(0x30);
   _delay_cycles(300);
   LCD_command(0x38);  // function set: 8 bit/2-line
   LCD_command(0x10);  // set cursor
   LCD_command(0x0F);  // display on/cursor on
   LCD_command(0x06);  // entry mode set
   LCD_command(0x01);  // clear display
   _delay_cycles(3000);
}
```

Program 9.1. LCD test program.

There are three subroutines. They are *LCD_command*, *LCD_write*, and *LCD_init*. For *LCD_command*, it is related to sending a command to the LCD module. *LCD_write* is related to sending character data. *LCD_init* is to initialize the LCD. After running this code successfully, users can see "Test" characters on their LCD module.

Chapter 10. Analog to Digital Converter

Analog signals can be converted to digital signals. Digital signals have a finite set of possible levels. An Analog to digital converter (ADC) can perform this conversion. For instance, an analog audio signal can be converted to a digital signal, and it can be stored in a portable SD memory card. This ADC component is useful in various microcontroller applications. A majority of modern MCUs have at least one integrated ADC. An MSP430FR5994 MCU has a 12-bit ADC module that supports multiple input channels. In this chapter, we will study basics of ADCs, and the use of the ADC module in an MSP430FR5994 MCU.

Sampling and Quantization

The ADC conversion process can be understood as the steps of sampling and quantization. Sampling converts an analog signal into a discrete time signal. This discrete time signal is defined at discrete times, and the amplitude of the signal is continuous. The discrete time signal can be obtained at uniformly spaced times. The period of the uniformly spaced times is related to a sampling rate. Next, the sequence of the finite numbers from the continuous amplitude signal can be obtained by a quantization process. This sequence of the finite numbers is relevant to a digital signal. Some of the relevant quantization levels are 256 (8 bit), 1,024 (10 bit), and 4,096 (12 bit).

Nyquist Sampling Theorem

A sufficient sampling rate (f_s) for a band limited signal (B) is higher than $2B$ according to the Nyquist sampling theorem [15]. For instance, an audible frequency range can be about 20 to 20 kHz. In this case, based on the Nyquist sampling theorem, the sampling frequency needs to be higher than 40 kHz. In digital audio, 44.1 kHz is a common sampling frequency, which is used in CD (compact disc) digital audio. Some ADCs have implemented a sampling (f_s) rate close to $2B$. These are Nyquist ADCs. However, practically, it is common to find ADCs to perform oversampling by choosing higher frequency than $2B$.

12-bit SAR ADC

One of the common ADCs that can be found in an MCU is a successive approximation (SAR) ADC. A SAR ADC is a reasonable choice for a microcontroller application that needs a decent resolution and conversion speed. It is suitable for a low power application, and the size of the SAR ADC on a chip is relatively small. Therefore, SAR ADC modules can be found in integrated with many modern MCU ICs.

A SAR ADC has a DAC that can generate reference voltages in a binary fashion. A comparator unit can generate the output comparing the input voltage with these reference voltages in sequence. A SAR ADC implements a binary search algorithm.

The binary output values in sequence from the comparator can be converted to digital data.

A conceptual block diagram of a 12-bit SAR with 32 input channels is shown in Figure 10.1. Let us suppose the first channel is selected properly. Then, the analog signal passes an analog multiplexer (mux), and the signal will be sampled. The sampled value is compared to the reference voltage generated by the DAC. The output of the comparator gets stored in one of the bits in a 12-bit register. Let us assume this DAC can generate the relevant binary weighted voltages. This process will be repeated until it can fill the rest of the bits in the 12 bit-register. In this block diagram, there is one SAR ADC core, but it can receive 32 analog inputs through the analog mux component.

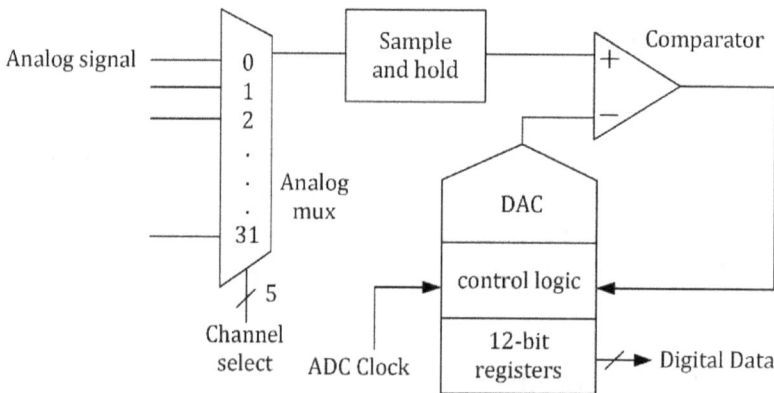

Figure 10.1. A conceptual block diagram of a 12-bit SAR with 32 input channels.

Sigma Delta Converter

An SAR ADC module is integrated with an MSP430FR5994 MCU. There are other ADC types such as a Sigma Delta Converter. This Sigma Delta Converter can typically provide a higher sampling frequency and higher resolution. If developers' targeted application needs a higher specification and requirement, they can choose a different MCU model with an integrated Sigma Delta Converter, or they can use an additional standalone Sigma Delta Converter IC. The key technique of a Sigma Delta Converter is Sigma Delta Modulation. The Sigma Delta modulator includes a quantizer and an integrator. The quantizer in the modulator generates a sequence of finite numbers for a digital signal.

ADC12_B

We have studied a generalized 12-bit SAR ADC module with multiple input channels. Now, let's study an ADC12 module in an MSP430FR5994 MCU. An ADC12_B module is a 12-bit SAR ADC with multiple input channels. Figure 10.2 shows the simplified functional block diagram of the ADC12_B module. The ADC core can convert analog signals to 12-bit digital signals. The programmable voltages of V_{R+} and V_{R-} are the upper and lower limits of the conversion. The full scale of the digital output (N_{ADC}) is 0x0FFF. V_{in} is an input analog voltage. Then, the conversion formula of the 12-bit ADC for a single-ended mode is as follows:

$$N_{ADC} = 4095 \times \frac{V_{in} - V_{R-}}{V_{R+} - V_{R-}}$$

Using this equation, a developer can estimate the digital output (N_{ADC}) from the input voltage (V_{in}). Likewise, the input voltage (V_{in}) can be estimated by the digital output (N_{ADC}).

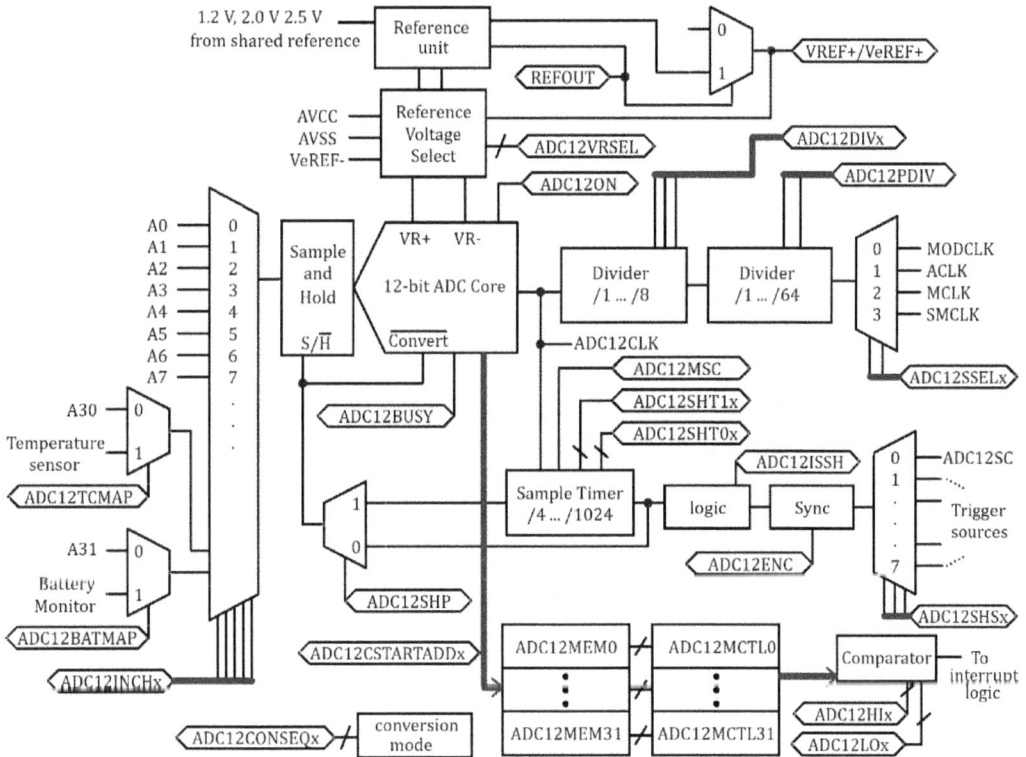

Figure 10.2. Simplified functional block diagram of ADC12_B [9].

The converted digital data can be stored in a memory buffer. The memory buffer has memory registers of ADC12MEM[0]~ ADC12MEM[31]. The ADC conversion process can be initiated by ADC12SC bit. In this section, we will study the "single-channel single-conversion mode." In order to perform the test, an ADC test circuit is configured as shown in Figure 10.3.

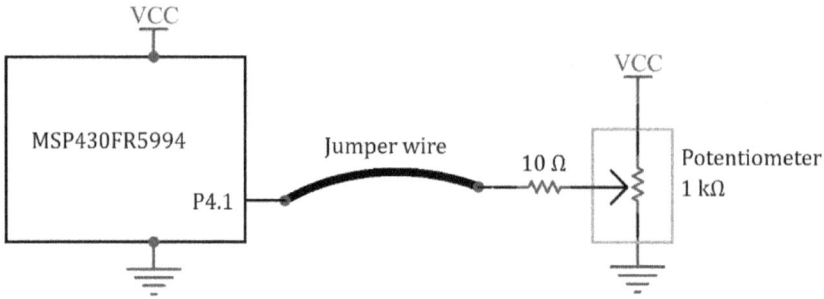

Figure 10.3. An ADC test circuit.

Readers can use a generic 1 kΩ potentiometer for an experiment. A 10 Ω resistor was added for protection. For a BH EDU board, this test circuit is already implemented. A user can simply connect P4.1 to a proper header on a BH EDU board using a breadboard jumper wire.

ADC Test Example (Polling)

Program 10.1 shows an ADC test example. P4.1 is configured for channel A9 by setting P4SEL1 and P4SEL0 bits. In the following line of the code, the ADC12CTL0 is configured to turn the ADC on, and it also configures the timing of the ADC unit.

ADC12RES_2 was chosen to obtain 12-bit converted data. Channel A9 was selected by configuring ADC12MCTL0. In the while loop, the ADC conversion is initiated by *ADC12SC*. There is another while loop that checks whether the ADC busy flag is set or not. The program stays in this while loop until the ADC conversion is completed. Then, the ADC result can be accessed using ADC12MEM[0], and it will be copied to *adc_raw*. Next, it can toggle a red LED. This behavior of the ADC conversion and toggling an LED will be repeated in the loop.

```
#include <msp430.h>
unsigned int adc_raw;
int main(void) {
  WDTCTL = WDTPW | WDTHOLD;  // hold watchdog timer
  PM5CTL0 &= ~LOCKLPM5; // clear LOCKLPM5 bit
  P1DIR |= 0x01; // output direction (P1.0)
  P4SEL1 |= BIT1; // alternate function (A9)
  P4SEL0 |= BIT1; // alternate function  (A9)
  ADC12CTL0 = ADC12SHT0_6 | ADC12ON; // ADC CTL0 set up
  ADC12CTL1 = ADC12SHP; // ADC CTL1 set up
  ADC12CTL2 = ADC12RES_2; // 12-bit conversion
  ADC12MCTL0 = ADC12INCH_9; // ADC channel selection
  while(1) {
    ADC12CTL0 |= ADC12ENC | ADC12SC; // ADC, Start conversion
    while ((ADC12IFGR0 & BIT0)==0); // flag check
    adc_raw=ADC12MEM0;  // read ADC
    P1OUT ^= 0x01; // toggle (P1.0)
```

```
      _delay_cycles(25000); // delay
   }
   return 0;
}
```

Program 10.1. ADC test example (Polling based).

Since the ADC result was copied to a global variable, *adc_raw*. There are many ways to check this value. One of them is to suspend the program in Code Composer Studio and move the cursor over the variable. Then, the value stored in this variable can be displayed in a small pop-up window.

ADC Test Example (Interrupt)

The test code in Program 10.1 was based on a polling method. It would be useful to write an interrupt-based program that can perform a similar task. In this reason, an interrupt-based ADC example code was written as shown in Program 10.2.

```
#include <msp430.h>
unsigned int adc_raw;
int main(void) {
   WDTCTL = WDTPW | WDTHOLD;  // hold watchdog timer
   PM5CTL0 &= ~LOCKLPM5; // clear LOCKLPM5 bit
   P1DIR |= 0x01; // output direction (P1.0)
   P4SEL1 |= BIT1; // alternate function (A9)
   P4SEL0 |= BIT1; // alternate function (A9)
   ADC12CTL0 = ADC12SHT0_6 | ADC12ON; // ADC CTL0 set up
   ADC12CTL1 = ADC12SHP; // ADC CTL1 set up
   ADC12CTL2 = ADC12RES_2; // 12-bit conversion
   ADC12MCTL0 = ADC12INCH_9; // ADC channel selection
   ADC12IER0 |= ADC12IE0; // enable interrupt, ADC
   _enable_interrupt(); // enable general interrupt
   while(1) {
      ADC12CTL0 |= ADC12ENC | ADC12SC; // ADC, Start conversion
      P1OUT ^= 0x01; // toggle (P1.0)
      _delay_cycles(25000); // delay
   }
   return 0;
}

#pragma vector = ADC12_B_VECTOR
_interrupt void ADC12_ISR(void) {
   if ((ADC12IFGR0 & BIT0)!=0) { // flag check
      adc_raw=ADC12MEM0; // read ADC
   }
}
```

Program 10.2. ADC test example (Interrupt).

A good portion of the code is similar; however, the major difference is related to an ISR set up and the ISR. The interrupt configuration for the ADC ISR was performed using the code lines as follows:

ADC12IER0 |= ADC12IE0;

The ADC interrupt is enabled by setting *ADC12IE0* bit in *ADC12IER0*, and the ISR name is "*ADC12_ISR*". In this ISR code, the ADC result will be copied to a global variable, *adc_raw*. As you have done in the previous example, you can check this variable to find out whether the ADC conversion was successful or not. Another indication of the completion of the ADC conversion is to check whether the red LED keeps bilking or not.

Chapter 11. ADC Applications

ADCs are commonly found in microcontroller applications. For instance, the ADCs can be used in processing analog signals from various sensors. It is typical to find sensor components providing variations in resistance values or voltage levels with respect to specific physical states of the sensors. Let us consider temperature sensor applications. The variations of the values in resistances or voltages can be observed when the sensors are exposed to different temperatures. With the use of proper interface circuits, these variations can be measured using ADCs. Let's say we have chosen to use MCUs with ADC modules. The MCUs can be used to provide digital communication interfaces; therefore, the digital sensor data can be transferred to other systems. This configuration can be found in temperature sensor applications. As we have studied previously, an MSP430FR5994 MCU has an ADC module. In this chapter, we will study temperature sensor and accelerometer applications using an MSP430FR5994 MCU. A generalized concept of these applications can be applied to other ADC applications.

Temperature Sensors

Temperature sensors are commonly used in many microcontroller applications. Developers may be able to obtain some temperature data easily from a temperature sensor using a programming example given by the manufacturer or by communities. For a better understanding of the obtained temperature data, it is important to understand the physical characteristics of temperature sensors and the considerations of the testing environment. To analyze the temperature data properly, it is recommended to obtain knowledge about the sensor characteristics and their limitations.

In this chapter, we will study four temperature sensor types. They are *Resistance Temperature Detector*, *Thermocouple*, *Thermistor*, and *Semiconductor-based temperature sensors*. They are briefly summarized in the following sections.

Resistance Temperature Detector (RTD)

A Resistance Temperature Detector (RTD) sensor can measure temperatures based on the resistance variations in a metal wire. The RTD wire is commonly made of a pure material such as platinum, nickel, or copper. Platinum RTDs can provide high accuracies, and a typical operating range is −200 °C to 600 °C.

Thermocouple

A Thermocouple temperature sensor typically consists of two wires that are made of different metals. There are several types of Thermocouples. Wires on one side have connected, and they form a hot junction. The wires on the other side connected form a cold junction. Typically, the hot junction is a measuring point. The varying voltages that can be measured due to the use of the different metals are associated with temperature variations. The measurements can be found to be nonlinear; therefore, it needs a proper conversion. The accuracy can be found a bit low, but the thermocouple sensors can be used in applications that need a wide temperature range. The temperature ranges vary by type, and an example operating range is −200 °C to 1750 °C.

Thermistor

A Thermistor is a thermally sensitive resistor that shows the value of resistance can change as the temperature changes. There are two types of thermistors, *Negative Temperature Coefficient (NTC) thermistor* and *Positive Temperature Coefficient (PTC) thermistor*. Typically, NTC thermistors are used as temperature sensors. The resistance of NTC thermistors will decrease as the temperature increases. NTC Thermistors show non-linear resistance variations with respect to temperature variations. NTC thermistors are suitable for various applications. An example operating temperature range is −50 °C to 250 °C.

PTC thermistors are also temperature sensitive, but the resistance will increase as the temperature increases. PTC Thermistors are typically used in circuit protection applications. A certain level of the overcurrent through a PTC can cause a high temperature on the PTC. The resistance of the PTC will increase significantly. When the cause of the overcurrent is eliminated and the PTC sensor is cooled down, the resistance will be decreased, and the circuit might work again. This is like a resettable fuse, and this can be used in a circuit protection application.

Semiconductor-based Temperature Sensor

Semiconductor-based temperature sensors can be designed and placed on IC wafers. These on-chip temperature sensors are often implemented by diodes and transistors. Types of temperature sensors can be categorized as *voltage output, current output, resistance output, digital output,* and *diode*.

Semiconductor temperature sensors are implemented on a chip, and the chip is placed inside IC packages. Some IC packages are not necessarily designed for thermal conduction. In this case, there can be limitations in making good thermal contact.

In general, semiconductor-based temperature sensors are found in many embedded systems. These temperature sensors are low-cost, and the sizes of the sensors are small. However, they may not be suitable for temperature applications that need high accuracy and/or a wide operating range. An example operating range of semiconductor-based temperature sensors is −40 °C to 120 °C.

Integrated Temperature Sensor in an MSP430FR5994 MCU

An MSP430FR5994 MCU has a built-in temperature sensor. The temperature sensor data can be accessed. This temperature sensor can be enabled by setting *ADC12TCMAP* bit in the *ADC12CTL3* register. On an MSP430FR5994 MCU, this integrated temperature sensor is connected to Analog channel 30 (A30). Therefore, the voltage that is relevant to the temperature sensor can be read through the A30.

The manufacturer provides calibration data measured at 30°C ±3°C and 85°C ±3°C under certain internal voltage reference states of 1.25 V, 2.0, and 2.5 V. The temperature in Celsius degree (°C) can be calculated using the characteristic equations as follows:

$$\text{Temp(°C)} = (\text{adc\_raw} - \text{Ref\_T30}) \times \left(\frac{85 - 30}{\text{Ref\_T85} - \text{Ref\_T30}}\right) + 30$$

The temperature data in Fahrenheit degree (°F) can be obtained by a simple mathematical formula as needed. An integrated temperature sensor test code is shown in Program 11.1.

In this code, the 2.5-V internal reference voltage is enabled. The temperature sensor calibration data for the 2.5-V reference voltage was read from the MCU. *ADC12RES_2* was chosen to obtain 12-bit data. *ADC12CTL0 ~ ADC12CTL3*, and *ADC12MCTL0* registers are configured as we have studied previously.

In the while loop, the ADC value is read, and the *adc_raw* value is converted. The value stored in "TempDegC" variable is a corresponding temperature in Celsius degrees (°C).

```
#include <msp430.h>
unsigned int adc_raw;
float TempDegC;
int main(void) {
  WDTCTL = WDTPW | WDTHOLD;   // hold watchdog timer
  PM5CTL0 &= ~LOCKLPM5;  // clear LOCKLPM5 bit
  P1DIR |= 0x01;  // output direction (P1.0)
  while(REFCTL0 & REFGENBUSY);  // wait until the busy flag is cleared
  REFCTL0 |= REFVSEL_2 | REFON;   // enable internal 2.5V ref.
  int Ref_T30=*((unsigned int *)(TLV_START+TLV_ADC12CAL+0x09));
                          // temperature calibration (30degC/12bit)
  int Ref_T85=*((unsigned int *)(TLV_START+TLV_ADC12CAL+0x0B));
                          // temperature calibration (85degC/12bit)
  ADC12CTL0 = ADC12SHT0_6 | ADC12ON;  // ADC CTL0 set up
  ADC12CTL1 = ADC12SHP;  // ADC CTL1 set up
  ADC12CTL2 = ADC12RES_2;  // 12-bit conversion
  ADC12CTL3 = ADC12TCMAP;  // select ADC12TCMAP channel
  ADC12MCTL0 = ADC12VRSEL_1 | ADC12INCH_30;  // VR+, ADC channel
  while(1) {
```

```
            ADC12CTL0 |= ADC12ENC | ADC12SC;  // ADC, Start conversion
            while ((ADC12IFGR0 & BIT0)==0);  // flag check
            adc_raw=ADC12MEM0;  // read ADC
            TempDegC = (((float) adc_raw - Ref_T30) * 55) / (Ref_T85 - Ref_T30) + 30.0;
                                                      // temperature conversion
            P1OUT ^= 0x01;  // toggle (P1.0)
            __delay_cycles(25000);  // delay
        }
    return 0;
}
```

Program 11.1. Integrated temperature sensor test example.

Accelerometers

An accelerometer sensor can measure acceleration. For instance, when an accelerometer is at rest on the surface of the earth toward upwards, the acceleration will be measured approximately as +g ($\approx$ 9.81 m/s). When an accelerometer is in free fall, the acceleration will be measured approximately as zero.

Accelerometers have been used in many applications such as vibration detection, tilt detection, and shock detection. Accelerometers are also used in flight control applications and robot applications. It is typical to find them as a part of an inertial measurement unit (IMU). An IMU can measure the force, angular rate, and orientation of an object. For instance, it can be a combination of accelerometers, gyroscopes, and magnetometers. There are several types of accelerometers. In the following sections, we will learn about accelerometer ICs.

Accelerometer ICs

MEMS stands for the micro-electromechanical system. It is a miniature mechanical and electro-mechanical element made by using microfabrication techniques. It has been merged with other technologies including integrated circuits. These techniques make it possible to create accelerometer ICs that are suitable for many compact-sized embedded systems. There are many standalone accelerometer IC models and IMU IC models.

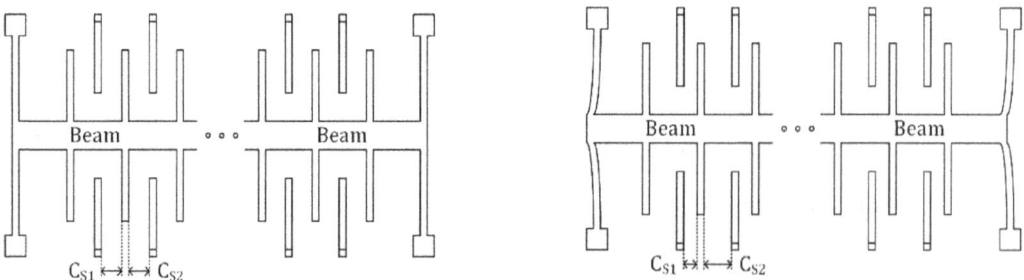

Figure 11.1. Simplified accelerometer MEM sensor example.

Let us consider a simplified accelerometer MEM sensor example as shown in Figure 11.1. The size of the sensor is assumed to be very small. On the left side, it shows the beam and finger structure. The gaps between the beam and the fingers are associated with the capacitors of C_{S1} and C_{S2}. In this case, the beam is in the middle, the capacitors of C_{S1} and C_{S2} are assumed to be equivalent. In this MEM sensor, the beam is a moving mass. On the right side, the beam was shifted to the left side. In this case, the capacitors of C_{S1} and C_{S2} show the variations that are related to the acceleration. These variations can be read and can be converted to the voltage output as shown in Figure 11.2. This figure shows a simplified accelerometer block diagram for one axis.

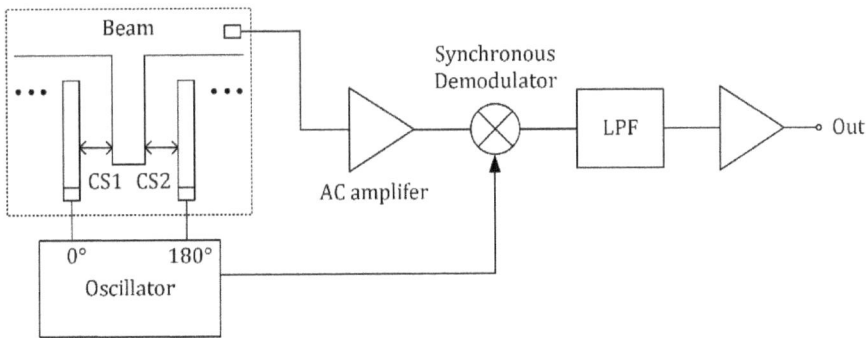

Figure 11.2. Simplified accelerometer block diagram for one axis.

It has an oscillator block that can generate two RF signals with a 180-degree phase difference. They are applied to the fingers and the beam. The output from the beam is amplified. This amplified signal is demodulated and filtered. Then, it is properly amplified to provide the proper output level to be read by other systems. This is a simplified and generic explanation for one axis. It can be extended to other axes with corresponding interface circuits.

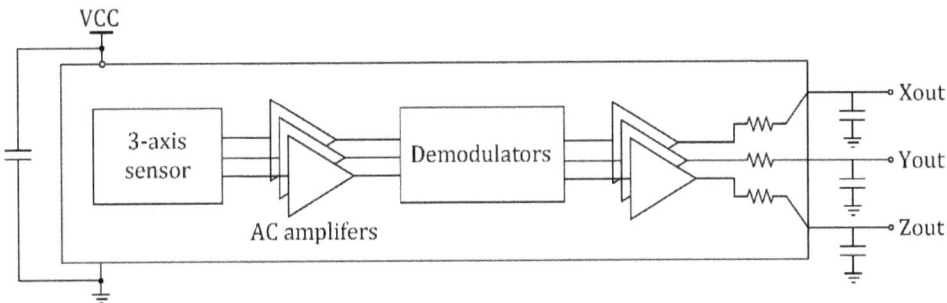

Figure 11.3. Simplified block diagram of ADXL355 accelerometer sensor IC [16].

For an experiment and further explanations, an ADXL335 module was chosen. A simplified block diagram of ADXL335 [16] accelerometer sensor IC is shown in

Figure 11.3. There is a 3-axis sensor block on the left side. The output signals are amplified and demodulated. Then, the amplifiers provide proper levels for Xout, Yout, and Zout. Typical zero g bias levels are almost half of the supply voltage. However, the actual value might vary by the sensor. The AXDL335 IC can be operated at 3.3 V. This sensor generates three output analog signals. They can be read through the ADC module in an MSP430FR5994 MCU.

Let us connect this ADXL335 IC and an MSP430FR5994 MCU. The connection diagram is shown Figure 14.4. The output signals of X, Y, and Z are connected to P4.1, P4.2, and P4.3, respectively. The selected functions of the P4.1, P4.2 and P4.3 are related to three analog channels of A9, A10, and A11. The directions of the X, Y, and Z are marked on the PCB. In the following sections, we will study how to read multiple channel ADC values.

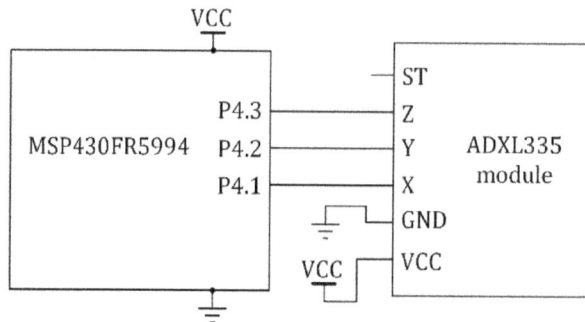

Figure 11.4. Connection example of an ADXL335 module [17].

There are several ADXL335 modules with ADXL335 ICs. Readers can find them from different vendors and companies for their experiments. If readers would like to use different but similar models of accelerometer ICs, they need to refer to the documents carefully from the manufacturer or the vendor to determine the proper connections. On a BH EDU board, one ADXL335 IC is placed. Users can access three pins for three axes of the accelerometer IC through the proper header pins.

ADC Conversion Modes

For an ADC module, there are four ADC conversion modes. They are *Single-channel single-conversion, Sequence-of-channels, Repeat-single-channel*, and *Repeat-sequence-of-channels.* Previously, we have used a *Single-channel single-conversion* mode.

A *sequence-of-channels* mode is also called *autoscan* mode. Multiple channels can be sampled and covered once in sequence. We will use this mode in the multiple channel conversion example in the following section.

Moreover, there are repeated modes for the continuous sampling and conversions. They are *Repeat-single-channel* mode and *Repeated-sequence-of-channels* (*Repeated autoscan*)

Multiple Channel Conversion

Depending on the embedded systems, we may need to access and read multiple ADC channels. Given the test setup in Figure 11.4, we can write a program that can read three ADC channels for X, Y, and Z axes. The example code is shown in Program 11.2.

```
#include <msp430.h>
unsigned int adc_raw[3]; // array
int main(void) {
  WDTCTL = WDTPW | WDTHOLD;  // hold watchdog timer
  PM5CTL0 &= ~LOCKLPM5; // clear LOCKLPM5 bit
  P1DIR |= 0x01; // output direction (P1.0)
  P4SEL1 |= 0x0E; // alternate function (A9, A10, A11)
  P4SEL0 |= 0x0E; // alternate function (A9, A10, A11)
  ADC12CTL0 = ADC12SHT0_6 | ADC12MSC | ADC12ON; // ADC CTL0 set up
  ADC12CTL1 = ADC12SHP | ADC12CONSEQ_1; // ADC CTL1 set up
  ADC12CTL2 |= ADC12RES_2; // 12-bit conversion
  // multiple sample conversion, sequence of channel mode
  ADC12MCTL0 = ADC12INCH_9;
  ADC12MCTL1 = ADC12INCH_10;
  ADC12MCTL2 = ADC12INCH_11 | ADC12EOS; // end of sequence
  while(1) {
    ADC12CTL0 |= ADC12ENC | ADC12SC; // ADC, Start conversion
    while ((ADC12IFGR0 & BIT2)==0); // flag check
    adc_raw[0]=ADC12MEM0; // read ADC
    adc_raw[1]=ADC12MEM1;
    adc_raw[2]=ADC12MEM2;
    P1OUT ^= 0x01; // toggle (P1.0)
    _delay_cycles(25000); // delay
  }
  return 0;
}
```

Program 11.2. Multiple channel conversion example.

The *ADC12CTL0* register is configured for a multiple sample conversion and *sequence of channel* mode. The multiple sample conversion is enabled by setting *ADC12MSC* bit and the sequence of channel mode is selected by configuring *ADC12CONSEQ* bits.

In order to store multiple values, the *adc_raw* variable is defined as an array. *ADC12MCTL0, ADC12MCTL1, ADC12MCTL2* registers are configured for A9, A10, and A11, respectively. *ADC12EOS* is added to the last channel of the sequence. In the while loop, the program waits until the ADC14BUSY flag is cleared to determine the completion of the conversion. Then, the converted data can be stored in the *adc_raw* array.

The raw reading of the ADC values may need to be converted to the corresponding voltages or angles as needed. Users can modify this code to perform their proper conversions of the values. This multiple channel example can be modified and applied to other microcontroller applications where it is necessary to read ADC values from multiple channels. For instance, a system may need to read multiple analog voltages for a temperature sensor, a battery level monitor, and an analog tuning knob. An MSP430FR5994 MCU can be configured to read many channels. Specific pin numbers associated with ADC channels can be found in the datasheet [2]. For an MSP430FR5994 Launchpad board, the pinout information can be found in the Launchpad board kit document [7].

Chapter 12. Embedded Software Architectures

In general-purpose computer systems, speed or throughput is one of the key performance parameters. You can imagine a typical laptop or a PC as an example of a general-purpose computer system. The speed or throughput is also a key performance parameter in embedded systems. Throughput is the amount of data that can be processed in a given amount of time. In addition, there are other key performance parameters such as response time and power consumption. Since embedded system is a special purpose system, the emphasis on performance parameters might vary depending on the applications. Moreover, in some embedded systems, performance parameters may not only be the major factors but, other factors can be important such as reliability of the system. In some cases, the cost associated with the production and development can be a major consideration in some embedded systems. Designers and programmers may need to understand the hardware and software requirements of the targeted project in development. Then, they can choose suitable hardware and an embedded software architecture for the project.

Embedded systems can be implemented without the use of any kernel or an embedded system operating system. In this case, these specific embedded systems simply do not have a kernel or a scheduler. In some of the other embedded systems, they are implemented using embedded system operating systems such as real-time operating systems (RTOSs). In this chapter, we will study five embedded systems architectures. They are *Round Robin, Round Robin with Interrupts, Function-Queue scheduling*, and *Real-time operating system* [18].

Some embedded systems are built based on a Linux kernel. Embedded Linux operating systems have been widely accepted in embedded systems. Embedded Linux operating systems may process complex tasks and provide user-friendly environments. For instance, an Android™ operating system that are used in smartphones is one of the examples of embedded Linux operating systems. An Android operating system is a mobile operating system, and it is based on a Linux kernel. Similarly, there are many embedded Linux systems.

Embedded systems are becoming more powerful and complex. Some of those complex embedded systems can be built using embedded Linux operating systems. And these embedded Linux systems may seem to be low performance general-purpose computers. However, embedded Linux systems and general-purpose computers are not the same because embedded Linux systems are targeted to service specific purposes. There are several embedded Linux systems that are suitable for educational environments. Educational Embedded Linux Systems will be briefly presented in Chapter 28.

Scheduler and Kernel

A *scheduler* is in charge of changing *ready* state to *running* of a task or process. When a task or a process is running, it means it is using the associated system resources. It is typical to manage multiple tasks. *Scheduling* is a method of assigning or distributing computer resources to perform tasks. There are many scheduling algorithms. A scheduler is typically a part of a *kernel*. A kernel is a part of an *operating system*. The kernel is a core of an operating system, and typically, it is the program loaded into the memory on boot, and it manages the process of starting up a system.

Round Robin

Some of the microcontroller applications can be implemented without the need for a kernel. They may have only several simple tasks to be performed. If the tasks do not need to be processed concurrently, they can be processed in sequence in an infinite loop. This embedded software system structure is called a *round robin* architecture. This structure can be seen as *cyclic executives or super loop*. This implementation is simple and easy. It may not suffer from a shared memory problem across multiple tasks.

Let us consider a pseudo code for the round robin architecture shown in Program 12.1. There are four tasks defined in the program. The first task is "*read-button*" task. The system reads the status of buttons. In this case, we assume the system has multiple buttons. The second task is "*read-ADC*" task. It reads the ADC values from the module and performs the associated calculations. The third task is "*control*" task. The program performs proper actions according to the system status including button and ADC status. The fourth task is "*display*" task. It manages to show data on a display module. The fifth task is "*send-data*" task. It sends data over a serial communication interface. In this program, a variable *function,* is used in switching a running task. Initially, this variable is configured to run the *read-button* task at the start. Then, in the while loop, all of the four tasks are running in sequence repeatedly. A *volatile* keyword is used for this *function* variable. The *volatile* keyword is used to try to prevent an unexpected optimization by the compiler.

```
#include <msp430.h>
volatile unsigned int function;
int main(void){
    # Initialization
    function=0;
    while (1) {
        if (function==0) {
            # read-button task
            function=1;
        }
        if (function==1) {
```

```
        # read-ADC task
        function=2;
    }
    if (function==2) {
        # control task
        function=3;
    }
    if (function==3) {
        # display task
        function=4;
    }
    if (function==4) {
        # send-data task
        function=0;
    }
    }
    return 0;
}
```

Program 12.1. Pseudo code for Round Robin.

In this program, each task can be processed one at a time. If there are data variables that are shared between the tasks, they do not suffer from shared memory problems. The shared memory is the memory area that can be accessed by multiple tasks. In this Round Robin architecture case, the shared memory is not accessed simultaneously by multiple tasks.

Since there can be other tasks to perform between the *read-button* task and the *control* task such as *read-ADC* task in this example, there is a chance that this program may suffer from a response-time problem. If the *read-button* task has a certain deadline like an emergency button and other tasks in-between could take longer time than the desired deadline. In this scenario, it may cause missing a targeted deadline. A missed deadline might cause a serious system failure. In order to overcome this issue, we can use interrupt service routines in this Round Robin architecture described in the following section.

Round Robin with Interrupts

There can be several variants of Round Robin Architecture. In this section, let us consider an architecture of Round Robin with Interrupts. For the *read-button* task and the *read-ADC* task, they can be processed in the interrupt service routines (ISRs) as shown in Program 12.2. These two tasks can be processed when they are requested. As they have higher priorities, these tasks may interrupt a running task in the while loop. In this while loop, the *control* task, *display* task, and *send-data* task are running in sequence repeatedly. When buttons are pressed, a running task in the while loop is going to be interrupted. Then, the associated ISR, *Port5_ISR_handler*, can be processed. This method may resolve the response time problem that we have considered in the Round Robin example. In addition, this program does not need to wait until the ADC conversion and the relevant calculation are completed. When the ADC interrupt service is requested, the *read-ADC* task can interrupt a task in the while loop. Then it can process the *read-ADC* task. After the *read-ADC* task is completed, the program can run *control* task, *display* task, and *send-data* task in sequence repeatedly.

```
#include <msp430.h>
volatile unsigned int function;
int main(void){
    # Initialization code
    function=3;
    while (1) {
        if (function==3) {
            # control task code
            function=4;
        }
        if (function==4) {
            # display task code
            function=5;
        }
        if (function==5) {
            # send-data task code
            function=3;
        }
    }
    return 0;
}

#pragma vector=PORT5_VECTOR
_interrupt void Port5_ISR_handler(void) {
    // function 1
    # read-button task code
}
#pragma vector = ADC12_B_VECTOR
_interrupt void ADC12_ISR(void) {
    // function 2
    # read-ADC task code
}
```

Program 12.2. Pseudo code for Round Robin with Interrupts.

This variant of Round Robin is a potential solution to resolve the response time problem. However, there are some other conditions to be considered. While the system is processing the *read-ADC* task, the other *read-button* task requests could be triggered multiple times. For an MSP430FR5994 MCU, an ADC12 ISR has a higher priority than a Port 5 ISR as we have studied previously. In this case, there is a chance to miss the multiple read-button task requests. In addition, these *read-button* or the *read-ADC* tasks have higher priorities than other tasks in the while loop. If ISRs were overly dominating the processor time, the other tasks in the while loop would not be running properly.

This would be related to the recommended practice of writing an ISR short to reduce the time spent in the ISR. Next, let us consider a scheduling system to tackle this problem in the following section.

Function-Queue Scheduling

We have studied simple examples of Round Robin and a variant of Round Robin in the previous sections. Using a circular queue, we can implement a simple scheduling system. A circular queue can store data, and its data structure is based on FIFO (First In First Out). The last position of the data is connected back to the first position of the data, and it forms a circular buffer. Function pointers for tasks can be stored in the circular queue. Let us say that there is a program routine that checks whether the function pointer has any data or not. If it has the data, then the program reads the queue and calls the associated function.

An example of this type of program with a circular queue is shown in Program 12.3. In this program, it is assumed that the circular queue is already implemented separately. This circular queue is not a part of a standard library; but a user can simply implement it, or a user can find relevant queue library found in a software package provided by a manufacturer. In this example program, there are five functions that were defined, and they are associated with five tasks we have studied previously.

```
#include <msp430.h>
void function1(void);
void function2(void);
void function3(void);
void function4(void);
void function5(void);
// Subroutine Header
void clearQueue(void);
void enQueue(unsigned int);
unsigned int deQueue();
unsigned char QueueIsNotEmpty();
// Circular queue is assumed to be already defined
void (*fcnPtr)(void); // function pointer with no parameter
int main(void){
    # Initialization
    clearQueue();
    enQueue(&function3);
    while (1) {
        while (QueueIsNotEmpty()) {
```

```
        fcnPtr = deQueue();
        (*fcnPtr)();
      }
    }
    return 0;
  }

  #pragma vector=PORT5_VECTOR
  _interrupt void Port5_ISR_handler(void) {
    # minimum actions to handle a read-button task
    enQueue(&function1);
  }
  void function1(void){
    # remaining actions to complete the read-button task
  }

  #pragma vector = ADC12_B_VECTOR
  _interrupt void ADC12_ISR(void) {
    # minimum actions to handle a read-ADC task
    enQueue(&function2);
  }
  void function2(void){
    # remaining actions to complete the read-ADC task
  }

  void function3(void){
    # control task
    enQueue(&function4);
  }
  void function4(void){
    # display task
    enQueue(&function5);
  }
  void function5(void){
    #send-data task
    enQueue(&function3);
  }
```

Program 12.3. Pseudo code for Function Queue Scheduling.

For the Port 5 ISR, it can process minimum actions to handle a *read-button* task, and the remaining actions to complete the *read-button* task can be processed in the *function1* sub-routine. This method can make the time to spend in an ISR short, and the rest of the process can be processed after exiting the ISR. Likewise, an ADC ISR is handling minimum actions for a *read-ADC* task, and the *function2* has the remaining actions for the *read-ADC* task to be performed. The *function3*, *function4*, and *function 5* are the sub-routines related to *control* task, *display* task, and *send-data* task, respectively. The *function3*, *function4*, and *function5* will be running in sequence in a normal condition repeatedly. If there is any interrupt request from the Port 5 or

ADC, this cycle can be interrupted, and the relevant code and function can be running first. This example program is capable of catching task requests reasonably fast, and it could resolve some of the problems discussed in the previous examples.

In Program 12.3, the function pointers that need to be executed are stored in the circular queue, and the program runs the relevant functions by reading function pointers from the queue. This is a function-queue scheduling, which is a simplified example of scheduling.

Let us consider a scenario. Let say *function3*, *function4*, or *funcion5* is desired to be low priority tasks and *function1* and *function4* are desired to be high priority. If there are too many requests of low priority tasks such as *function3*, *function4*, or *funcion5*, stored in the queue, then, the chance of running higher priority tasks properly such as *function1*, or *function4* gets lower. This might be relevant to the need for a capability to selectivity run a task from the requested tasks stored in the queue. In addition, this program treats all tasks as the same priority except the tasks related to ISRs.

In this function-queue example, the method of assigning different priorities was not implemented. But, these complex cases can be handled by using a real-time kernel that is a part of a real-time operating system (RTOS). In RTOS, developers can assign different priorities for the tasks, and RTOS can manage to put a lower priority task in a ready state and run a higher priority first. In the following section, we will study an RTOS example.

Real-time Operating System

A real-time kernel is the core of a real-time operating system. It manages booting, task scheduling, and resources of an MCU. A real-time operating system (RTOS) includes a real-time kernel and other higher level and additional services. An RTOS is designed to meet strict deadlines. In addition, an RTOS includes a large set of libraries that are suitable for various applications of embedded systems.

A pseudo code example for an RTOS is shown in Program 12.4. Five tasks were defined. *Task3*, *Task4*, and *Task5* are for a *control* task, *display* task, and *send-data* task, respectively. They are running in sequence repeatedly by synchronization using signaling. There are two more tasks that are configured to be triggered by hardware interrupt requests. They are *Task_GPIO_btn0* and *Task_ADC_callback0*. In the main program, it begins with the custom initializations including task definitions. Then, the BIOS (Basic Input Output System) gets started. Once the BIOS started, RTOS system will take over the system. As you can notice, this program style is different than the ones without an O/S. At the same time, it is also different from an application program for a general-purpose O/S because the application programing in a general-purpose O/S typically gets loaded and running after the booting process. However, in this RTOS, the initialization of the tasks run first. Developers can add their custom code to execute them first before the operating system is running. After this initialization, the kernel will be running, and it will run defined tasks.

```c
#include <msp430.h>
#include "stdbool.h"
void Task1(void) {
    while (true) {
        # wait for Signal T1
        # read buttons
        # clear Signal T1
    }
}
void Task2(void) {
    while (true) {
        # wait for Signal T2
        # read ADC
        # clear Signal T2
    }
}
void Task3(void) {
    #  set signal T3
    while (true) {
        # wait for Signal T3
        # control
        # clear Signal T3, set signal T4
    }
}
void Task4(void) {
    while (true) {
        # wait for Signal T4
        # display
        # clear Signal T4, set signal T5
    }
}
void Task5(void) {
    while (true) {
        # wait for Signal T5
        # send data
        # clear Signal T5, set signal T3
    }
}
void Task_GPIO_btn0 (void) {
    # set signal T1
}
void Task_ADC_callback0 (void) {
    # set signal T2
}
```

```
int main(void){
    Board_init();
    # custom initialization including task definitions
    BIOS_start();
    return 0;
}
```

Program 12.4. Pseudo code for RTOS.

RTOS supports task scheduling and multitasking as discussed previously. In this example, the method of synchronization using signaling was used. RTOS provides various methods for a multitasking environment such as mutexes. Mutexes are objects that can be used as signaling and they may be used in resolving a conflict in shared resources. Mutexes are binary semaphores with a method to resolve priory inversions. In addition, RTOS provides more methods that are suitable for a multitasking environment.

There are many Real-time operating systems available, and the license options may vary depending on Real-time operating systems. Texas Instruments provides TI-RTOS. TI-RTOS has a TI-RTOS kernel that was formerly called SYS/BIOS. Later in Chapter 24, we will study simple TI-RTOS examples.

Architecture Selection

An embedded system is a special purpose system, and it is up to developers to choose a proper embedded system architecture for their targeted system. The decision is typically dependent on the project requirements and specifications.

In this respect, developers may need to understand their project requirements and specification in order to choose proper hardware and software architectures for their embedded systems. At the same time, they need to understand the limitations of their choice of software architecture. In some applications, their embedded systems are relatively simple, and they can be implemented without the use of any scheduler or operating system. In some other applications, they may need to use an embedded operating system such as RTOS.

As mentioned, for some embedded systems, it is allowed to use rich resources. In this case, embedded systems can be built using a Linux kernel, Microsoft's Windows kernel, or a macOS® kernel. In high-end embedded systems, the programming environment is similar to an application program in general-purpose computing systems. These systems can be still considered embedded systems since they are designed to perform specific tasks and for the specific purposes.

Chapter 13. Pulse Width Modulation

Pulse Width Modulation (PWM) can be understood as a method of generating analog signals using digital data. A PWM signal can control the duration of logical high or low states of a periodic digital signal. PWM signals are useful in many applications such as controlling DC motors, valves, pumps, and the brightness of LEDs. There are two major parameters determining the behavior of a PWM signal. These parameters are duty cycle and frequency. Previously, we could vary the frequency of periodic digital signals. In this section, we will learn how to control the duty cycle of the digital signals.

PWM signals

A duty cycle of a PWM signal can be determined by the percentage obtained by the fraction of the "ON" time and the period of the PWM signal. Let us suppose that a logical high level is ON state. Now, a duty cycle (%) can be obtained as follows:

$$Duty\ Cycle\ (\%) = \frac{T_{ON}}{T_{Period}} \times 100 = \frac{T_{ON}}{T_{ON} + T_{OFF}} \times 100$$

PWM signal examples with different duty cycles are shown in Figure 13.1. It shows the duty cycle of 50% at the top. In this case, the ON time is assumed to be half of the period of the signal.

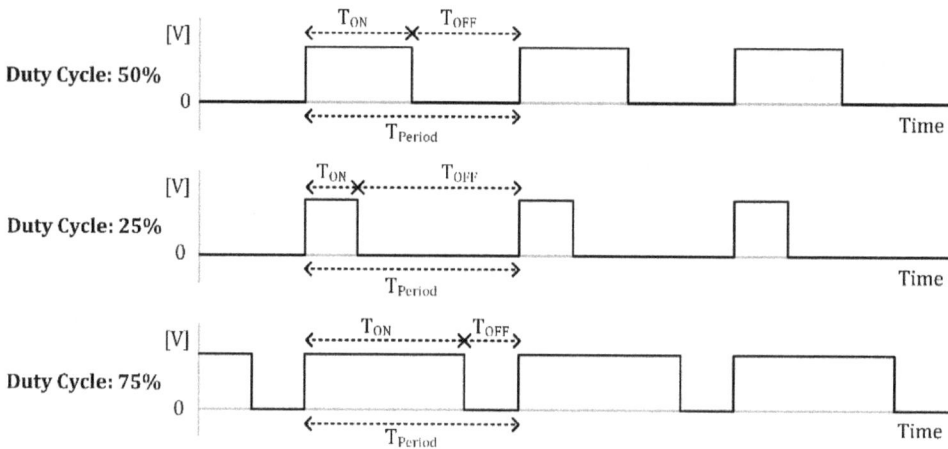

Figure 13.1. PWM signals.

In the middle of Figure 13.1, the duty cycle of a PWM signal is 25%. In this case, the ON time is less than half of the period. The ON time is 1/4 of the period. At the bottom of Figure 13.1, it shows the case of the duty cycle of 75%. In this case, the ON time is bigger than half of the period. The ON time is 3/4 of the period.

We have studied variable frequency generator examples in earlier chapters. The duty cycles were 50% and they were not variable. In this chapter, we are going to learn a method that can control the duty cycles.

PWM signals can be generated using an MSP430FR5994 MCU. In order to generate a PWM signal, let us use CCR0 and CCR1 of a Timer_A1 module. At the top of Figure 13.2, it shows a case where TA1CCR1 is half of TA1CCR0. The timer mode is configured as *Up mode*. Let us say that we can generate a logical high level (set) when the counter reaches TA1CCR0, and we can generate a logical low level (reset) when the counter reaches TA1CCR1. Then, an output signal alternating ON/OFF states can be generated. Since TA1CCR1 is half of the TA1CCR0, the duty cycle of the generated signal is close to 50%.

For reference, this method is different than the one we used in Chapter 7. Previously, the output signals were simply toggled at each time when the counter reaches at TA1CCR0. The frequency generated by the method shown in this chapter would be two times higher than the one in Chapter 7.

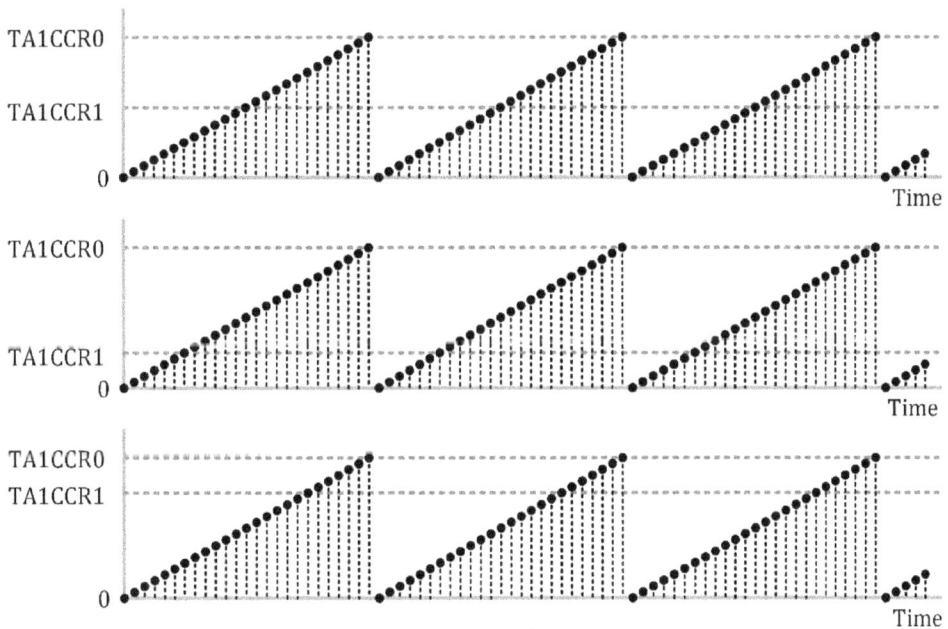

Figure 13.2. PWM generation using TA1CCR0 and TA1CCR1.

In the middle of Figure 13.2, it shows the case where TA1CCR1 is smaller than half of the TA1CCR0. In this case, the duty cycle of PWM signals is less than 50%. If TA1CCR1 is 1/4 of TA0CCR0, the duty cycle is close to 25%.

At the bottom of Figure 13.2, it shows the case where TA1CCR1 is bigger than half of the TA1CCR0. In this case, the duty cycle of a PWM signal is higher than 50%. If TA1CCR1 is 3/4 of TA1CCR0, the duty cycle is close to 75%.

As described, using TA1CCR0 and TA1CCR1, we can generate PWM signals and the duty cycles of PWM signals can be varied. In the following sections, we are going to study in more detail about generating PWM signals using an MSP430FR5994 MCU.

Software PWM

Using a timer_A1 and a GPIO port, we can write a program that can generate PWM signals. We call this technique "Software PWM" in this section. The code example of the Software PWM using CCIFG flag is shown in Program 13.1. In this program, the values of TA1CCR0 and TA1CCR1 are configured as 2000 and 500, respectively. Both TA1CCTL0 and TA1CCTL1 interrupt services are enabled.

```
#include <msp430.h>
int main(void) {
    WDTCTL = WDTPW | WDTHOLD;   // hold the watchdog timer
    PM5CTL0 &= ~LOCKLPM5;  // clear LOCKLPM5 bit
    P1DIR |= BIT0; // output direction (P1.0)
    P1DIR |= BIT2; // output direction (P1.2)
    TA1CCR0 = 2000; // TA1CCR0 value
    TA1CCR1 = 500; // TA1CCR1 value
    TA1CTL = TASSEL_2 | MC_1 | TACLR; // TA1CTL setup
    TA1CCTL0 = CCIE;  // enable CCIE
    TA1CCTL1 = CCIE; // enable CCIE
    _enable_interrupt();  // enable general interrupt
    while(1) {
        P1OUT ^= BIT0; // toggle (P1.0)
        _delay_cycles(250000);  // delay
    }
    return 0;
}


#pragma vector = TIMER1_A0_VECTOR
_interrupt void Timer1_A0_ISR(void) {
        P1OUT |= BIT2; // set (P1.2)
}


#pragma vector = TIMER1_A1_VECTOR
_interrupt void Timer1_A1_ISR(void) {
    if((TA1CCTL1 & CCIFG)!=0) { // check CCIFG flag
        P1OUT &= ~BIT2; // clear (P1.2)
        TA1CCTL1 &= ~CCIFG; // clear CCIFG flag
    }
}
```

Program 13.1. S/W PWM program using CCIFG flag (Interrupt).

Timer1_A0_ISR and *Timer1_A1_ISR* are the interrupt service routines. If the CCIFG for TA1CC0 is set, *Timer1_A0_ISR* can be executed, and the output of P1.2 can be set. Moreover, the code in *Timer1_A1_ISR* can check whether the CCIFG for TA1CCR1 is set or not. If the CCIFG is set, the output of P1.2 can be cleared.

Depending on the values of TA0CCR1 and TA0CCR0, a PWM signal can be generated. The duty cycle of the generated PWM signal can be about 25%, and the frequency of the generated PWM signal is about 500 Hz.

Another program example of the software PWM using TAIFG flag is shown in Figure 13.2. The set-up process is similar; but there are some differences such as in the use of timer flags and interrupt configurations. In this program, TA1CTL and TA1CCTL1 interrupt services are enabled. Only *Timer_A1_ISR* interrupt service routine (ISR) is used. In the ISR, it can check whether the TAIFG is set or not. If the TAIFG is set, the output of P1.2 can be set. Moreover, it can check whether the CCIFG of TA1CCR0 is set or not. If the CCIFG is set, the output of P1.2 can be cleared.

```
#include <msp430.h>
int main(void) {
  WDTCTL = WDTPW | WDTHOLD;  // hold the watchdog timer
  PM5CTL0 &= ~LOCKLPM5; // clear LOCKLPM5 bit
  P1DIR |= BIT0; // output direction (P1.0)
  P1DIR |= BIT2; // output direction (P1.2)
  TA1CCR0 = 2000; // TA1CCR0 value
  TA1CCR1 = 500; // TA1CCR1 value
  TA1CTL = TASSEL_2 | MC_1 | TAIE | TACLR; // TA1CTL setup
  TA1CCTL1 = CCIE;  // enable CCIE
  _enable_interrupt(); // enable general interrupt
  while(1) {
    P1OUT ^= BIT0; // toggle an LED
    _delay_cycles(250000); // delay
  }
  rcturn 0;
}

#pragma vector = TIMER1_A1_VECTOR
_interrupt void Timer1_A1_ISR(void) {
  if((TA1CTL & TAIFG)!=0) { // check TAIFG flag
    P1OUT |= BIT2; // set (P1.2)
    TA1CTL &= ~TAIFG; // clear TAIFG flag
  }
  if((TA1CCTL1 & CCIFG)!=0) { // check CCIFG flag
    P1OUT &= ~BIT2; // clear (P1.2)
    TA1CCTL1 &= ~CCIFG; // clear CCIFG flag
  }
}
```

Program 13.2. S/W PWM program using TAIFG flag (Interrupt).

Similar to the previous example, depending on the values of TA1CCR1 and TA1CCR0, PWM signals can be generated. The duty cycle of the generated PWM signal can be about 25%, and the frequency of the generated PWM signal is about 500 Hz.

Both Software PWM example programs can generate PWM signals with similar duty cycles and frequencies; however, internal processing and operations are different. One of the benefits of a software PWM generator is that developers can apply their own custom operation pattern using any of GPIO pins. However, in order to provide more stable PWM signals, a hardware based PWM signal generation method can be used instead. Hardware based PWM signals can be generated using an MSP430FR5994 MCU.

Hardware PWM

We have studied Software PWM methods, and PWM signals can be generated. However, there can be a chance that some of interrupt services with higher priorities may need to be running. If this instance occurs frequently, the accuracy of the PWM signals might suffer.

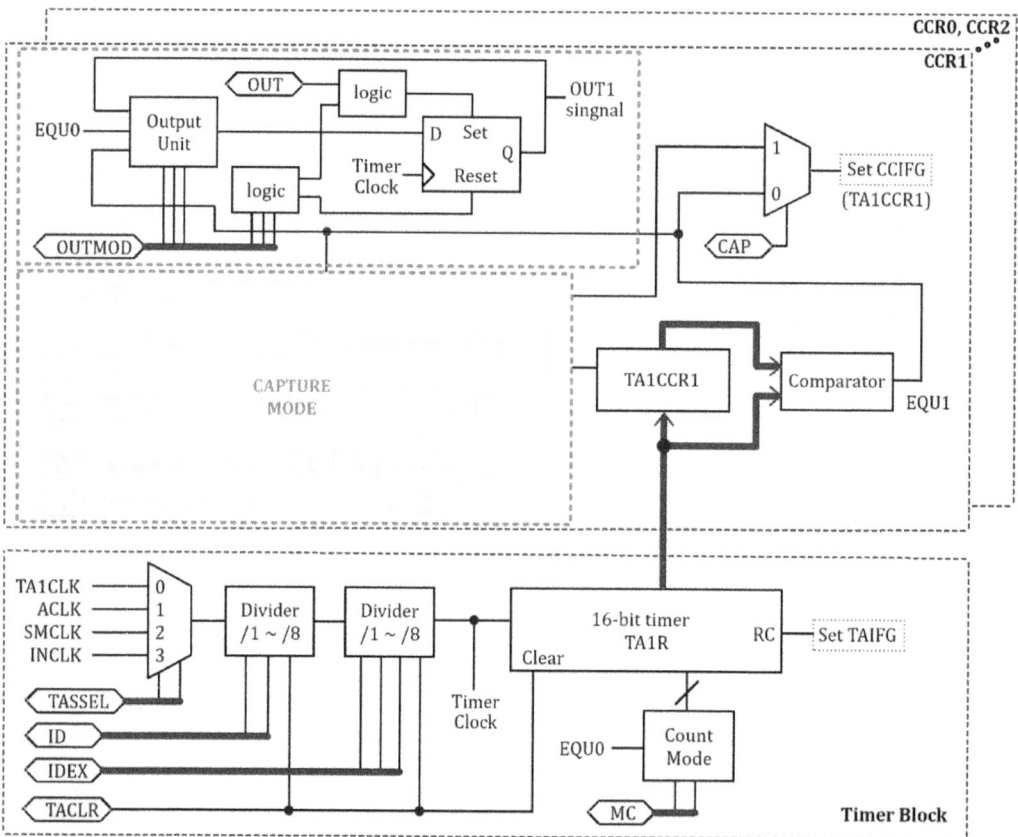

Figure 13.3. Simplified Timer_A1 block diagram showing CCR1 block [1].

For some applications such as motor control applications, stable and accurate PWM signals can be critically important. In this reason, hardware based PWM signals can be preferred choices. An MSP430FR5994 MCU can provide hardware based PWM signals using a timer. We will use Timer A1 module in this chapter.

Timer_A1 modules in an MSP430FR5994 MCU have output units and relevant components that can be used in hardware PWM generations. A simplified Timer_A1 block diagram displaying CCR1 block is shown in Figure 13.3. In this figure, the OUTPUT MODE box is uncovered. And it is still enclosed with a thick dotted line. This block shows the output unit and relevant components. Each capture/compare block has these output unit and the relevant components.

Output Unit and Output Modes

There are multiple capture and compare blocks in the Timer_A1 module. Each capture/compare block has an output unit. The output unit can be used in generating PWM signals. There are eight operating modes supported by the output unit as shown in Table 13.1. This table shows a specific case of TA1CCR0 and TA1CCR1. However, users can extend it to other cases such as TA1CCR0/TA1CCR2. One of the output modes can be selected by the configuration of OUTMOD bits.

Mode	OUTMOD Bits	Description
Output	0	Output signal is updated according to the corresponding OUT bit.
Set	1	Output signal is set when the counter reaches TA1CCR1.
Toggle/Reset	2	Output signal is toggled when the counter reaches TA1CCR1, and it is reset when the counter reaches TA1CCR0.
Set/Reset	3	Output signal is set when the counter reaches TA1CCR1, and it is reset when the counter reaches TA1CCR0.
Toggle	4	Output signal is toggled when the counter reaches TA1CCR1.
Reset	5	Output signal is reset when the counter reaches TA1CCR1.
Toggle/Set	6	Output signal is toggled when the counter reaches TA1CCR1, and it is set when the counter reaches TA1CCR0.
Reset/Set	7	Output signal is reset when the counter reaches TA1CCR1, and it is set when counter reaches TA1CCR0.

Table 13.1. OUTPUT modes (TA1CCR0/TA1CCR1) [9].

We have used a specific signal generation pattern in the previous Software PWM examples. This pattern was based on Output mode 7. In this Output mode 7, the output signal is reset when the counter reaches TA1CCR1, and the output signal is set when the counter reaches TA1CCR0. When it is properly configured, the hardware units and components can function to perform in generating a similar signal pattern. In addition to this pattern, users can generate different signal patterns by using these Output modes.

Output signal examples in *Up mode* using Timer_A1 are shown in Figure 13.4. In this example, TA1CCR1 is smaller than half of the TA1CCR0. Given the configuration, Output modes of 2, 3, 6, or 7 can generate PWM signals. However, the patterns and the duty cycles are different. The duty cycles can be varied by changing the value of TA1CCR1. Also, it is worth mentioning that we have examined the case of the *Up mode* only in this chapter. This is simply one configuration of many combinations. The other cases include a case of using other timer modes such as *continuous* mode and *up/down* mode.

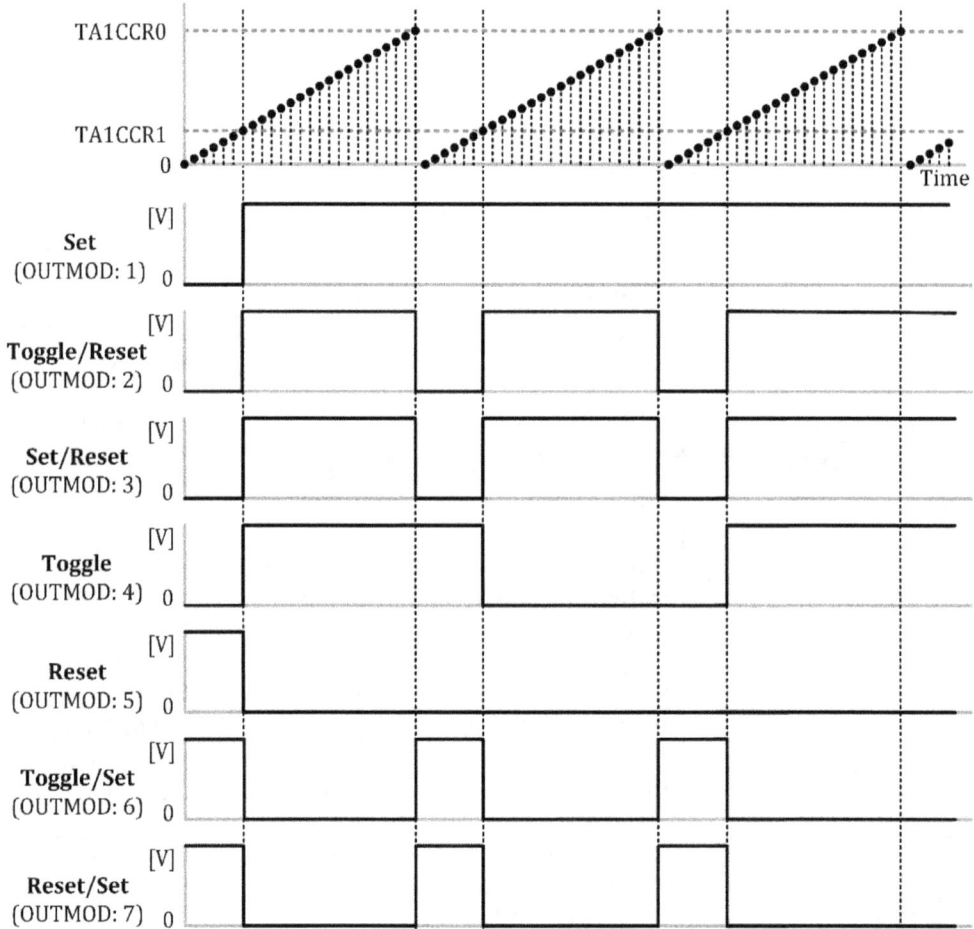

Figure 13.4. Output Signals – Up mode [9].

Pin Functions

The pin function needs to be configured properly in order to generate an output signal. Specific pins that are interconnected to the output units were pre-defined by the manufacturer. Table 13.2 shows the selected pin functions of P1.2 in an MSP430FR5994 MCU.

Pin	P1SEL1	P1SEL0	P1DIR	Description
P1.2	0	0	0	GPIO (Input)
	0	0	1	GPIO (Output)
	0	1	0	TA1.1 (Input/CC1A)
	0	1	1	TA1.1 (Output)

Table 13.2. Selected pin functions of P1.2 in an MSP430FR5994 MCU [9].

In order to generate an output signal using the corresponding output unit and the relevant components, the P1SEL1 and P1SEL0 registers need to be configured properly to provide proper alternate function for TA1.1. The output direction needs to be configured properly as well. Then, an output signal associated with the Timer A1 and the corresponding output unit can be generated properly through the pin of P1.2.

Hardware PWM Example

The hardware PWM example is shown in Program 13.3. The registers related to P1.2 are configured to provide an output signal associated with the Timer A1 and the relevant output unit. The TA1CCTL register is configured for Output mode 7. Compared to the previous Software PWM programs, this Hardware PWM program is simpler, and the MCU is less occupied with the tasks to be routinely processed.

```c
#include <msp430.h>
int main(void) {
    WDTCTL = WDTPW | WDTHOLD;  // hold the watchdog timer
    PM5CTL0 &= ~LOCKLPM5; // clear LOCKLPM5 bit
    P1DIR |= BIT0; // output direction (P1.0)
    P1DIR |= BIT2; // output direction (P1.2)
    P1SEL1 &= ~BIT2; // alternate function (TA1.1)
    P1SEL0 |= BIT2; // alternate function (TA1.1)
    TA1CTL = TASSEL_2 | MC_1 | TACLR; // TA1CTL setup
    TA1CCR0 = 2000; // TA1CCR0 value
    TA1CCR1 = 500; // TA1CCR1 value
    TA1CCTL1 = OUTMOD_7; // output mode selection
    while(1){
        P1OUT ^= BIT0; // toggle (P1.0)
        __delay_cycles(250000); // delay
    }
    return 0;
}
```

Program 13.3. Hardware PWM generation program.

This hardware PWM program example can generate a hardware PWM signal, and we can control the PWM frequency and duty cycle. In the following chapter, we will use this method to con a DC motor.

Chapter 14. DC Motor Control

A DC motor is an electromechanical component that transforms direct current electrical energy into mechanical energy in the form of rotation. DC motors are used in a wide range of microcontroller applications. Small-sized motors are used in handheld tools, toys, and small electronics. Large-sized DC motors are used in electric vehicles and industrial equipment. In this chapter, we will learn about a DC motor control method that is suitable for embedded systems.

DC Motor Control and Practical Consideration

An electronics circuit with a DC motor and a switch is shown on the left side of Figure 14.1. This switch is open. In the middle of the figure, it shows the case where the switch is closed. In this state, the current flows through the motor. It causes the DC motor to rotate. Next, when it is rotating, the switch can be controlled to be open as shown on the right side of the figure. Then, it will cut off the power and the rotation of the DC motor will eventually be stopped. However, there would be a possible status that a high voltage could be induced, and it might cause an arc through the air gap. This voltage spike could occur because the current flowing through the inductance of the motor would change suddenly. We can consider an equation of an inductor as follows:

$$V_L = L \frac{di_L}{dt}$$

As it can be seen from the equation, the induced voltage of an inductor can be very high, if there is a sudden current change for a very short time. This voltage spike or an arc is not desired because any spark can be hazardous, and the high voltage could damage electronics components. Therefore, a protection method is needed due to the potential arc and unwanted high voltage. One of the methods is to use a flyback diode.

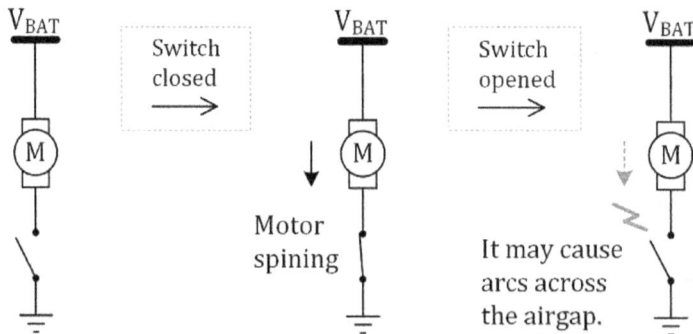

Figure 14.1. Simplified DC motor control and the practical consideration.

Flyback diode

A flyback diode is a diode connected in parallel to an inductor, and the flyback diode is placed with the reverse polarity from the power. The inductor could be a relay or motor. A flyback diode can be used in tackling the described practical problem of an arc or a high voltage. This flyback diode also has other names such as a kickback diode and snubber diode. Let us consider a case shown on the left side of Figure 14.2. This is a similar condition when the current is flowing, and the motor is operating as shown in Figure 14.1. However, the difference is that this circuit in Figure 14.2 has a diode connected across the motor.

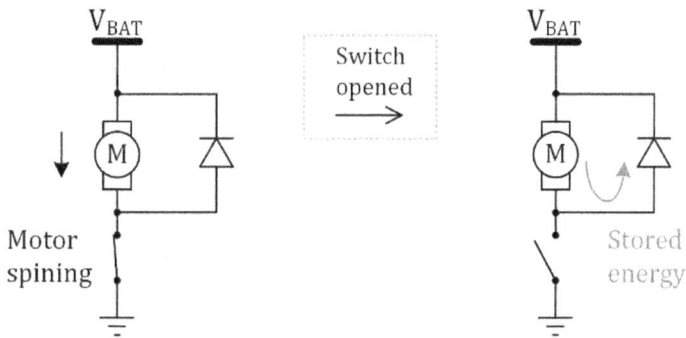

Figure 14.2. Simplified DC motor control circuit with a flyback diode.

When a motor is rotating, counter-electromotive force also known as back electromotive force (EMF) can be induced. This is because the motor is also like a generator. Back EMF can be measured as a voltage that appears in the opposite direction to the current flow. The voltage of the back EMF is related to the speed of the motor. Back EMF is not necessarily bad because the current consumption of a motor drops while the motor is spinning. Now, the switch can be turned off as shown on the right side of the figure. In this case, there is a still path through the diode. Therefore, the remaining current can flow through the path of the flyback diode. In this reason, it could reduce a possibility of an unwanted arc or high voltage. Flyback diodes can also be used in circuits such as relay switch applications.

Basic DC Motor Control Circuit

A switch for the motor control can be implemented using a power transistor. A basic DC motor control circuit using an NPN power transistor is shown in Figure 14.3. A base resistor is used between a GPIO pin and the base of a transistor. The base resistor is an essential component in this control circuit. When the logical output level of the GPIO pin is high, a significant current can flow through the motor. It causes the motor to spin. When the logical level of the GPIO pin is low, the current across the motor is very small. It can make the motor stop eventually. During the transition from ON to OFF state, the remaining current has a path through the diode.

Then, the motor current can decay. This is a practical circuit example of controlling a DC motor in embedded systems. For instance, one of the GPIO pins of an MSP430FR5994 MCU can be used to control a DC motor as a vibration motor.

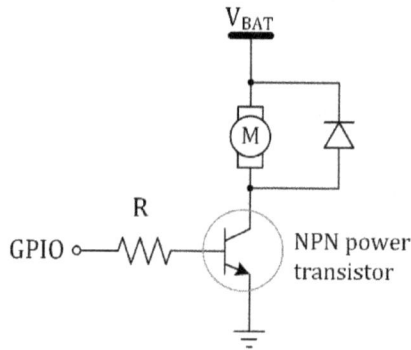

Figure 14.3. Basic DC motor control circuit.

This basic DC motor control circuit can control a motor to spin. However, it cannot change the direction of the rotation. If developers want to control the direction of the rotation, an H-bridge motor control driver can be used.

H-bridge Motor Control Driver

An H-bridge is a circuit configuration that can switch the polarity of the voltage across a load. Let us say the load in this section is a DC motor. An H-bridge circuit with ideal switches is shown on the left side of Figure 14.4. Four ideal switches and one motor components are used. As you can see, the graphical representation of the circuit due to the arrangement of the four switches is similar to the letter H.

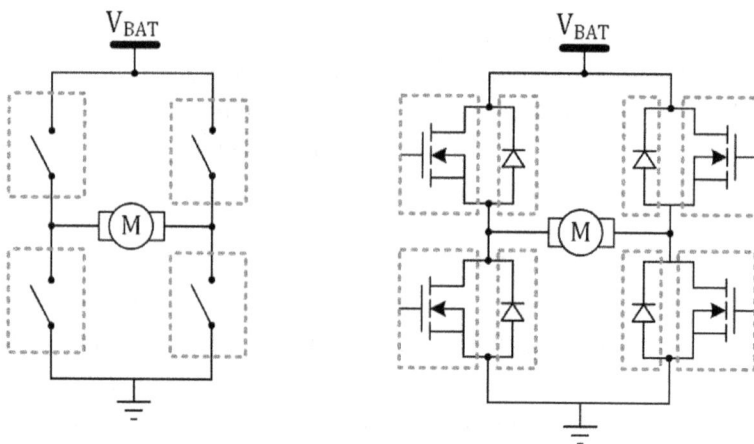

Figure 14.4. H-bridge circuits.

An ideal switch can be implemented by replacing it with a N-channel power MOSFET (metal–oxide–semiconductor field-effect) transistor and a diode as a flyback diode. All switches were replaced with this N-channel MOSFET power transistors and diodes as shown on the right side of Figure 14.4. To compare the cases of an NPN power transistor and a N-channel MOSFET, a resistor at the gate of the MOSFET transistor is not necessary. This H-bridge circuit is a basic H-bridge configuration that we will study in more detail in the following sections.

Let us consider the case where two transistors are turned ON and the rest of transistors are remained turned OFF as shown on the left side of Figure 14.5. In this case, the current can flow through the motor and two of the transistors at each side. On the right side of the figure, it shows the other case where the other two transistors are turned ON instead. In this case, the current can flow through the motor as well. However, the current directions in these two cases are different. Thus, the direction of the rotation of a motor can be switched by controlling these transistors. Let us say that the first case is a forward direction, the other case is a reverse direction for ease of explanation in this chapter.

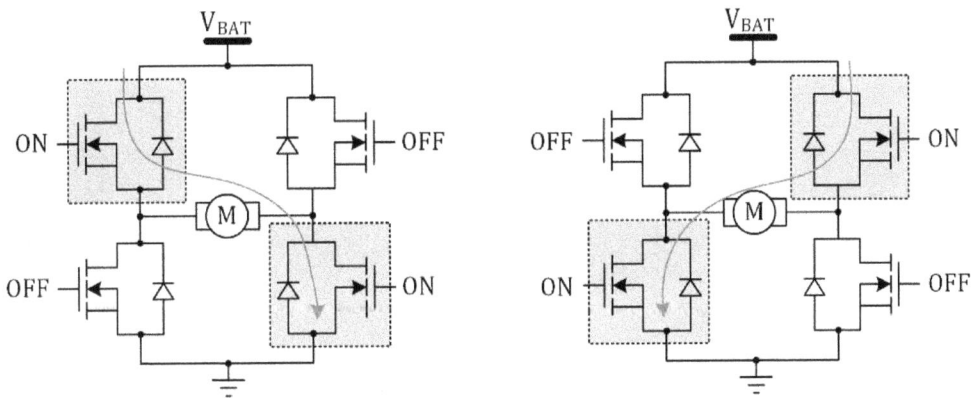

Figure 14.5. Forward and reverse directions.

Decay Modes

As shown on the left side of Figure 14.6, if the H-bridge driver is configured for the forward direction, the motor can spin. Then, let us say we want to control it to stop. The figure in the middle shows the condition that all of the transistors are turned OFF. In this case, as we have discussed earlier, there is a path of the current through the flyback diodes. Let us assume that this behavior of turning all transistors OFF is the state during the dead time in this example. However, the behavior during the dead time can be implemented differently by the manufacturer. Next, there can be further steps of decay modes that are implemented for stop conditions depending on the H- bridge motor drivers. Let us examine different decay modes for stop conditions.

One of the decay modes is a *fast decay* mode. In order to stop the motor, the motor driver can turn the opposing transistors ON as shown at the top right side of Figure 14.6. These transistors are turned ON until the current decays to zero or during a fixed short amount of time. The current in this mode is made to decay faster than the other decay mode.

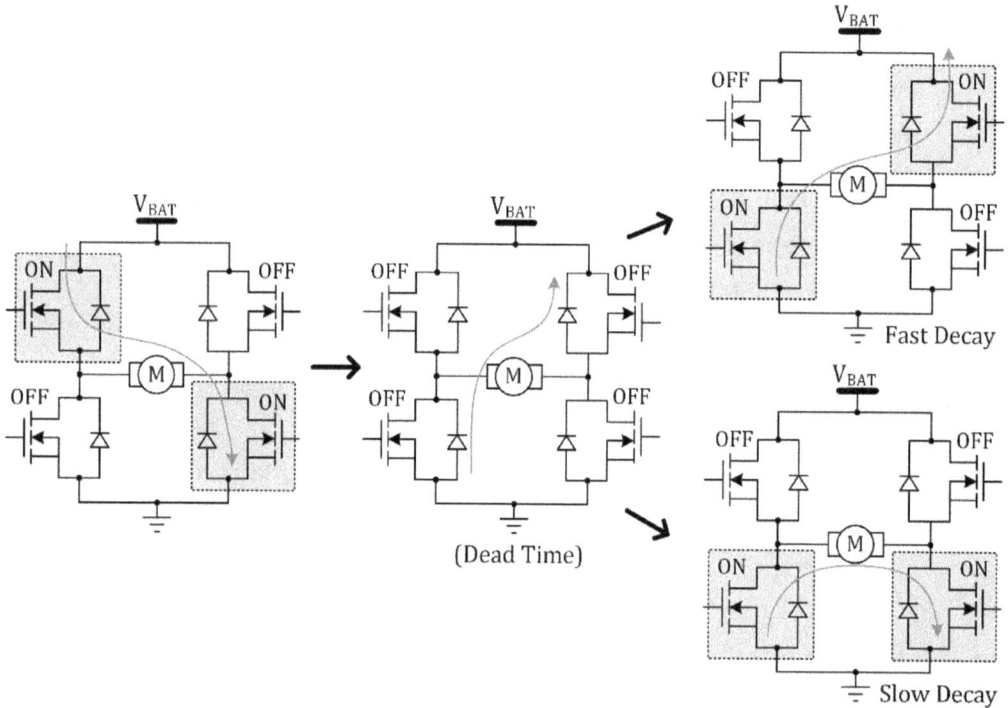

Figure 14.6. Decay modes.

Another decay mode is a *slow decay* mode. To stop a motor, the motor driver can turn ON two transistors that are located at the lower side as shown at the bottom right side of Figure 14.6. In this configuration, there would be a back EMF involved across the motor. Shorting the back EMF can cause a very quick rotor stop. This is also known as *short brake*.

In some motor drivers, they support *mixed decay* mode. For instance, a fast decay mode can be applied for a certain duration of time. Then, a slow decay mode can be applied for another duration of time. The ratio of the durations in these two modes may vary depending on the motor driver. The *mixed decay* mode can be useful in some applications such as stepper motor driver applications.

Shoot-through

When the transistors are controlled, *shoot-through* should be avoided. An example of *shoot-through* is shown in Figure 14.7. If both of two transistors are turned ON at the same side as shown in the figure, it might cause an excessive current flow and catastrophic damage. It is common to use an H-bridge motor driver IC instead of using individual components. One of the advantages in using an H-bridge motor driver IC is that some of the H-bridge driver IC models support the shoot-through protection or prevention features.

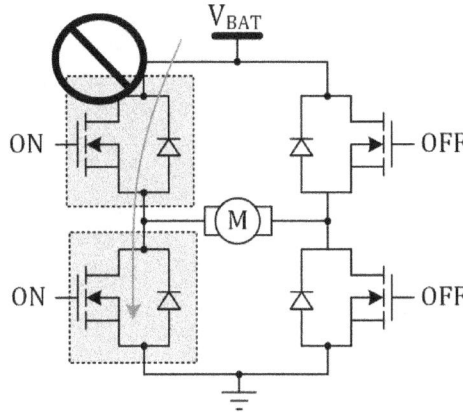

Figure 14.7. Shoot-through.

DRV8833 H-bridge Motor Driver

There are many H-bridge motor driver ICs. Developers need to find a suitable one for their given project. In this book, as an example, a TI DRV8833 H-bridge motor driver IC is chosen [19]. A DRV8833 IC can be powered with the supply voltage of 2.7 V to 10.8 V. A DRV8833 IC includes two H-bridge drivers. Each H-bridge driver can provide the current up to 1.5-A RMS and 2A peak.

A simplified block diagram of this motor driver IC is shown in Figure 14.8. Two H-bridge drivers can be found on the right side, and they are connected to two DC motors. Input pins of AIN1 and AIN2 are used to control the state of one of the H-bridge drivers. The other input pins of BIN1 and BIN2 can control the other DC motor. Moreover, a DRV8833 IC provides protection features such as over-current protection and over-temperature protection. A DRV8833 IC can be controlled using a MCU such as an MSP430FR5994 MCU.

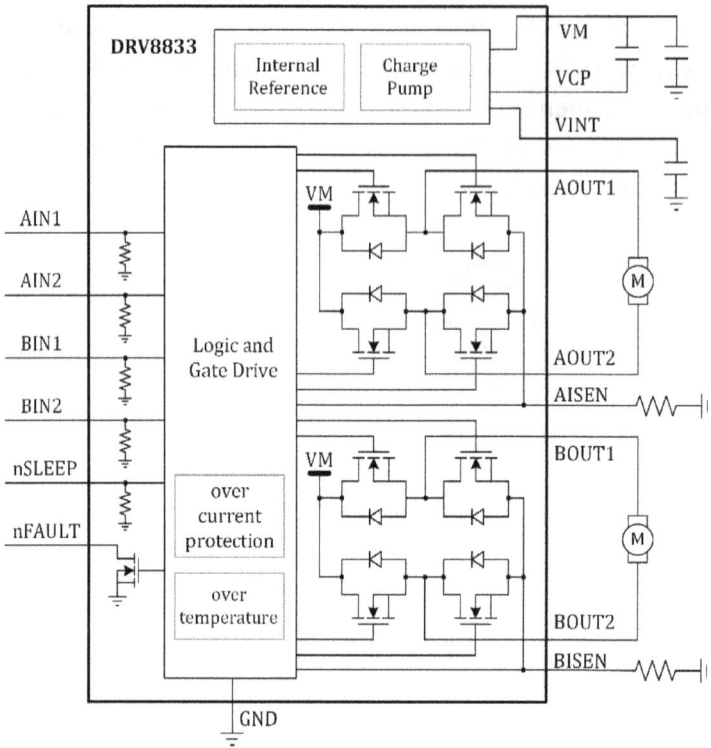

Figure 14.8. Simplified block diagram of a DRV8833 IC [19].

There is a logic and gate driver block that controls the behavior of the H-bridge drivers including decay modes. The H-bridge logic for a DRV8833 IC is shown in Table 14.1.

AIN1(BIN1)	AIN2 (BIN2)	Description
0	0	Fast decay
0	1	Reverse
1	0	Forward
1	1	Slow decay (Short brake)

Table 14.1. H-bridge logic.

The H-bridge logic table shows the relevant functions according to the input signals. If the logic levels of AIN1 and AIN2 are high and low, respectively, the motor will spin. Let us say this is a forward direction. If the logical levels of AIN1 and AIN2 are low and high, respectively, the motor will spin but, the direction of the rotation will be the opposite. This is a reverse direction.

When the motor is spinning, logical levels of both AIN1 and AIN2 can be controlled to be either low or high. Then, the motor is going to stop spinning. If the logical levels of both AIN1 and AIN2 are low, the current gets decayed in a *fast decay* mode. On the other hand, if the logical levels of both AIN1 and AIN2 are high, the current gets decayed in a *slow decay* mode. In comparison, in the fast decay, the current decays faster. However, in the slow decay, due to the effect of shorting back EMF, the rotor stops quickly.

In order to control the speed of the motor, PWM (Pulse Width Modulation) signals can be applied. Table 14.2 shows the functions when the PWM signals are applied.

AIN1(BIN1)	AIN2 (BIN2)	Description
0	PWM	Reverse (PWM) / fast decay
PWM	0	Forward (PWM) / fast decay
1	PWM	Forward (PWM) / slow decay
PWM	1	Reverse (PWM) / slow decay

Table 14.2. PWM control.

If the logical level of AIN1 is low and a PWM signal is applied to AIN2, the reverse and fast decay states will be alternating. By controlling the average power delivered to the motor, the motor speed can be controlled. Then, if the input signals of AIN1 and AIN2 are switched, the direction of the motor will be reversed.

Likewise, if the logical level of AIN1 is high and a PWM signal is applied to AIN2, the forward and slow decay states will be alternating. Next, if the input signals of AIN1 and AIN2 are switched, the direction of the motor will be reversed.

As it was explained, the speed and rotation of the motor can be varied by providing different a PWM signal and a logical signal, and it can control the average power delivered to the motor.

A simplified DRV8833 IC connection example is shown in Figure 14.9. An DRV8833 motor driver IC is connected to an MSP430FR5994 MCU.

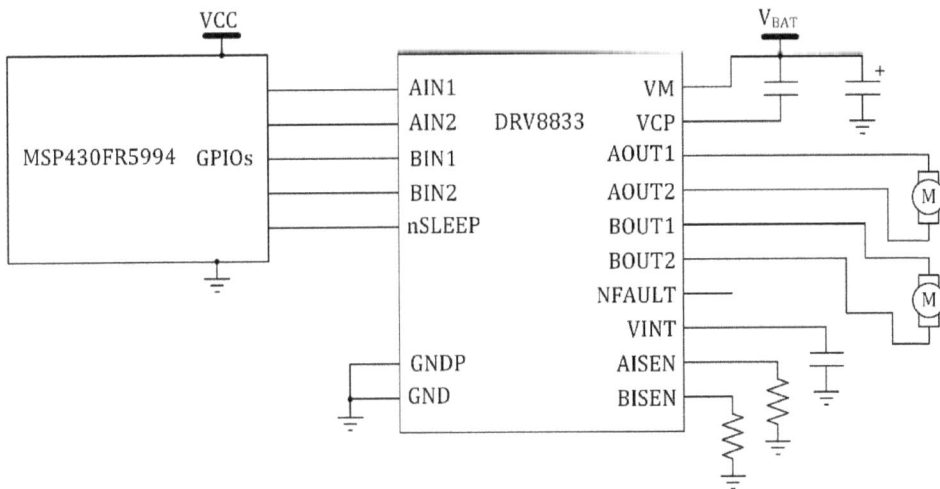

Figure 14.9. Simplified DRV8833 connection diagram for two DC motors.

This circuit example shows a case of controlling two DC motors. As it can be seen, the supply voltage of a DRV8833 IC can be higher than the supply voltage of an MSP430FR5994 MCU. A DRV8833 motor driver IC is connected to five GPIO pins of an MSP430FR5994 MCU. Four GPIO pins are connected to AIN1, AIN2, BIN1, and BIN2 pins, and one more GPIO pin is connected to the nSLEEP pin. If the logic level of this pin is high, the motor driver will be activated. However, if the logical level of this pin is low, the motor driver enters a low-power sleep mode.

DRV8833 Motor Driver Module

In order to reduce the complexity, instead of using an individual DRV8833 IC, a PCB module with an DRV8833 motor driver IC can be used. There are several modules available from different vendors. Readers can choose their own DRV8833 module. One of the modules shown in this section is an Adafruit® DRV8833 module. Using this module, the connection can become simpler.

The connection diagram is shown in Figure 14.10. In this example, only one motor is connected. There is "VM" pin in the module. This pin is internally connected to the VM pin of the DRV8833 IC on the PCB. In this module, there is a small screw fixed terminal block. This module supports reverse polarity protection through this terminal block. VM pin can be also connected through this terminal block. Either the terminal block or directly VM pin would be fine in supplying the power. However, if it would be a good idea to supply the power through the terminal block due to the reverse polarity protection function.

For test and safety purposes, a DC power supply can be used instead of batteries. A power supply can provide additional protection by limiting the supply current. Using the power supply, a proper supply voltage can be provided. The supply voltage to the DRV8833 module has to meet the specification of a chosen DC motor. For instance, a DC gearbox motor may have a recommended operating range such as 3 V to 6 V DC. A user can choose the supply voltage as 5 V.

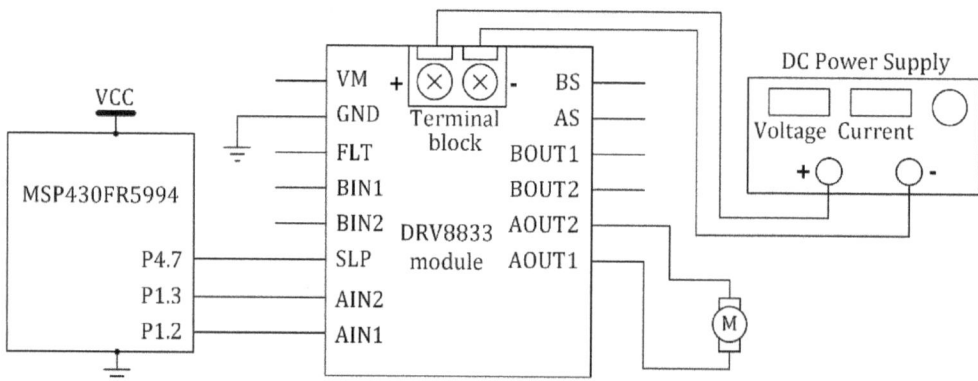

Figure 14.10. DRV8833 module connection diagram [20].

In this diagram, three pins are connected to an MSP430FR5994 MCU. The AIN1 and AIN2 pins are connected to the pins of P1.2 and P1.3, respectively. The SLP pin is the internally connected to nSLEEP pin of the DRV8833 IC. The SLP pin is connected to the pin of P4.7.

On a BH EDU board, a DRV8833 IC is placed. Users need to connect to the proper headers to access pins of the motor driver IC.

Pin functions

The selected pin functions of P1.2 and P1.3 are shown in Table 14.3. As we have studied in the previous chapter, P1SEL1, P1SEL0, and P1DIR need to be configured properly for a proper alternate function. As shown in the table, the alternate functions for P1.2 and P1.3 are chosen. They are related to TA1.1 and TA1.2, respectively, and they can generate PWM signals.

Pin	P2SEL1	P2SEL0	P2DIR	Description
P1.2	0	0	0	GPIO (Input)
	0	0	1	GPIO (Output)
	0	1	0	TA1.1 (Input/CC1A)
	0	1	1	TA1.1 (Output)
P1.3	0	0	0	GPIO (Input)
	0	0	1	GPIO (Output)
	0	1	0	TA1.2 (Input/CC2A)
	0	1	1	TA1.2 (Output)

Table 14.3. Selected pin functions of P1.2 and P1.3 in an MSP430FR5994 MCU [9].

DC Motor Control Example

A DC motor control program is shown in Program 14.1. This is based on the connection shown in Figure 14.10. In this program, the GPIO ports and the Timer_A1 are configured properly for the hardware PWM signals through P1.2 and P1.3. In the previous chapter, we studied the program that can generate PWM signals through one pin. The program in this chapter can generate hardware PWM signals through two separate pins.

```
#include <msp430.h>
int main(void) {
    WDTCTL = WDTPW | WDTHOLD;  // hold the watchdog timer
    PM5CTL0 &= ~LOCKLPM5; // clear LOCKLPM5 bit
    P1DIR |= BIT0; // output direction (P1.0)
    P4DIR |= BIT7; // output direction (P4.7)
    P4OUT |= BIT7; // set (P4.7)
    P1DIR |= BIT2 | BIT3; // output direction (P1.2, P1.3)
    P1SEL1 &= ~(BIT2 | BIT3); // alternate function (TA1.1, TA1.2)
    P1SEL0 |= (BIT2 | BIT3); // alternate function, (TA1.1, TA1.2)
    TA1CTL = TASSEL_2 | MC_1 | TACLR; // TA1CTL setup
    TA1CCR0 = 2000; // TA1CCR0 value
```

```
  TA1CCR1 = 1000; // TA1CCR1 value
  TA1CCTL1 = OUTMOD_7; // Output mode 7
  TA1CCR2 = 2000; // TA1CCR2 value
  TA1CCTL2 = OUTMOD_7; // Output mode 7
  while(1){
    P1OUT ^= BIT0; // toggle (P1.0)
    _delay_cycles(250000);  // delay
  }
  return 0;
}
```

Program 14.1. PWM DC motor control example.

The duty cycles of the PWM signals can be controlled by tweaking TA1CCR1 and TA1CCR2 values. In this case, TA1CCR1 and TA1CCR2 values are configured as 1000 and 2000, respectively. Since TA1CCR0 is 2000, the duty cycles for the PWM signals at P1.2 and P1.3 are about 50% and 100%. The ideal 100% PWM signal is simply like a logical high level. It is worth mentioning that it is not the same as a solid logical high signal. The signal may show some periodic glitches. Referring to Table 14.2, this program example will demonstrate the operations of the reverse motor rotation and slow decay.

Users can change the TA1CCR1 and TA1CCR2 values in order to create various conditions shown in Table 14.2. The value of TA1CCR0 can be tweaked and it may vary the frequency. While any of the PWM frequency can be chosen, it is preferred to choose a frequency that is above audible frequency range. This is because an audible noise in a motor could be problematic in some applications. However, if the PWM frequency gets too high, the motor driver may not be able to handle the control signals properly. This may also be relevant to the choice of decay mode.

In Chapter 22, we will study a system integration topic and a simple educational robot will be shown as an example. This robot is a differential wheeled robot platform, which has two separately driven wheels with one or more caster wheels. In order to operate the two motors, users can modify this example program to add two more pins that can generate PWM signals.

Chapter 15. Servo Motor

A servo motor is a component that can produce a rotary motion typically for precise control of angular position. Servo motors have been utilized in many microcontroller applications. Servo motors are also used in industrial robotics, manufacturing equipment, and CNC (Computer Numerical Control) machines. Moreover, they can be small in size, and they are used in radio-controlled (R/C) cars, airplanes, and boats. In this chapter, we will learn about servo motors.

Open Loop Control System

A gear motor can be controlled by an open loop system as shown in Figure 15.1. In this open loop control system, an input is simply fed to a controller, and the controller controls a gear motor accordingly. To make it clear, the output of a system is not used as an input back to the system to determine whether the output has achieved a goal or not.

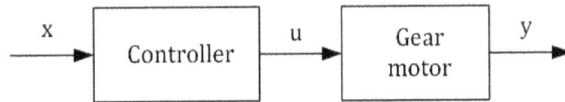

Figure 15.1. Open loop control.

The advantage of the open loop control is the reduction of system complexity. However, this open loop system cannot correct errors that may have been caused by any disturbances. In a normal condition, the output behavior may be close to the desired behavior or goal. However, in the presence of disturbances, there is a chance that the output behavior can be deviated from the goal.

Closed Loop Control

A gear motor can be controlled by a closed loop system as shown in Figure 15.2. In a closed loop control system, the output of a system has a feedback loop to the system and the output is used as an input to the system to determine whether the output has achieved a goal.

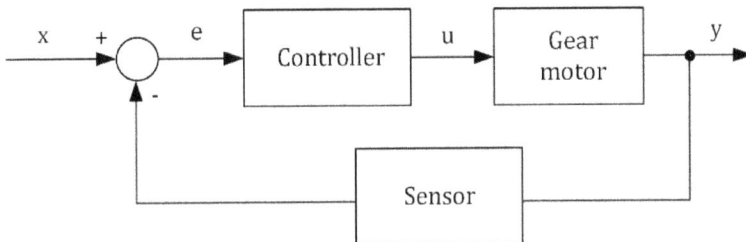

Figure 15.2. Closed loop control.

A feedback controller controls the gear motor. The difference between the variable "x" and the sensor block output is going to be used as an input for the feedback controller. The sensor block converts the behavior of the gear motor such as rotation or angle to a proper format of a voltage, a current, or a signal. This closed loop system is more complex than the open loop system. However, in the presence of disturbances, the output behavior can be corrected in order to meet the goal and for the desired behavior. A servo motor is an example of closed loop control systems.

PID Control

A simplified PID control block diagram is shown in Figure 15.3. The block diagram includes proportional (P), integral (I), and derivative (D) blocks. The controller block is related to these PID blocks. This is a conceptual representation of the controller. Their outputs of PID blocks are summed to provide the input to the motor. This is an example of a proportional integral derivative controller (PID) controller. A PID controller continuously calculates an error between the goal and the measured value, and it applies corrections based on proportional, integral, and derivative terms. A PID controller has been widely used in control applications.

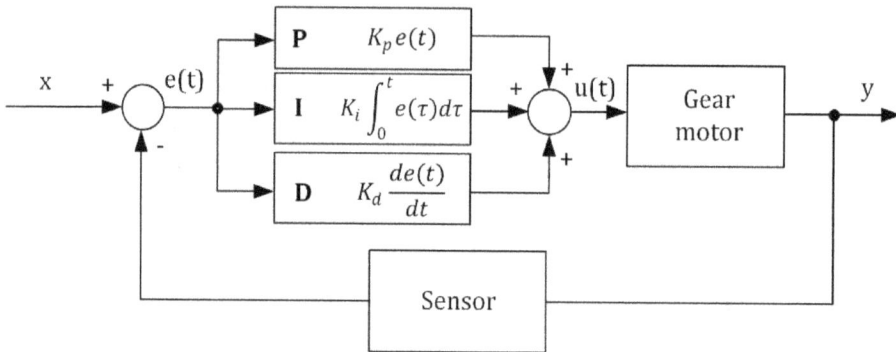

Figure 15.3. Simplified PID control.

The control function can be expressed by the equation as follows:

$$u(t) = K_p e(t) + K_i \int_0^t e(\tau)d\tau + K_d \frac{de(t)}{dt}$$

The first term is the proportional term. It contributes to the output that is proportional to the current error value. The rate of the change can be adjusted by a constant K_p. The second term is the integral term. The contribution to the output can be determined by the sum of instantaneous errors over time. The rate of the change can be adjusted by a constant K_i. The third term is the derivative term. The contribution is determined by the slope of the error over time. The rate of the change can be adjusted by a constant K_d. There are three control terms. In some applications, only one or two terms can be used depending on the application. Proportional and integration terms are chosen, which is known as a PI controller.

PID controllers can be found in many control applications including servo control systems. For instance, a servo control system can include a feedback loop and a PID controller that can provide tuning of a control loop.

Servo Motor

Servo motors are used in industrial applications including industrial robots and industrial automation systems. Servo motors can provide high precision positioning. A servo motor is shown in Figure 15.4, and the servo motor is paired with an encoder. The encoder can determine the speed and position. Depending on the servo motor model, a servo motor may provide several connectors including encoder and power connectors.

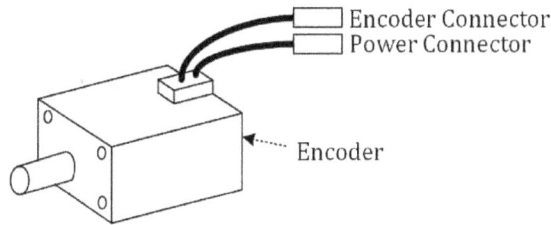

Figure 15.4. Servo motor.

Using this servo motor, a servo control system is configured as shown in Figure 15.5. The servo motor is connected to a block with servo amplifier and motion controller units. This block is connected to a computer. A custom application on the computer can control the speed and position of the servo motor. For instance, a servo control system can be applied to a conveyor system of manufacturing applications.

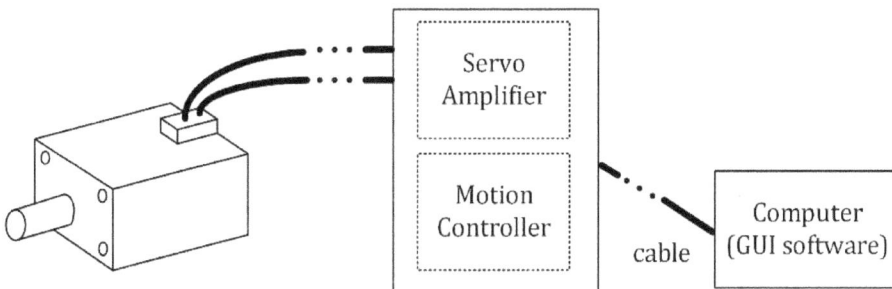

Figure 15.5. Servo control system.

Hobby/RC Servo Motor

In some small or simple electronics projects, "hobby" or "RC" servo motors are used to provide motion control. Hobby or RC servo motors are often simply called servo motors. In this book, they could be also called servo motors. However, hobby servo motors are clearly different from the described typical servo control systems. Hobby servo motors are inexpensive, and easier to control. They can be found useful in small sized electronic systems. Now, let us study more about hobby servo motors and how to control them in the following sections.

A micro servo and standard servo motors are shown in Figure 15.6. As described, hobby servo motors are called RC servo motors or RC servos, and they are widely used in small sized R/C cars and R/C airplanes. Standard servo motors are bigger than micro servo motors; however, typically, they can deliver higher torque. Hobby or RC servo motors have been used in small-sized robotics projects.

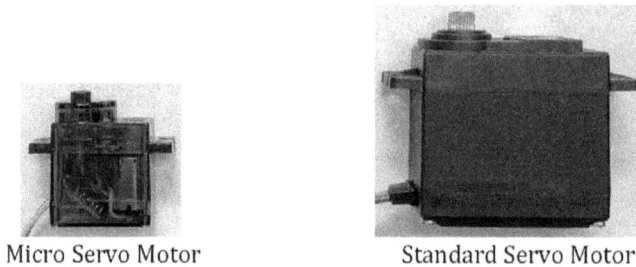

Micro Servo Motor   Standard Servo Motor

Figure 15.6. Hobby servo motors.

A simplified block diagram of a hobby servo motor is shown in Figure 15.7. The hobby servo motor has a smaller closed loop system than the industrial servo motor system we have studied previously. A hobby servo motor has a feedback control, and the shaft position is measured by a potentiometer. A PWM signal can be applied to a hobby servo motor, and the shaft of the hobby servo motor can hold a corresponding angular position.

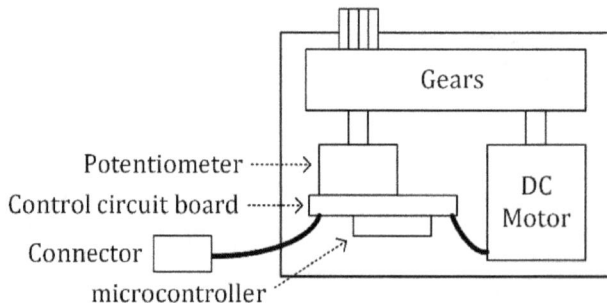

Figure 15.7. Simplified block diagram of a hobby servo motor.

Control of a Hobby/RC Servo Motor

It is typical to find a 3-pin female header that is attached to a hobby servo motor. One of the pins is a control signal line. A digital signal can be applied through this pin to control the shaft position of the servo motor. Examples of control signal patterns are shown in Figure 15.8. It shows the neutral position case in the center of the figure. The ON time is 1.5 ms, and the period of the signal is 20 ms. When the servo motor receives this control signal pattern, the shaft of the hobby servo motor attempts to stay at the neutral position. This control signal can be generated by an MCU. An MCU can generate a PWM signal with the frequency of 50 Hz and a proper duty cycle for the 1.5 ms ON time.

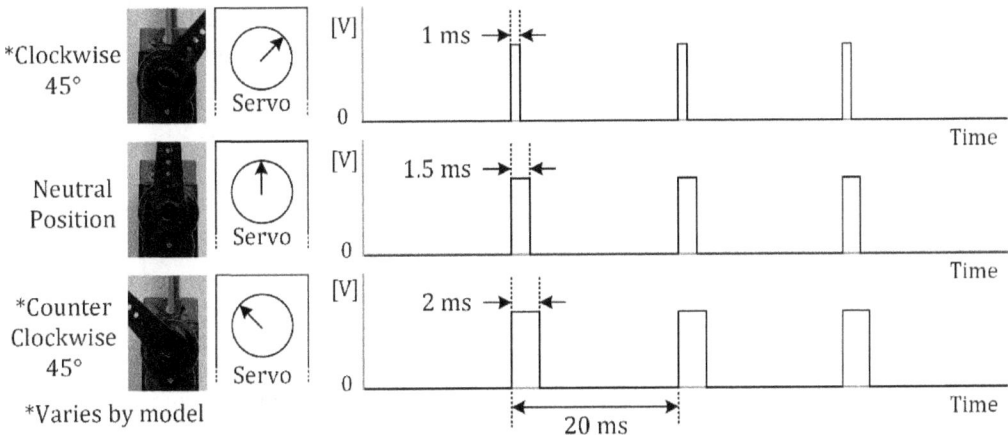

Figure 15.8. Control signal pattern examples.

Next, the duty cycle can be varied to generate a 1-ms ON time pattern as shown in the case at the top of the figure. Then, the shaft of the servo motor will be rotated by 45 degrees.

Let us suppose we set the shaft of the servo motor back to the neutral position. Next, we can change the duty cycle to generate the 2-ms ON time pattern as shown in the case at the bottom of the figure. Then, the shaft of the servo motor will be rotated to the other direction by 45 degrees. In this way, the servo motor position can be varied by applying proper PWM signals.

A typical range of the ON time is 1 ms to 2 ms. However, depending on the model of servo motors, the servo motor position can travel further by applying a lower than 1-ms or higher than 2-ms ON time pattern. For instance, some of the servo motors can provide a 180-degree range of motion.

If the ON time is out of the operating range, the servo motor may not respond. The specifications of servo motors may vary depending on manufacturers. Developers need to refer to the documents from the manufacturers for more information such as operating ranges.

There are continuous rotation servos. While a regular servo motor can rotate the shaft within only a certain rotation range, the shaft of the continuous rotation servos can spin the shaft continuously. In this case, the PWM control signal can control the speed and direction of the servo motor.

Micro Servo Motor Example

There are a wide range of selections of servo motor models. One of them is the SG90 servo motor. There are several similar models with different specifications. As an example, in this chapter, a SG92R servo motor is chosen, the connection diagram is shown in Figure 15.9. A SG92R servo motor is similar to a SG90 servo motor; However, a SG92R has a higher torque.

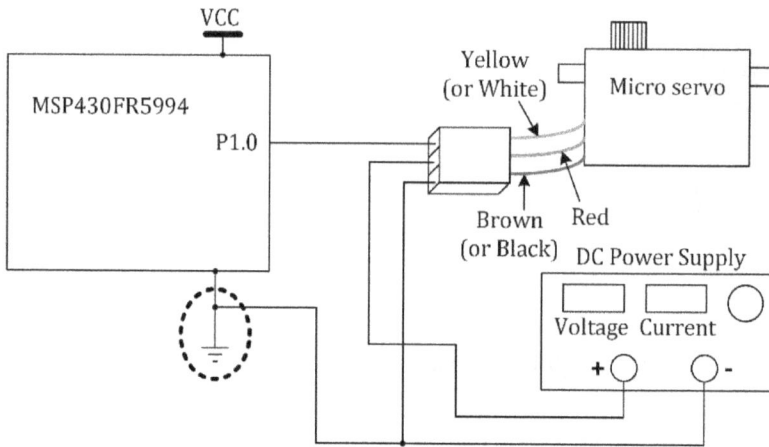

Figure 15.9. micro servo motor connection example.

The color of the control signal is yellow or white depending on the servo motors. This control line is connected to the pin of P1.0 of an MSP430FR5994 MCU. The red color line is connected to the positive terminal and the brown line is connected to the negative terminal of a power supply. The brown line is a ground signal line, and the color of this line can be found black depending on the model. The supply voltage for this servo motor is 5 V. It is worth mentioning that the ground lines for an MSP430FR5994 MCU and the servo motor may need to be connected to each other.

In this example, the pin of P1.0 is used to control the servo motor. On the Launchpad, this P1.0 pin is pre-configured to be connected to a red LED. However, this P1.0 pin can be disconnected from the LED and the P1.0 pin can be accessible directly by removing the shunt jumper (JP7) as shown in Figure 5.10.

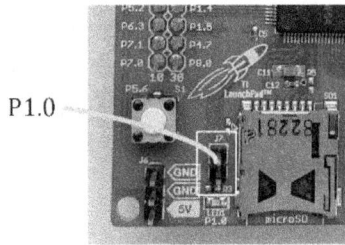

P1.0

Figure 15.10. Shunt jumper removal for P1.0.

After removing this shunt jumper, you can see two pins. The exposed pin close to the MCU is the breakout pin of P1.0. After the experiment in this chapter, this removed shunt jumper may need to be placed back for other experiments. In Chapter 20, this P1.0 pin needs to be directly accessed again for timer capture examples.

Hobby Servo Motor Control Example

A hobby servo motor control example is shown in Program 15.1 The selected alternate function for P1.0 is associated with TA0.1. The function selection registers are configured properly as shown in the program. Previously, we have used the Timer_A1. In this program, Timer_A0 is used instead. The timer register configuration for Timer_A0 is very similar to the one for Timer_A1.

```
#include <msp430.h>
int main(void) {
    WDTCTL = WDTPW | WDTHOLD;  // hold the watchdog timer
    PM5CTL0 &= ~LOCKLPM5; // clear LOCKLPM5 bit
    P1DIR |= BIT0 | BIT1; // output direction (P1.0, P1.1)
    P1SEL1 &= ~BIT0; // alternate function (TA0.1)
    P1SEL0 |= BIT0; // alternate function (TA0.1)
    TA0CTL = TASSEL_2 | MC_1 | TACLR; // TA0CTL setup
    TA0CCR0 = 20000; // set the value of TA0CCR0
    TA0CCR1 = 1500; // set the value of TA0CCR1
    TA0CCTL1 = OUTMOD_7; // output mode selection
    while(1){
        P1OUT ^= BIT1; // toggle (P1.1)
        _delay_cycles(250000); // delay
    }
    return 0;
}
```

Program 15.1. Servo motor programming example.

The value of TA0CCR0 is calculated and the specific value is used to generate a 50-Hz PWM signal. Output mode 7 is selected. TA0CCR1 is calculated and the proper value is entered to generate a 1.5 ms ON time pattern.

Using this program, the position of the servo motor can be set to a neutral position initially. Users can change the value of the TA0CCR1 register. The duty cycle can be varied depending on the value of the TA0CCR1 register, and the shaft of the servo motor position can change accordingly.

Chapter 16. Basics of Serial Communications and UART

Data communication refers to the transmission of data between systems. The communication links can be a point-to-point link or point-to-multiple links. Embedded systems typically utilize one or more communication modules to exchange data between microcontrollers and other external devices. In this chapter, we will learn about serial communications and a UART module on an MSP430FR5994 MCU.

Serial and Parallel

In digital communications, serial and parallel communications can be used to exchange data between devices. Data can be transmitted and received over a single channel in serial communication. Or data can be transmitted and received simultaneously over multiple channels in parallel communication.

Examples of serial communication for computer applications are USB, Firewire, and SATA. Examples of parallel communication for computer applications are IDE (Integrated Drive Electronics) and PCI (Peripheral Component Interconnect).

Intuitively, it would seem parallel communication might offer faster speed of data transfer compared to serial communication. However, practically, this is not the case in modern systems. Serial communication offers faster speed of data transfer. There are many reasons. Firstly, the signals that travel along the multiple wires may not arrive at the destination at the same time. This difference may get more significant as the frequency gets higher. It may cause a problem in synchronization, and, eventually, it will affect and limit the data transmission speed. Secondly, the parallel wires may suffer from crosstalk as well as inter symbol interference (ISI) due to noise. For these reasons, parallel communication may result in lower speed than serial communication.

Types of Communication Systems

Types of communications systems can be defined in several ways. Let us consider three types with respect to communication channels between two systems as shown in Figure 16.1. A simplex communication system is shown at the top. *System A* can send the data over a channel to *System B,* while *System B* is unable to send data back to *System A.* A simplex communication system transmits data in one direction only. An example is the communication between a radio broadcast station and a listener.

Duplex communication systems transmit data and receive data in both directions. In duplex communications, there are half-duplex and full-duplex communication systems. A half-duplex communication system is shown in the middle of Figure 16.1. A half-duplex system can send and receive data between two systems but not simultaneously. *System A* and *System* B in the duplex system of the figure can exchange data, but it does not send and receive the data simultaneously. An example is a walkie-talkie, which is a two-way radio transceiver and only one radio on the channel can transmit at a time.

Simplex Communication

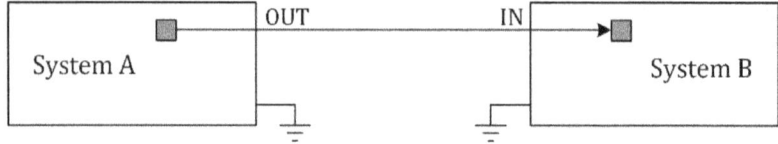

Duplex Communication

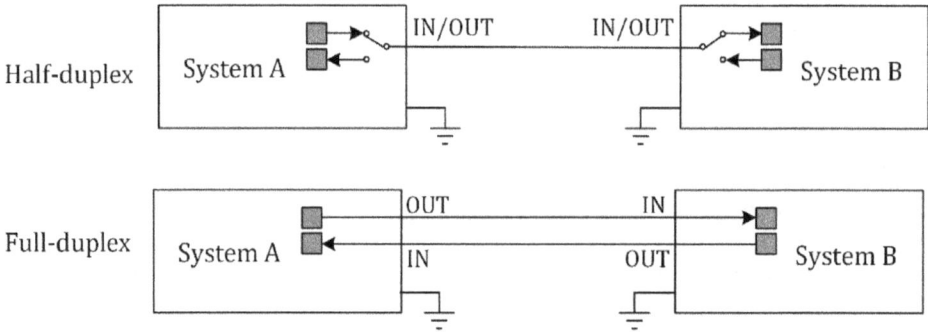

Figure 16.1. Types of communication systems.

A full-duplex communication system is shown at the bottom of Figure 16.1. A full-duplex system can send and receive data between two systems simultaneously. *System A* and *System* B in the full duplex system of the figure can exchange simultaneously. An example of duplex communication is mobile phone communication.

Universal Asynchronous Receiver/Transmitter

Universal asynchronous receiver-transmitter (UART) peripherals are useful in microcontroller applications. There can be multiple UART modules integrated on an MCU. A UART provides asynchronous serial communication. It has been widely used in data communications between external ICs. An example is the UART communication between a MCU and a USB-to-UART IC. In this configuration, the MCU can communicate with a computer over a USB interface through the USB-UART IC. An MSP430FR5994 Launchpad board includes an on-bard eZ-FET debug probe. This eZ-FET debug probe provides a "backchannel" UART-over-USB connection. The backchannel term is used to differentiate the UART channel that is provided through the booster pack header pins. The backchannel UART can be referred to as *Application UART* in this book. The microUSB connector on the Launchpad board is not only used to supply power to the MSP430FR5994 Launchpad board, but also to provide serial communication between an MSP430FR5994 MCU and a computer.

UART Data Transmission

A baud rate is one of the important parameters, and it needs to be matched between systems in UART communication. A baud rate is used to determine the speed of serial communication. A baud rate is usually expressed in bits-per-second (bps). Standard baud rates include 1200, 2400, 4800, 9600, 19200, 38400, 57600, and 115200. Let us say that 9600 bps is chosen for a certain system. Each bit for the UART data transmission has a fixed time duration. If we calculate 1 divided by 9600 bps, we can obtain 104 μs per bit. This is the value associated with the time duration for a single bit to be sent or received.

A UART data frame format is shown in Figure 16.2. One bit is allocated for the start bit. The logic level of the start bit is low. One bit or two bits can be allocated for the stop bit(s). The logic level of the stop bit is high. Between the start and stop bits, there are data bits and a parity bit. The number of bits for data can be any choice between 5 and 9. A common choice is 7 or 8. Typically, data can be transmitted least significant bit (LSB) first. The use of the parity bit is selectable, which is expressed as the "0~1 bit" in the frame format.

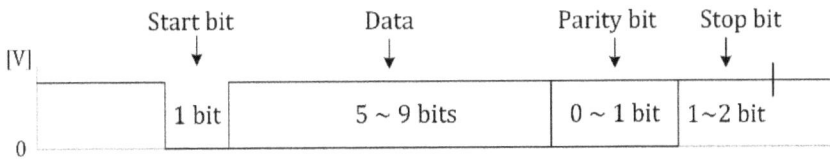

Figure 16.2. UART data frame format.

Let us consider a 9600 7E1 case. In this 9600 7E1 setting, the baud rate is 9600 bps. The number of data bits is 7, and the parity bit is enabled. The setting for the parity bit is even. One bit of the stop bit is selected. The 7E1 UART data frame case is shown in Figure 16.3.

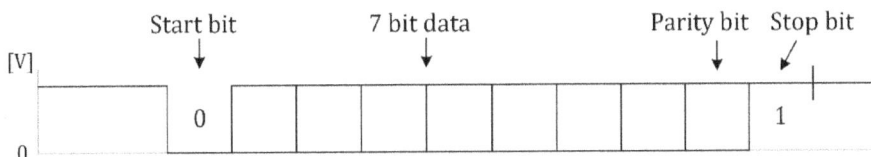

Figure 16.3. 7E1 UART data frame.

Now, let us suppose we want to send character **T**. Let us create this UART data packet. The ASCII (American Standard Code for Information Interchange) code for the character T is 0x54. We can send the bits of data. LSB can be sent first. The value of the parity bit is 1 because it can make the even number of 1s in the data packet excluding start and stop bits. One bit is used for the stop bit. This UART data packet is shown in Figure 16.4.

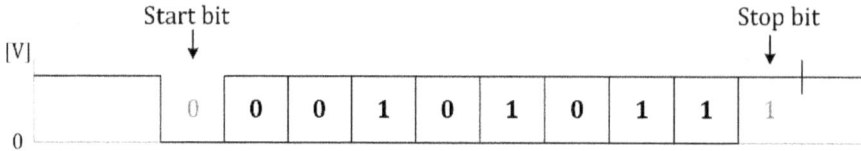

Figure 16.4. 7E1 UART data frame example for the character of T.

Another common choice is 8N1. In this 8N1 setting, the number of data bits is 8 and the parity bit is not used. The 8N1 UART data frame for the character T is shown in Figure 16.5. This is similar to the 7E1 case, but the difference is related to the parity bit. In this 8N1 setting, the bit that was for the parity bit in the 7E1 case is used as the bit for a part of data.

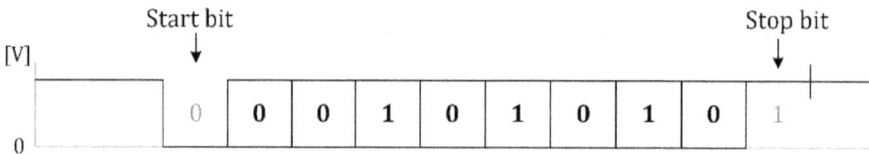

Figure 16.5. 8N1 UART data frame example for the character T.

UART Device Connection

A UART device connection example is shown in Figure 16.6. UART devices are typically connected using a crossover cable. The TX pin in *System A* is connected to the RX pin in *System B*, and the RX pin in *System A* is connected to the TX pin in *System B*.

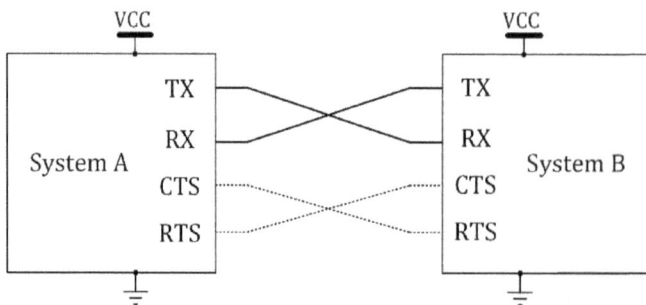

Figure 16.6. UART device connection.

Additionally, we may need VDD and GND wires. Power line configuration may vary depending on systems. The wires for RX and TX pins and additional power wires can be used for a basic connection via UART communication.

There are two more pins, RTS and CTS. They are used for hardware flow control. In some applications, a handshaking process is needed to ensure communication between systems or devices. RTS means *Request to Send*, and CTS means *Clear to Send*. RTS pin in *System A* is connected to CTS in *System B*, and CTS pin in *System A* is connected to RTS in *System B*. This is a typical connection of the hardware flow control. However, in some implementations, it can be found that RTS is connected to RTS and CTS is connected to CTS depending on their configuration.

UART connections are typically used in a point-to-point configuration as shown in Figure 16.6. There can be variants including a one-to-multiple configuration. However, the one-to-multiple configuration is not a typical connection scheme.

Software UART

Without dedicated hardware, serial communications can be implemented simply using timers and GPIO pins. This technique is called *bit-banging*. Using a *bit-banging* technique, we can implement a UART using two GPIO pins for transmit and receive channels. This can be called Software UART. We will learn about hardware UART in the following section. A hardware UART approach can be a preferred choice. However, there could be cases where software UART approaches are needed depending on the applications.

Asynchronous communication is relatively easier to implement compared to synchronous communication. UART communication is an asynchronous communication because there is no external clock signal line used for synchronization.

Software UART Programming Example

Software UART program example is shown in Program 16.1. This program keeps sending the character T over a backchannel UART. The pin of P2.0 is used as TX in this program. This matches with the TX pin configuration in the backchannel UART. This means that data will be sent to a computer. The data can be read using a terminal window in Code Composer Studio or using other serial terminal software such as PuTTY.

An array of *TX_buf* includes the pattern for the character T. It also includes the start and stop bits. This program reads the bit in sequence from this array, then, it sets or clears the output of the pin of P2.0. Since it keeps repeating, the terminal will keep receiving the character T.

The time duration between each bit is controlled by the timer_A1. The target time delay is 104 µs. This code line can result in roughly 104 µs. As it was described, the time delay of 104 µs is related to 9600 bps. In order to receive the characters successfully, the terminal setting on a computer needs to be configured properly to match with 9600 8N1.

```c
#include <msp430.h>
unsigned char TX_buf[10]={0,0,0,1,0,1,0,1,0,1}; // UART TX pattern for T
int main(void) {
    WDTCTL = WDTPW | WDTHOLD;  // hold the watchdog timer
    PM5CTL0 &= ~LOCKLPM5;  // clear LOCKLPM5 bit
    P1DIR |= 0x01; // output direction (P1.0)
    P2DIR |= 0x01; // output direction (P2.0)
    TA1CCR0 = 72;  // TA1CCR0 value, for delay
    TA1CTL = TASSEL_2 | MC_1 | TACLR;  // TA1CTL setup
    unsigned char kp; // variable
    while(1){
        for (kp=0; kp<10; kp++) { // sending the pattern
            if (TX_buf[kp]!=0) P2OUT |= 0x01; // set (P2.0)
            else P2OUT &= ~0x01; // clear (P2.0)
            TA1CTL |= TACLR; // clear (TA1R)
            TA1CCTL0 &= ~CCIFG; // clear CCIFG
            while ((TA1CCTL0 & CCIFG)==0);  // wait until CCIFG is set
        }
        P1OUT ^= 0x01; // toggle (P1.0)
        _delay_cycles(250000); // delay
    }
    return 0;
}
```

Program 16.1. Software UART program (Sending characters).

This software UART programing example does not process received data from a terminal. If a user sends data over a terminal, it will be sent to the pin of P2.1. This pin of P2.1 is related to RX in the back channel UART. However, as described, this program does not process received data. If desired, users write a code that supports an RX function.

An MSP430FR5994 MCU supports hardware UART communication. Hardware UART modules can be used to provide good communication between UART devices. Using the hardware UART modules, we can process both TX and RX data. The MSP430FR5994 UART communication module will be covered in the following sections. We will learn how to send data and how to process received data using the hardware UART modules.

Hardware UART

An MSP430FR5994 MCU has eUSCI (Enhanced Universal Serial Communication Interface) modules. An eUSCI module includes eUSCI_A and eUSCI_B modules. An eUSCI_A supports UART and SPI modes. A simplified block diagram of eUSCI_A0 in UART mode is shown in Figure 16.7. On the left side, it shows a baud rate generator. The setting of these parameters is important in UART communication. BRCLK can be found in the figure. It is used in the baud rate generator. The baud rate generator in an eUSCI_A module can provide signals for standard and non-standard baud rates. It supports two modes of operation that can be selected by a UCOS16 bit. The two modes are low-frequency baud rate and oversampling baud rate generation modes.

At the bottom of the figure, it shows the blocks associated with the transmit functions. The major blocks are *transmit state machine*, *transmit shift register*, and *transmit buffer*. The name of the transmit buffer is UCA0TXBUF. At the top of the figure, it shows the blocks associated with the receive functions. The major blocks are *receive state machine, receive shift register*, and *receive buffer*. The name of the receive buffer is UCA0RXBUF.

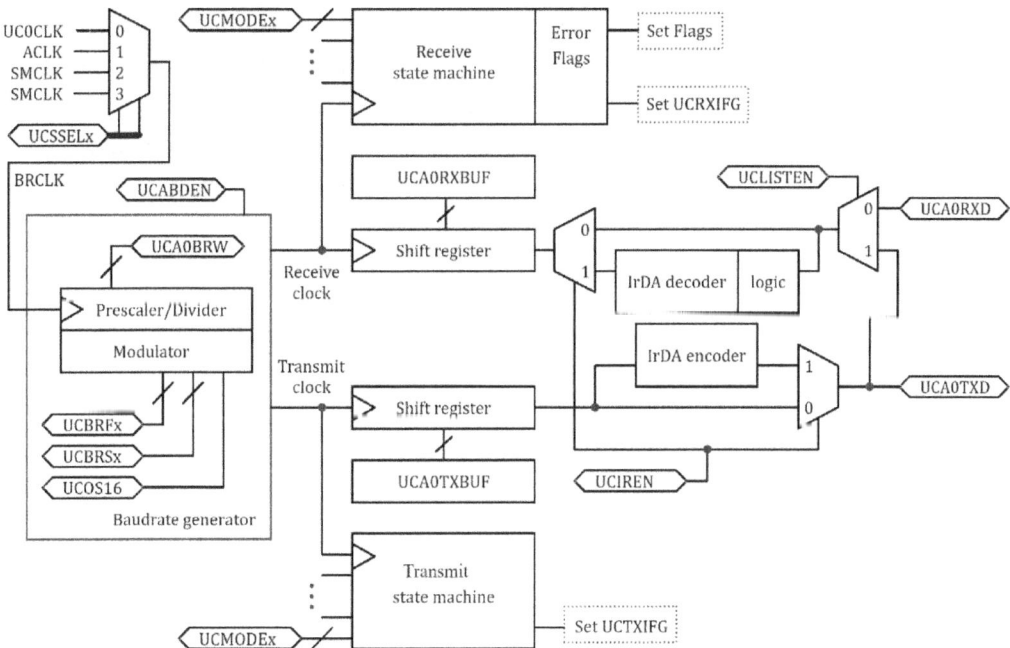

Figure 16.7. Simplified block diagram of eUSCI_A0 in UART mode [9].

There are registers related to interrupt and interrupt flags in the USCI_A0 module. *UCA0IE* register is an interrupt enable register, and it includes *UCTXIE* and *UCRXIE* bits. *UCA0IFG* register is an interrupt flag register, and it includes *UCTXIFG* and *UCRXIFG* bits.

eUSCI_A0 Initialization

Setting *USCWRST* bit can reset the eUSCI_A0 module. While keeping this bit set, we can configure the eUSCI_A0 module by changing eUSCI_A0 registers. The port configuration can be processed. Once it is completed, eUSCI_A0 can operate in a normal mode by clearing *USCWRST* bit. This step of configuring eUSCI_A module is recommended to avoid unexpected behavior. The initialization step is summarized below.

    (a) Set USCWRST
    (b) Initialize eUSCI_A0 registers (while USCWRST bit is set)
    (c) Port configuration
    (d) Clear USCWRST
    (e) If applicable, enable interrupts such as UCRXIE and UCTXIE

UART Baud Rate Generation

One of the low frequency baud rate and oversampling baud rate generation modes can be selected by a *UCOS16* bit. If the *UCOS16* bit is cleared, it operates in low frequency baud rate generation mode. This mode is suitable if the BRCLK is selected from a low frequency clock source such as a 32.768 kHz crystal. If the *UCOS16* bit is set, it can operate in an oversampling frequency baud rate generation mode. This mode is suitable for higher frequency generation. It uses a modulator to generate an internal clock that is 16 times faster, and it results in a factor of 1/16 in UART baud rate parameter calculations. We will study how to determine parameters in the following sections.

Setting a Baud Rate

Using the parameters of BRCLK and baud rate, a division factor of N can be determined using the equation as follows:

$$N = \frac{f_{BRCLK}}{baud\ rate}$$

If N is equal to or greater than 16, it is recommended to use an oversampling frequency baud rate generation mode. In this case, let us say *UCOS16* is 1. It means UCOS16 bit is set.

Low-frequency Baud rate Generation

In low-frequency mode, *UCOS16* is 0. It means the UCOS16 bit is cleared. We can obtain the integer portion of the divisor N that is relevant to the prescaler parameter as shown in the following equation.

$$UCBRx = Integer\ of\ N$$

Since *UCOS16* is 0, the UCBRFx is ignored. The fractional portion of N is relevant to the modulator parameter.

The value of *UCBRSx* can be obtained by using the table of "*UCBRSx Settings for Fractional Portion of N...*" from the manufacturer's technical manual document [9], or performing an detailed error calculation based on the recommendation from the manufacturer.

For the determination of the UCBRSx values, this book introduces another method as an option. The method is to begins with multiplying the fraction portion of N by 10^4, and the parameter *FN* can be obtained by taking integer portion of the product. The equation of *FN* is shown as follows:

$$FN = Integer\ of\ \big((fractional\ portion\ of\ N) \times 10^4\big)$$

Next, using the calculated value of FN, the value of UCBRSx can be obtained from Table 16.1.

FN	UCBRSx	FN	UCBRSx	FN	UCBRSx
0 ~ 528	0	3335 ~ 3574	73	7001 ~ 7146	183
529 ~ 714	1	3575 ~ 3752	74	7147 ~ 7502	187
715 ~ 834	2	3753 ~ 4002	82	7503 ~ 7860	221
835 ~1000	4	4003 ~4285	146	7861 ~ 8003	237
1001 ~1251	8	4286 ~ 4377	83	8004 ~ 8332	238
1252 ~ 1429	16	4378 ~ 5001	85	8333 ~ 8463	191
1430 ~ 1669	32	5002 ~ 5714	170	8464 ~ 8571	223
1670 ~ 2146	17	5715 ~6002	107	8572 ~ 8750	239
2147 ~ 2223	33	6003 ~ 6253	173	8751 ~ 9003	247
2224 ~ 2502	34	6254 ~ 6431	181	9004 ~ 9169	251
2503 ~ 2999	68	6432 ~ 6666	182	9170 ~ 9287	253
3000 ~ 3334	37	6667 ~ 7000	214	9288 ~ 9999	254

Table 16.1. UCBRSx settings for FN [9].

The obtained parameters can be used as an initial value. However, these parameters are not necessarily fixed numbers, but they can be tweaked depending on a system for better performance. Specifically, modulator parameters such as UCBRFx and UCBRSx can be tweaked to achieve better performance depending on a system.

To assist the understanding of determining parameters for low-frequency baud rate mode, the baud rate calculation example is shown in Exercise 16-1.

Exercise 16.1) *If the value BRCLK is selected as 32.768 kHz and the targeted baud rate is 9600 bps, what are the reasonable parameter values for UCOS16, UCBRx, UCBRFx, and UCBRSx?*

Explanation) *We can obtain the division factor as follows:* $N = \frac{f_{BRCLK}}{baud\ rate} = \frac{32768}{9600} =$ *3.4133. Since this is lower than 16, UCOS16 is selected as 0. This is a low-frequency baud rate generation mode setting. UCBRx can be obtained by the equation as follows: UCBRx = Integer of* N *= 3. UCBRFx is ignored because USCO16 =0. The fractional portion of N is 0.4133, and the value of FN is 4133. According to Table 16.1, UCBRSx is 146.*

Oversampling Baud rate Generation

In oversampling mode, UCOS16 is 1. It means that UCSO16 bit is set. We can obtain the value of *UCBRx* using the equation as follows:

$$UCBRx = Integer\ of\ \frac{N}{16}$$

The first stage modulator parameter can be obtained by the equation as follows:

$$UCBRFx = round\left(\left(fractional\ portion\ of\ \frac{N}{16}\right) \times 16\right)$$

For the value of UCBRSx, it can be obtained from the same method described int the previous section, Low-frequency baud rate Generation. One of the methods to obtain UCBRSx was to obtain the value of FN. Using the value of FN, we can obtain the value of UCBRSx from Table 16.1.

The baud rate calculation example for the case of the oversampling baud rate generation shown in Exercise 16-2. The explanation is as follows.

Exercise 16.2) *If the value of BRCLK is selected as 1 MHz and the targeted baud rate is 9600 bps, what are the reasonable parameter values for UCOS16, UCBRx, UCBRFx, and UCBRSx?*

Explanation) *We can obtain the division factor as follows:* $N = \frac{f_{BRCLK}}{baud\ rate} = \frac{1 \times 10^6}{9600} =$ *104.1667. Since this is higher than 16, UCOS16 is selected as 1. This is an oversampling baud rate generation mode setting. UCBRx can be obtained by the equation as follows: UCBRx = Integer of* $(N/16)$ *= 6. UCBRFx can be obtained by the equation described above. The fractional portion of* $(N/16)$ *is 0.5104, and the* number is multiplied by 16. Next, the number after rounding is 8. Thus, *UCBRFx = 8.* For UCBRSx, FN is 1667 because the fractional portion of N is 0.1667. According to Table 16.1, UCBRSx is 32.

Hardware UART Program

In the previous UART example program, we used the software UART method. In this section, we can write a program that can perform a similar task using a hardware UART module. This hardware UART program example is shown in Program 16.2.

As you can see, there are code lines that initialize the eUSCI module. It starts with setting *USCWRST* bit. The UART configuration is for 9600 8N1. We have studied this case in Exercise 16.2. The SMCLK is selected as a clock source. In this setting, the value of BRCLK is 1MHz. The parameters of this configuration were shown previously. UCBRx was calculated as 6, and we can put "UCA0BRW" as 6. UCBRFx and UCBRSx were calculated as 8 and 32, respectively. The UCOS16 was 1. Thus, "UCA0MCTLW" is configured as follows: "UCOS16 | (8 << 4) | (32 << 8)". Next, the port configuration for the UART function is described.

```
#include <msp430.h>
int main(void) {
  WDTCTL = WDTPW | WDTHOLD;  // hold the watchdog timer
  PM5CTL0 &= ~LOCKLPM5; // clear LOCKLPM5 bit
  P1DIR |= 0x01; // output direction, P1.0
  UCA0CTLW0 = UCSWRST; // eUSCI reset state
  UCA0CTLW0 |= UCSSEL_2; // eUSCI clock source: SMCLK
  UCA0BRW = 6; // BRx
  UCA0MCTLW = UCOS16 | (8 << 4) | (32 << 8); // UCOS16, BRFx, BRSx
  P2SEL1 |= BIT0 | BIT1; // UART function (P2.0, P2.1)
  P2SEL0 &= ~(BIT0 | BIT1); // UART function (P2.0, P2.1)
  UCA0CTLW0 &= ~UCSWRST; // eUSCI operation state
  __delay_cycles(200); // delay
  while(1){
    UCA0IFG &= ~UCTXIFG; // clear UCA0TXIFG flag
    UCA0TXBUF = 'T'; // store 'T' on TXBUF
    while ((UCA0IFG & UCTXIFG)==0); // wait until UCA0TXIFG is set
    P1OUT ^= 0x01; // toggle (P1.0)
    __delay_cycles(200000); // delay
  }
  return 0;
}
```

Program 16.2. Hardware UART program (Sending characters).

After the UART initialization, *USCWRST* bit is cleared. In the while loop, the *UCXIFG* flag is cleared. The character T is going to be stored in the *transmit buffer*. The name of the *transmit buffer* is UCA0TXBUF. The data is going to be transmitted by the UART hardware module. If the transmission is completed, the *UCTXIFG* flag will be set. Then, the program waits until *UCTXIFG* flag is set. Next, it is going to toggle an LED. This pattern keeps repeating, and it will result in sending the T characters to the computer through the back channel UART. You can check whether you can receive the T characters through a serial terminal in Code Composer Studio, or through any other serial terminal software such as PuTTY.

UART Echo Program (Polling)

A UART "echo" program can be useful in testing UART communication between systems or devices. This is a loopback test. It can simply send received data back. Once the communication channel is established and verified, the program can be modified to describe more complicated tasks. The UART echo program example is shown in Program 16.3. This code is based on a polling method.

```
#include <msp430.h>
unsigned char UCA0_UART_RX_data(void);
void UCA0_UART_TX_data(unsigned char);
volatile unsigned char ch;  // byte variable
int main(void) {
    WDTCTL = WDTPW | WDTHOLD;  // hold the watchdog timer
    PM5CTL0 &= ~LOCKLPM5;  // clear LOCKLPM5 bit
    P1DIR |= 0x01;  // output direction, P1.0
    UCA0CTLW0 = UCSWRST;  // eUSCI reset state
    UCA0CTLW0 |= UCSSEL_2;  // eUSCI clock source: SMCLK
    UCA0BRW = 6;  // BRx
    UCA0MCTLW = UCOS16 | (8 << 4) | (32 << 8);  // UCOS16, BRF, BRSx
    P2SEL1 |= BIT0 | BIT1;  // UART function (P2.0, P2.1)
    P2SEL0 &= ~(BIT0 | BIT1);  // UART function (P2.0, P2.1)
    UCA0CTLW0 &= ~UCSWRST;  // eUSCI operation state
    _delay_cycles(200);  // delay
    while(1){
        ch=UCA0_UART_RX_data();  // receive a character
        UCA0_UART_TX_data(ch);  // send a character
        P1OUT ^= BIT0;  // toggle (P1.0)
        _delay_cycles(200000);  // delay
    }
    return 0;
}

unsigned char UCA0_UART_RX_data(void){
    volatile unsigned char data;
    while ((UCA0IFG & UCRXIFG)==0);  // wait until UCA0RXIFG is set
    data = UCA0RXBUF;  // read UCA0RXBUF
    UCA0IFG &= ~UCRXIFG;  // clear UCA0RXIFG flag
    return data;
}
void UCA0_UART_TX_data(unsigned char data){
    UCA0IFG &= ~UCTXIFG;  // clear UC0TXIFG flag
    UCA0TXBUF = data;  // store 'T' in TXBUF
    while ((UCA0IFG & UCTXIFG)==0);  // wait until UCA0TXIFG is set
}
```

Program 16.3. UART Echo Example (Polling).

As a result, for instance, when a user types a character on a serial terminal window, this character can be sent to an MSP430FR5994 MCU. Then, the data can be sent back to the computer so that it will be displayed on the serial terminal. This UART echo test is useful in checking and verifying the serial communication between the device and the computer.

UART Echo Program (Interrupt)

As described, a UART echo program can be useful in testing a serial port. We have studied a polling based UART echo program previously. An interrupt based UART echo program can be written as shown in Program 16.4. The UART initialization is similar to the one in a polling based UART echo program. But, in this interrupt based UART echo program, the UART interrupt is enabled, and the relevant configuration for interrupt service requests is added. In the while loop, it simply toggles the pin of P1.0 to blink an LED.

```
#include <msp430.h>
int main(void) {
  WDTCTL = WDTPW | WDTHOLD;  // hold the watchdog timer
  PM5CTL0 &= ~LOCKLPM5; // clear LOCKLPM5 bit
  P1DIR |= 0x01; // output direction (P1.0)
  UCA0CTLW0 = UCSWRST; // eUSCI reset state
  UCA0CTLW0 |= UCSSEL_2; // eUSCI clock source: SMCLK
  UCA0BRW = 6; // BRx
  UCA0MCTLW = UCOS16 | (8 << 4) | (32 << 8); // UCOS16, BRFx, BRSx
  P2SEL1 |= BIT0 | BIT1; // UART function (P2.0, P2.1)
  P2SEL0 &= ~(BIT0 | BIT1); // UART function (P2.0, P2.1)
  UCA0CTLW0 &= ~UCSWRST; // eUSCI operation state
  UCA0IE |= UCRXIE; // Set UCRXIE
  _delay_cycles(200); // delay
  _enable_interrupt(); // enable general interrupt
  while(1){
    P1OUT ^= 0x01; // toggle (P1.0)
    _delay_cycles(200000); // delay
  }
  return 0;
}

#pragma vector=EUSCI_A0_VECTOR
_interrupt void USCI_A0_ISR(void) {
  if ((UCA0IFG & UCRXIFG)!=0) { // check whether UCRXIFG is set
  UCA0TXBUF = UCA0RXBUF; // read the data and send it back
  while ((UCA0IFG & UCTXIFG)==0); // waits until UCTXIFG is set
  UCA0IFG &= ~(UCTXIFG | UCRXIFG); // clear UCTXIFG & UCRXIFG flags
  }
}
```

Program 16.4. UART echo example (Interrupt).

The code lines to process the UART data are located in *USCI_A0_ISR*. In the ISR, it executes a relevant code block, if the *UCRXIFG* in the *UCA0IFG* register is set. This code block contains several lines of code. First, data is read from *UCA0RXBUF*. The data is going to be stored back in *UCA0TXBUF*. Then, it waits until the *UCATXIFG* flag in the *UCA0IFG* register is set. After the transmission is completed, both *UCTXIF* and *UCRXIFG* flags are cleared. As a result, a UART echo program can perform a similar task as shown in the previous polling-based example. This UART echo code can be modified for embedded system applications that need communication between an MSP430FR5994 MCU and a computer.

ASCII control character

When we use a serial terminal, readers may experience or may wonder why it shows a different behavior than what you actually type on the serial terminal.

For instance, you can send "\n" expecting that it may work similar to "enter key" on your keyboard. It may move the position to the next line on the serial terminal. But, the position may stay in the same row. This is related to the control characters. There are pre-defined control characters in ASCII. Some of the useful control characters are summarized below.

8 is a backspace. It can be used by adding backslash; thus, it is "\b".

10 is a line feed. It can be used as "\n".

13 is a carriage return. It can be used as "\r".

27 is an escape. It can be used as "\e".

In order to move the position to the first line, "\r" can be used. Therefore, if a user wants to perform the function that is similar to "enter key" on a keyboard, two control characters can be used, and they are "\n" and "\r".

Chapter 17. RS-232, RS-485, and USB

Digital output signals directly from GPIO pins of an MCU are not typically suitable for long-distance communication due to the noise. For instance, UART signals from an MCU are typically for short-distance communication. To extend the distance of communication, line drivers and buffers can be used to improve signal reliability and noise immunity. To extend the communication distance, RS-232 and RS-485 can be used in personal computers and industrial applications. In modern systems, many of these applications have been largely replaced by USB technology. In this chapter, we will learn about the drivers and buffers including RS-232, RS-485, and USB.

RS-232

RS-232 is a standard protocol for serial communication. The RS-232 standard was introduced in 1962 and revised in 1969. EIA-232-D standard was developed in 1986. Many modern RS-232 ICs are based on TIA/EIA-232-E (1991) or TIA/EIA-232-F (1997). But, this not the latest version, and there is a more recent version of the RS232-standard. Physical serial ports on computers used to be widely used for RS-232 communication; but they are not used in typical personal PCs or laptops these days. However, serial COM ports can be found in industrial equipment and instrumentations that are designed to be compatible with old models or devices. For RS-232, TXD and RXD pins are for transmitter and receiver, respectively. In addition to these pins, RS-232 provides flow control functions using RTS and CTS as well as DCD, DTR, DSR, and RI.

Signal lines are unbalanced. The signals are voltages referring to the ground. For TXD and RXD signals, Logic 1 is represented as a negative voltage, and it is named "mark". On the other hand, Logic 0 is represented as a positive voltage, and it is named as "space". For control signals, they are defined differently. The "asserted" is a positive voltage and the "de-asserted" is a negative voltage.

The maximum speed can be about 20kbit/s at a 50 ft cable length. Practically, some of the RS-232 devices can be operated faster these days. In addition, the length of the cable can play a role in the speed of communication.

RS-232 ICs are available, and the operating voltage for a majority of the RS232 IC models such as MAX232 is +5 V [21]. In order to this IC and to interface with a 3.3-V MSP430FR5994 MCU, it may need extra circuits such as a logic level converter. Instead, we choose to use RS232 IC models that can be operated at +3.3 V. A MAX3232 IC is an example of this 3.3-V RS232 device [22]. This IC supports 2 receivers and 2 drivers. Internal regulated charge pumps generate output voltages of ±5.5V.

RS-485

RS-485 is a standard protocol for serial communication. RS-485 is also known as EIA-485. The EIA-485 standard was approved in 1983. RS-485 support multipoint interconnections, and electrical signaling is balanced. RS-485 can be used in communication over a long distance in electrically noisy environments.

The maximum data rate can be about 10 Mbit/s at a 40 ft cable length. This is a much higher data rate than RS-232. Practically, some of the RS-485 devices can achieve higher data rate these days. The maximum cable length is 4000 ft.

RS-485 uses a balanced interface. Differential singling provides noise immunity because a majority of the common mode noise can be rejected. For instance, the virtual ground can be shifted, and noise signals can be nullified.

RS-485 can form a network, and it supports up to 32 transceivers on the bus. Depending on the model of RS-485 ICs, it can be found that it can support more than 32 transceivers on the bus. Unlike a RS-232 case, RS-485 application configuration needs termination resistors to avoid reflected signals. The typical resistor value is 120 Ω.

RS-485 can be either a half-duplex or full-duplex system. If it is used in a half-duplex system, there are "enable" control pins. They need to be controlled properly. In a certain RS-485 IC, the pin names are DE and $\overline{RE}$.

RS-485 is used as a physical layer of industrial control systems. One of the examples is Modbus. It is a serial communication protocol and was originally published by Modicon® (now Schneider Electric®) in 1979 for programmable logic controllers (PLCs). It is commonly used in industrial electronic devices.

The operating voltage of a majority of RS-485 ICs is +5 V. For instance, a MAX485 is a transceiver for the RS-485 communication [23]. There are also RS-485 ICs that can be operated at +3.3 V. A MAX3485 IC is an example of this 3.3-V RS485 device. This IC supports up to 32 transceivers on the bus [24].

Performance comparison

The performance comparison between RS-232 and RS-485 for selected parameters is shown in Table 17.1. If a simple configuration for communication between two systems is needed, RS-232 can be selected. However, if the network between multiple systems is needed, RS-485 may be suitable because RS-485 can be used to connect up to 32 transceivers.

RS-232 signaling is unbalanced. It may have less noise immunity than RS-485. Thus, RS-232 can be found useful in the short distance communication application between two systems. For the systems that are separately more than 50 ft, RS-485 can be a reasonable choice.

	RS-232	RS-485
Number of devices	1 transmitter, 1 receiver	32 transmitters, 32 receivers
Maximum cable length	50 feet	4000 feet
Signaling	Unbalanced	Balanced
Typical maximum data rate	~20 kbit/s at 50 ft cable length	~10 Mbit/s at 40 ft cable length

Table 17.1. Summarized characteristics of RS232 and RS485.

As it was mentioned, some of RS-232 and RS-485 communication modules are replaced by USB technology. A brief introduction of the USB technology will be followed in the next section.

USB

Universal Serial Bus (USB) is an industry standard that provides a serial bus for connecting devices. USB 1.0 specification was introduced in 1996. USB became popular a few years later. USB 2.0 was introduced in 2001. USB ports are commonly found in desktop and laptop computers these days. The data rate has been improved significantly in USB 2.0. The summary of USB specifications is shown in Table 17.2.

	Release date	Maximum data rate	*Typical voltage	*Typical maximum current
USB 1.0	1996	12 Mbit/s	5 V	0.5 A
USB 2.0	2000	480 Mbit/s	5 V	0.5 A
USB 3.0	2008	5 Gbit/s	5 V	0.9 A
USB 3.1	2013	10 Gbit/s	5 V	0.9 A
USB 3.2	2017	20 Gbit/s	5 V	3.0 A
USB 4.0	2019	40 Gbit/s	5 V	-

Table 17.2. USB specifications. (*It excluded USB power delivery specification).

In USB 3.0, the data rate has been improved significantly. The power capacity has also increased. There are separate USB power delivery specifications since some of the USB ports are used primarily for supplying power. These were not included in Table 17.2. In USB 3.1, the speed has increased. In USB 3.2, both speed and power have improved. This power improvement is because of the use of USB-C connectors and cables.

USB-C can carry significantly more power, and USB-C can supply power to decent size electronics devices. The latest USB standard is USB 4.0. It is even faster than USB 3.2.

USB signaling is balanced. For instance, there are four wires in a USB 2.0 cable. There are +5V and ground wires. In addition, there are D+ and D- wires. They are for data signals, and the signaling is balanced. In USB 2.0 technology, the data encoding and decoding is based on NRZI (Non Return to Zero Inverted).

USB protocol layers are sophisticated. There are several ways to provide serial communication over USB in an embedded system. One of the easy methods is to use a USB-UART IC and to communicate over a virtual COM port. Then, the system sends and receives data in a way that is similar to UART communication.

USB-to-UART IC

We will learn about open-source electronics development platforms in Chapter 25. One of the popular open-source electronics platforms is Arduino® [25]. Arduino Uno is one of the hardware models. In the earlier model of Arduino Uno, a FT232RL IC was used as an USB-to-UART IC. Recent Arduino Uno model uses an ATMEGA16U2 IC. The FT232RL IC is a dedicated IC for a USB-to-UART bridge function. The ATMEGA16U2 IC used in an Arduino Uno is an 8-bit MCU with an internal USB controller. Once the proper firmware is loaded on this MCU, ATMEGA16U2 IC can work as a USB-to-UART bridge IC. A benefit of this approach is that it could be used to provide additional functions.

An MSP430FR5994 Launchpad board has an on-board eZ-FET debug probe. The core of this on-board eZ-FET debug probe is an MSP430F5528 MCU. The MSP430F5528 MCU is one of the MSP430F552x MCUs. One of the important features of this MCU is the USB controller. It supports USB 2.0 standard.

If an MSP430FR5994 MCU sends a character over the backchannel UART, data can be processed in the MSP430F5528 MCU, and it can be sent over USB to a computer. In addition, the MSP430F5528 IC is used to debug and program the MSP430FR5994 IC through JATG pins.

Chapter 18. Serial Peripheral Interface (SPI)

Various serial interfaces, buses, and protocols have been used in embedded systems. The serial peripheral interface (SPI) and Inter-integrated Circuit (I²C) bus are widely adopted in embedded systems. In this chapter, we will learn about the SPI bus and the SPI communication in an MSP430FR5994 MCU.

Serial Peripheral Interface

The serial peripheral interface (SPI) was introduced by Motorola® in the late 1970s. It is one of the simple synchronous communication protocols. It has been widely accepted in microcontroller applications. The connection of the master and slave SPI devices is shown in Figure 18.1.

The serial data out (SDO) pin of a master device is connected to the serial data in (SDI) pin of a slave device. This line is called MOSI, which stands for "Master Out, Slave In." The SDI pin of the master device is connected to the SDO pin of the slave device. This line is called MISO, which stands for "Master In, Slave Out." The master device provides clock signals through a serial clock (SCK) line to the slave device. The master device also provides a chip select signal for the $\overline{CS}$ pin, or a slave select signal for the $\overline{SS}$ pin through a control line. The pin of the $\overline{CS}$ pin or the $\overline{SS}$ pin is active low. This means the slave device can be selected by providing a logical low signal through this control line.

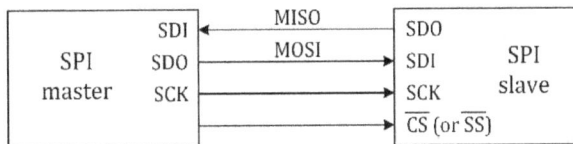

Figure 18.1. SPI, Master-Slave connection.

A simple SPI bus can be understood conceptually as serial communication using two shift registries as shown in Figure 18.2. Let us suppose that data, 0x81, is going to be transmitted from a master device to a slave device. First, this data needs to be stored in the 8-bit shift register of the master device. In this block diagram, the most significant bit (MSB) is passed first. The data bits are transmitted to the input of the 8-bit shift register of the slave device through the MOSI line. Once the data transfer is completed, it can be seen that the data stored in the slave device is 0x81. Likewise, the data in the slave device can be sent to the master device. This is a simple conceptual description for ease of understanding. However, an actual SPI unit is more complicated, and an internal state machine provides micro-operations that are needed for the SPI module.

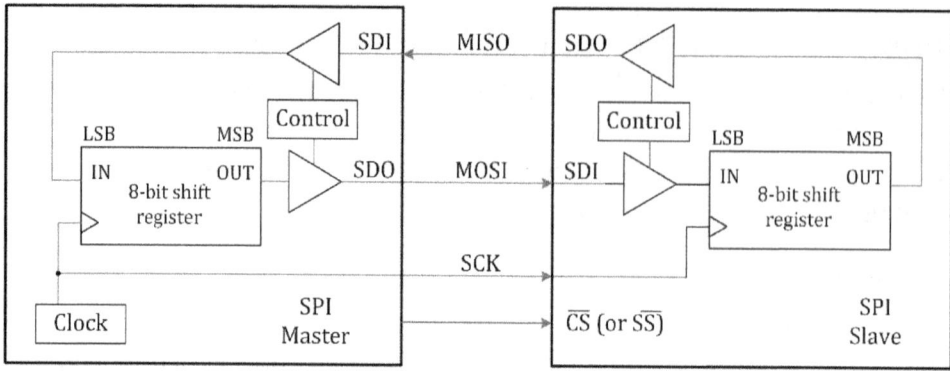

Figure 18.2. Simplified block diagram of an SPI bus.

SPI communication is relatively simple compared to other serial communication interfaces and buses. An SPI bus can achieve higher throughput than an I2C bus. An SPI protocol is more flexible than an I2C protocol.

SPI Device Connection

Multiple slave devices can be connected to one master device. A typical SPI bus connection is shown in Figure 18.3. In this setting, one master SPI device can communicate with two slave SPI devices. The slave-A device can be selected by providing a logical low signal for the $\overline{CS}$ pin of *SPI Slave A*. Next, the slave-B device can be selected instead by providing a logical low signal for the $\overline{CS}$ pin of *SPI Slave B*. This connection requires one *chip select* pin per slave device. As the number of slave devices increases, this connection scheme may increase the hardware complexity due to the increasing number of *chip select* pins that are needed for the master device.

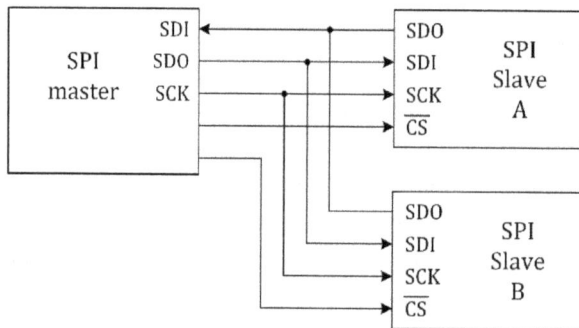

Figure 18.3. Typical SPI bus connection.

In order to reduce the number of *chip select* pins, a daisy-chained connection can be considered as shown in Figure 18.4. The daisy-chained SPI bus method does not require to use additional *chip select* pin. The signal for a *chip select* pin from the master device can be shared through the multiple slave devices.

As shown in the figure, data from the slave-A device can be transferred to the master directly. However, the data from the slave-B device needs to be transferred to the slave-A device first. Then, the data can be transferred to the master. In order to configure a daisy-chained SPI connection, the slave devices should meet daisy-chain requirements. You can check the datasheet to see whether your selected SPI device can support a daisy chain connection or not.

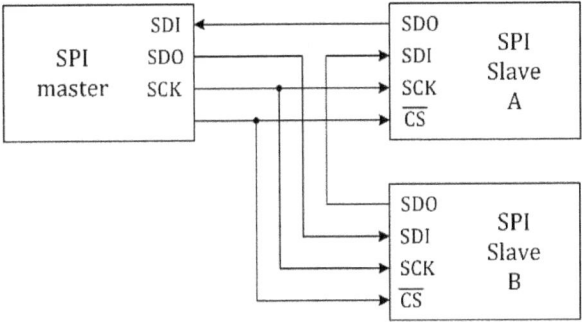

Figure 18.4. Daisy-chained SPI bus connection.

SPI Mode

In an SPI bus, there are a few key parameters such as clock polarity (CPOL) and clock phase (CPHA). They are used to determine the clock format and the associated timing of the data signals. These CPOL and CPHA as well as the waveforms are shown in Figure 18.5. The CPOL parameter determines whether the clock is active high or active low. CPHA determines whether the clock is out of phase with the data or in phase with the data. There are four SPI modes depending on the configurations of the CPOL and CPHA parameters.

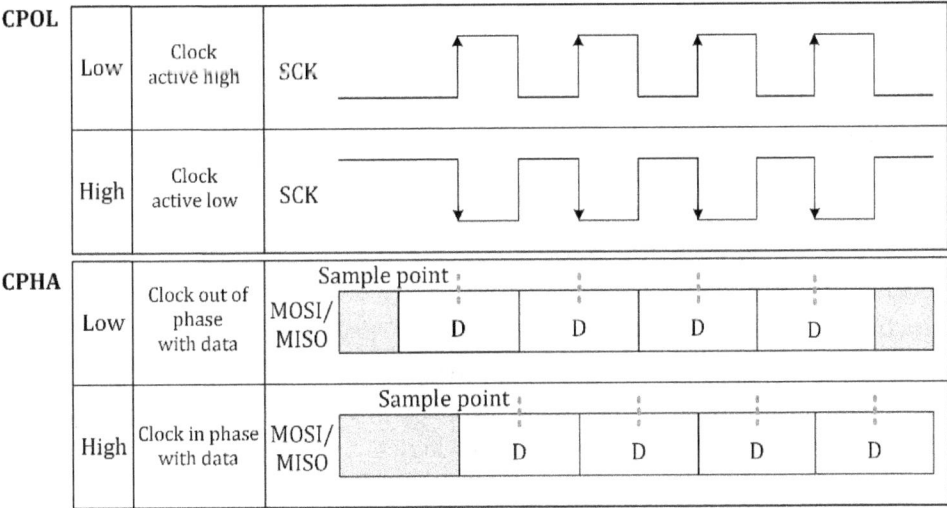

Figure 18.5. CPOL, CPHA, and waveforms.

The SPI transfer modes are shown in Table 18.1. The SPI mode in an MSP430FR5994 MCU is configurable and programmable. For the slave SPI ICs, the information related to the default SPI mode can be found in the datasheet, or it can be determined by examining the timing diagram in the datasheet.

CPOL	CPHA	SPI Mode
Low	Low	0
Low	High	1
High	Low	2
High	High	3

Table 18.1. SPI modes.

SPI Transactions

A simple SPI write transaction example is shown in Figure 18.6. This shows the case that sends instruction and one-byte data. The transaction begins with providing a logical low *chip select* signal. For the MOSI line, an instruction byte is sent. Next, a data byte is sent. The MISO line in the slave device can be controlled to be in a high-impedance state. The transaction ends with providing a logical high *chip select* signal.

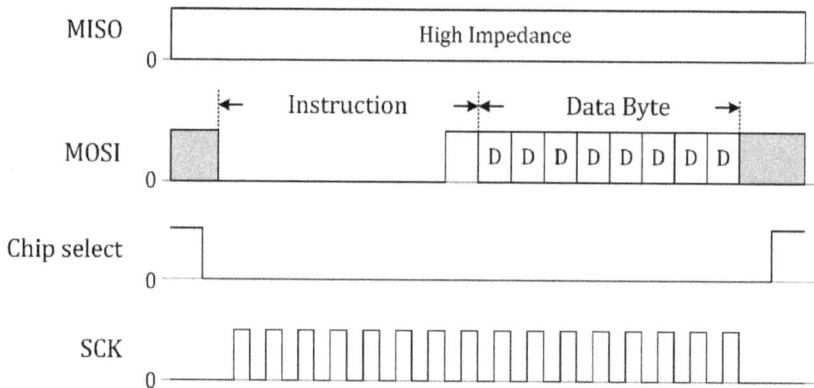

Figure 18.6. Simple SPI write transaction.

A simple SPI read transaction example is shown in Figure 18.7. This is the case that sends an instruction byte and receives one data byte. Similarly, the transaction begins with providing a logical low *chip select* signal. For the MOSI line, the instruction byte is sent. Since this is a read instruction, a data byte is sent from the slave device to the master device through the MISO line. While receiving the data, the MOSI line for the master device side can be controlled to be in a high-impedance state. The transaction ends with providing a logical high *chip enable* signal.

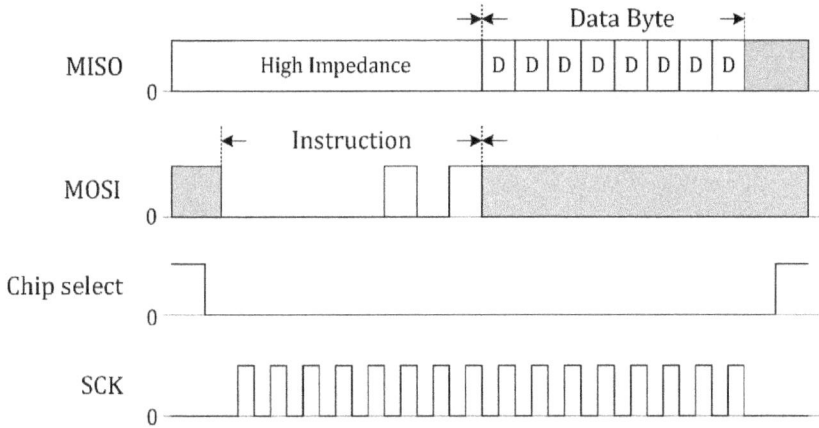

Figure 18.7. Simple SPI read transaction.

eUSCI – SPI Mode

Let us examine an SPI communication module in an MSP430FR5994 MCU. The SPI mode is supported by both eUSCI_A and eUSCI_B. There are several SPI modules available in an MSP430FR5994 MCU. In this chapter, we have chosen a eUSCI_B1 unit. The simplified block diagram is shown in Figure 18.8.

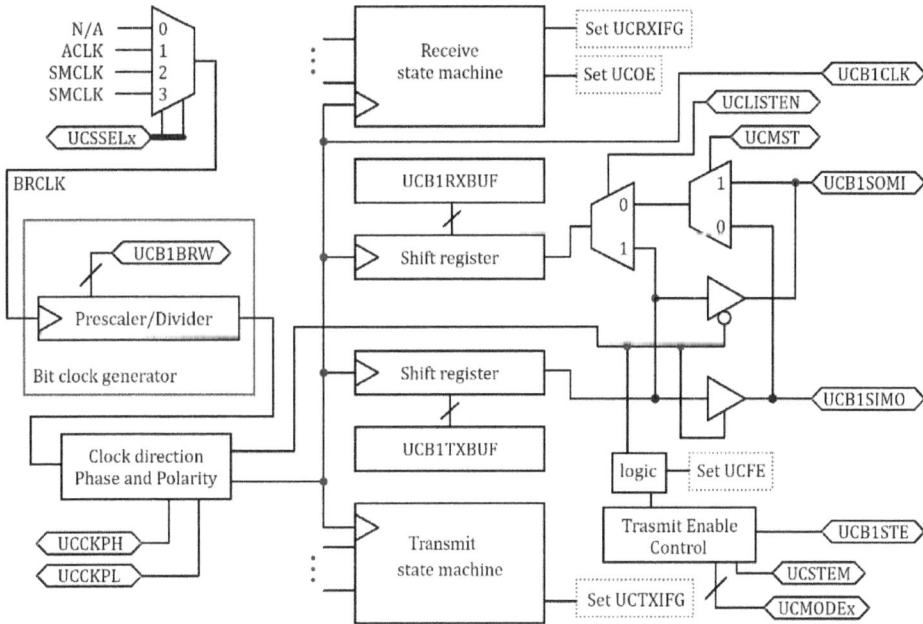

Figure 18.8. Simplified block diagram of eUSCI_B1, SPI mode [9].

There are four pins related to the SPI mode. They are *UCB1SIMO*, *UCB1SOMI*, *UCB1CLK*, and *UCB1STE* pins. The SPI mode parameter can be configured by *UCMODE* bits. Either a 3-pin or 4-pin SPI operation can be chosen. For the 4-pin SPI operation, all four pins are used. However, for the 3-pin SPI operation, *UCB1STE* is not used. *UCB1STE* is a slave transmit enable. In this SPI module, master or slave modes are programmable. The master can be selected by setting the *UCMST* bit. The parameter in data transmission whether the LSB or MSB first can be configured by *UCMSB* bit.

The clock direction phase can be configured by the *UCCKPH* bit. This is related to *CPHA*. The clock polarity can be configured by the *UCCKPL* bit. This is related to *CPOL*. These are the parameters that can configure the SPI mode.

MCP3008 SPI Example

An MCP3008 IC is an 8-channel 10-bit A/D converter with an SPI serial interface [26]. There are several IC packaging options. One of them is a Plastic DIP (PDIP) package. The PDIP model of the MCP3008 IC can be mounted on a prototyping breadboard. Readers can perform their experiments using a prototyping breadboard. On a BH EDU board, this MCP3008 IC is placed, and the pins of the IC are accessible through the proper header pins.

The connection diagram is shown in Figure 18.9. Since the MSP430FR5994 MCU has a 12-bit SAR ADC with many channels, an additional external 10-bit ADC IC may not be really necessary. However, this configuration using an external ADC is for an educational purpose to demonstrate SPI communication. In general, this 10-bit ADC IC can be found useful for microcontrollers with 8-bit ADC modules or for microprocessors that do not have any built-in ADC module. However, in some cases, it can be found that more ADC channels are necessary where there are many analog sensors or analog voltages to read.

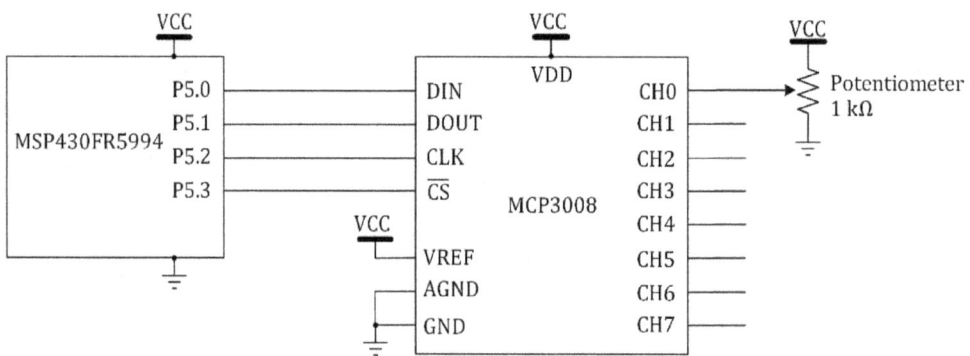

Figure 18.9. MCP3008 connection diagram.

The MCP3008 IC has eight ADC channels. In this section, we will study an example program to read a voltage level through channel 0. A potentiometer is connected to channel 0. The voltage level can be varied by tweaking the knob of the potentiometer.

The input pin of the IC (DIN) is related to the MOSI line. It is connected to the pin of P5.0. The choice of the function is *UCB1SIMO*. Moreover, the output pin of the IC (DOUT) is related to the MISO line. It is connected to the pin of P5.1. The choice of the function is *UCB1SOMI*, The CLK pin of the IC is connected to the pin of P5.2. The choice of function is *UCB1CLK*. For the slave select pin, the P5.3 is used as a custom chip select pin, and it is connected to the $\overline{CS}$ pin.

The MCP3008 SPI example program is shown in Program 18.1. The selected SPI mode is 0. The SMCLK is selected as a clock source, and the SCK is configured to be about 100kHz. In the while loop, it reads data from the IC, and stores it in *ADC_buf*. The pattern of receiving data from the IC over SPI communication keeps repeating.

```c
#include <msp430.h>
unsigned int ADC_buf;
unsigned char RXdata;
void UCB1_SPI_TX_data(unsigned char);
unsigned char UCB1_SPI_RX_data(void);
int main(void) {
    WDTCTL = WDTPW | WDTHOLD;  // hold the watchdog timer
    PM5CTL0 &= ~LOCKLPM5; // clear LOCKLPM5 bit
    P1DIR |= 0x01; // output direction, P1.0
    UCB1CTLW0 = UCSWRST; // eUSCI reset state
    UCB1CTLW0 |= UCMST | UCMODE0 | UCSYNC | UCMSB | UCSSEL_2;
                                       // eUSCI, 3-pin SPI mode, master
    UCB1BRW = 10; // ~100kHz
    P5DIR |= BIT3; // custom SS pin
    P5OUT |= BIT3; // set (P5.3)
    P5SEL1 &= ~(BIT0 | BIT1 | BIT2); // SPI mode (P5.0, P5.1, P5.2)
    P5SEL0 |= BIT0 | BIT1 | BIT2; // SPI mode (P5.0, P5.1, P5.2)
    UCB1CTLW0 &= ~UCSWRST; // eUSCI operation state
    _delay_cycles(2000); // delay
    while(1) {
        P5OUT &= ~BIT3; // set (P5.3); custom SS pin
        UCB1_SPI_TX_data(0x01); // send start bit
        RXdata=UCB1_SPI_RX_data(); // receive data
        UCB1_SPI_TX_data(0x80); // send data with channel info.
        RXdata=UCB1_SPI_RX_data(); // receive data
        ADC_buf = (RXdata & 0x03) << 8; // store data in ADC_buf (highest 2 bits)
        UCB1_SPI_TX_data(0x00); // send data
        RXdata=UCB1_SPI_RX_data(); // receive data
        ADC_buf |= RXdata; // store data in the variable (the rest of 8 bits)
        P5OUT |= BIT3; // clear (P5.3)
        P1OUT ^= 0x01; // toggle (P1.0)
        _delay_cycles(50000); // delay
    }
    return 0;
```

```
}
void UCB1_SPI_TX_data(unsigned char data) {
  UCB1IFG &= ~UCTXIFG; // clear UCB1TXIFG flag
  UCB1TXBUF = data; // store data in UCB1TXBUF
  while ((UCB1IFG & UCTXIFG)==0); // wait until UCB1TXIFG is set
}
unsigned char UCB1_SPI_RX_data(void) {
  unsigned char data; // variable
  while ((UCB1IFG & UCRXIFG)==0); // wait until UCB1RXIFG is set
  data = UCB1RXBUF; // read data from UCB1RXBUF
  UCB1IFG &= ~UCRXIFG; // clear UCB1RXIFG flag
  return data; // return data
}
```

Program 18.1. MCP3008 SPI example program.

The method of SPI communication varies by IC. It is recommended to refer to the datasheet of the manufacturer. For the MCP3008 IC, it needs to perform several transmit and receive operations to read an ADC value from the IC. In the example program, *EUSCIB1_SPI_TX_data* and *EUSCIB1_SPI_RX_dat*a subroutines are used to transmit or receive data.

Chapter 19. Inter-integrated Circuit (I^{2}C)

The Inter-integrated Circuit (I^{2}C) bus is versatile, and it is widely used in embedded systems. There are several variants of I^{2}C serial communication interfaces; however, they are typically compatible with each other. Many sensor ICs provide I^{2}C serial interfaces. In this chapter, we will learn about an I^{2}C peripheral in an MSP430FR5994 MCU.

Inter-integrated Circuit

Inter-integrated Circuit (I^{2}C) technology was developed by PHILIPS®. This is a serial communication based on two wires. The patent for this two-wire bus system was filed in 1981, and the date of the patent is August 25, 1987 [27]. The original I^{2}C patent was already expired. The hardware and the software protocol structures are relatively simple, and the I^{2}C technology provides a simple universal bus.

Each device on the I^{2}C bus is identified by its own address. The master device initiates communication by providing the clock signal. There can be a maximum clock frequency. However, the minimum clock speed may not be provided.

The master device can "poll" the device with a specific address. It can be used to check whether a specific device is present or not. This allows designers to build a system that can support easily adding or removing I^{2}C slave devices.

System Management Bus (SMBus) is also a two-wire interface, which is based on the principles of operation of the I^{2}C bus. The SMBus was defined by Intel® in 1995. The SMBus and I^{2}C are similar, and they can be compatible in general. However, there are a few differences in specifications including *VDD & threshold voltage* and *address acknowledge*, and etc.

Two Wire Interface (TWI) was introduced by Atmel® and other companies. Atmel was acquired by Microchip Technology in 2016. This TWI bus and I^{2}C are also similar, but there are a few differences such in high-speed mode. Generally, TWI devices are compatible with I^{2}C devices.

A simple I^{2}C bus example is shown in Figure 19.1. There are two I^{2}C devices. Any of these two can be used as either master or slave device. It is typical to assign one master device on an I^{2}C bus. However, it is not common; but it is possible to assign multiple masters on an I^{2}C bus. A master device can initiate I^{2}C communication.

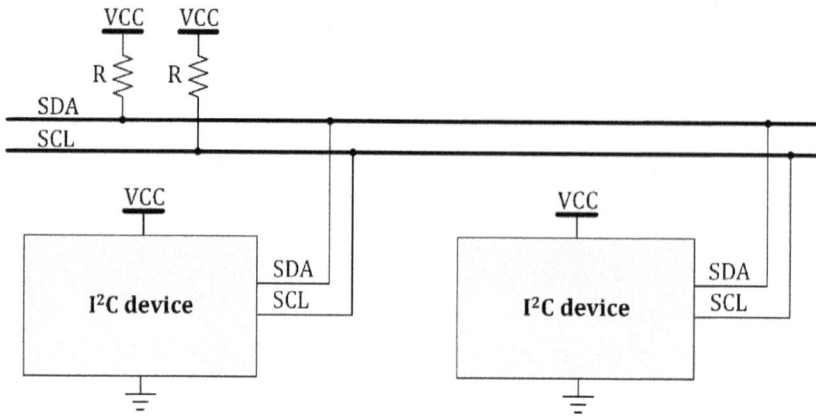

Figure 19.1. Simple I²C bus example.

In Figure 19.1, you can see SDA and SCL lines. SDA represents the "serial data." This line is used to send and receive data. SCL represents the "serial clock." This line is used to provide a clock signal. There are two pull-up resistors connected to these lines. These resisters are required components. The value of the resisters may not need to be precise. Common choices of the values are 1 kΩ, 4.7 kΩ, and 10 kΩ. Designers can choose a reasonable value. The values of the resistors may affect the communication speed; therefore, the choice of the values can be important depending in some applications.

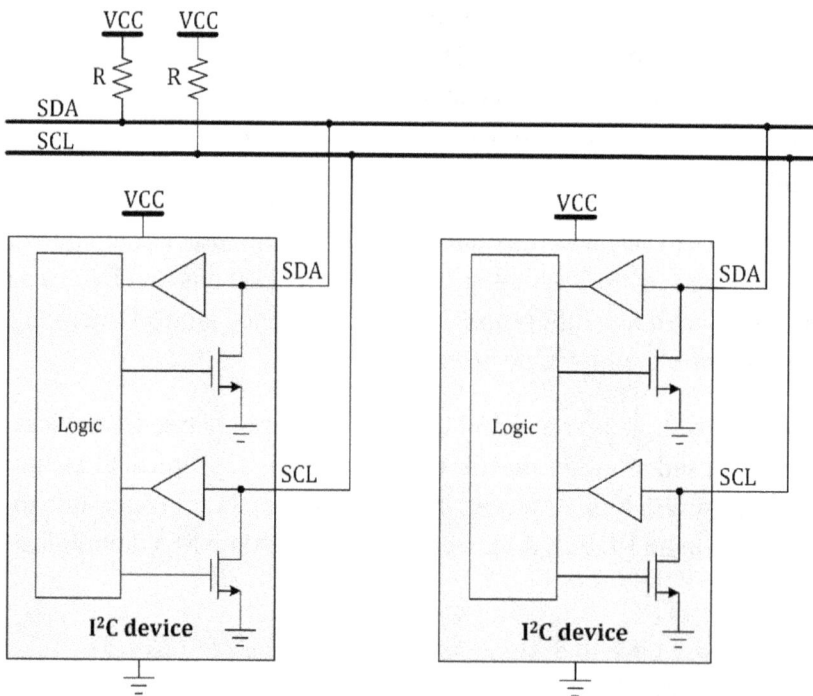

Figure 19.2. Simplified I²C block diagram on the I²C bus.

A simplified I²C block diagram on the I²C bus is shown in Figure 19.2. This conceptual I²C device block includes buffers, Field effect transistors (FETs), and control logic. This is an open-drain configuration, and it is the reason that external pull-up resistors are essential.

Each I²C device can read the digital values on the bus. Each device can pull the bus lines low, or it can release the bus lines. The example of pulling the bus line down or releasing the bus is shown in Figure 19.3. The figure on the left shows the case of controlling the FET to be the ON state from the OFF state. When the FET is OFF, the bus line generates a logical high level since the bus is released. When the FET is controlled to be ON, the bus line is pulled down, and the logical output is low. Next, as shown on the right side of the figure, the FET is controlled to be OFF. In this case, the bus line is released, and the logical level of the output is back to high. This bus configuration is applied to both SDA and SCL lines.

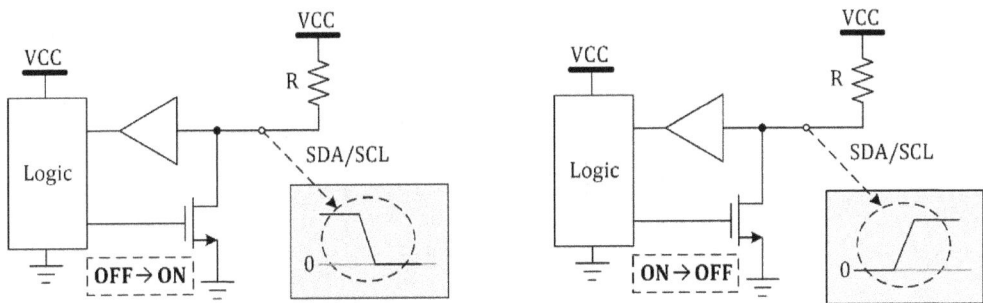

Figure 19.3. An open-drain driver.

In the previous example, it shows only two devices. You can connect multiple I²C devices. The connection example is shown in Figure 19.4.

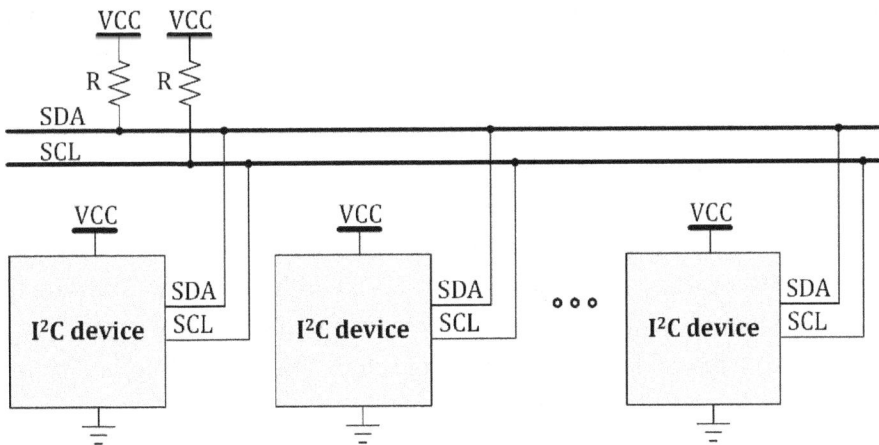

Figure 19.4. Multiple devices on the I²C bus.

Multiple I²C devices can share the SDA and SCL lines, and the connection of multiple I²C devices is straightforward and simple. However, the designers need to make sure to use pull-up resisters properly. Moreover, each device needs to have a unique address on the bus.

In embedded system applications, it is common to find a system with multiple supply voltage levels such as 3.3 V and 5V. Let us suppose there are two 3.3-V I²C devices and two 5-V I²C devices, and we want them to be the I²C bus. One of the example connections, in this case, is shown in Figure 19.5.

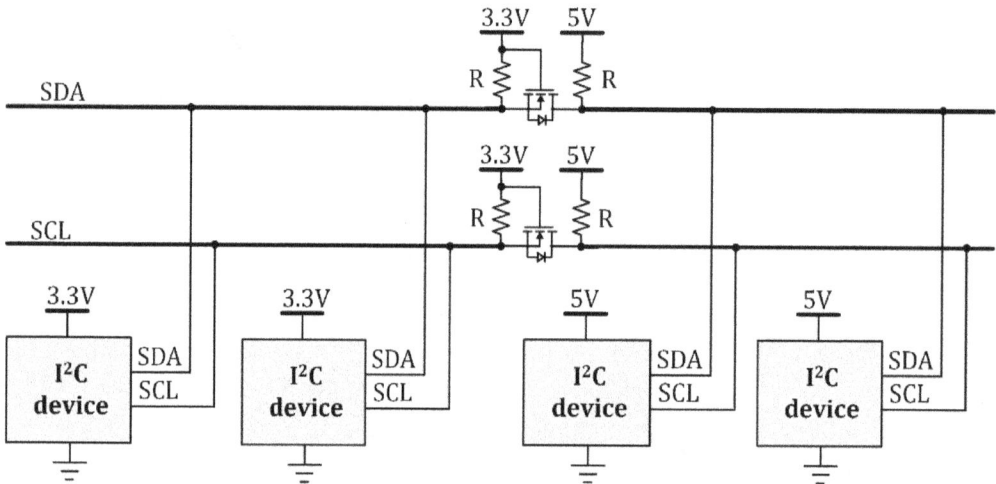

Figure 19.5. 3.3-V and 5-V I²C devices on the I²C bus.

We can use a bi-directional logic converter that is at the top of the figure. It can provide an interface between 3.3-V and 5-V bus signals. One channel of the bi-directional logic converter consists of one N-channel MOSTFET and two pull-up resistors. There are several "bidirectional logic level converter" modules available. One of bidirectional logic level converters module will be used for interfacing 3.3-V and 5-V signals in the next chapter.

I²C Message Format and Transactions

An I²C message example is shown in Figure 19.6. The message starts from the "start condition (ST)." It can be generated when the SDA line is pulled down while the logical level of the SCL line is held high. Next, a 7-bit address is sent. The data is valid, while the logical level of the SCL line is held high. The change of the data is possible, while the logical level of the SCL line is low. The 8th bit is R/$\overline{W}$. It indicates whether it is a read or write operation.

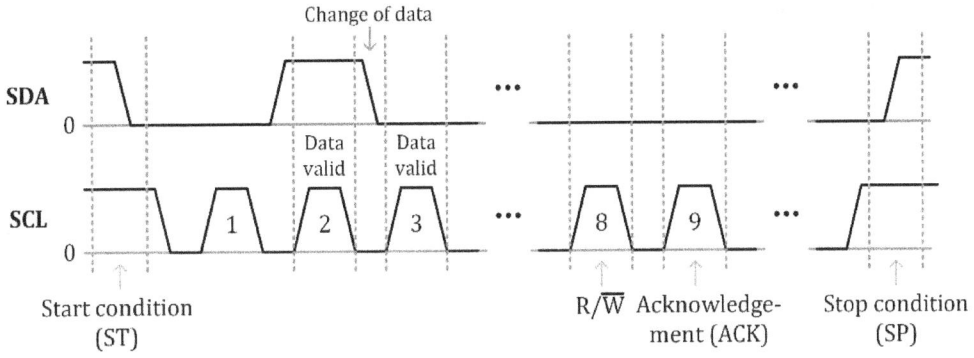

Figure 19.6. I²C message example.

The 9th bit is acknowledgment (ACK) signal. For this acknowledgment bit, the logical level of the SDA line is low. This ACK is generated by the receiver side. It can be used to check whether the data is sent successfully or not. If not, NACK bit can be sent instead. NACK means "Not Acknowledgment." In this case, the logical level of the SDA line is high. NACK can be used in other cases including the condition to halt communication followed by the stop condition in a repeated start transaction. The stop condition (SP) is shown at the end of the message. It can be generated when the SDA line is released while the logical level of the SDA line is held high.

An I²C write transaction example is shown in Figure 19.7. The start condition is sent. Next, 8 bits are sent, which consist of a 7-bit address and one bit of R/$\overline{W}$. In this case, the logical level of R/$\overline{W}$ bit is low. It is followed by receiving acknowledgment. Next, 8-bit data is sent, and it receives an acknowledgment signal. Then, it generates a stop condition. This transaction initiates communication and sends one-byte data to the slave device.

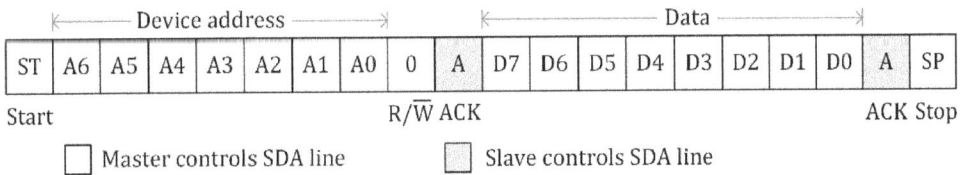

Figure 19.7. I²C write transaction example.

Next, an I²C read transaction example is shown in Figure 19.8. As it was done in the previous case, the start condition is sent. Next, 8 bits are sent, which consist of a 7-bit address and one bit of R/$\overline{W}$. This is a read operation. Thus, the logical level of R/$\overline{W}$ bit is high. Then, it is followed by receiving an acknowledgment signal. Now, 8-bit data will be sent from the slave device, and the master receives the 8-bit data.

Next, the master device sends acknowledgment and stop condition signals. This transaction initiates communication and receives a byte data from the slave device.

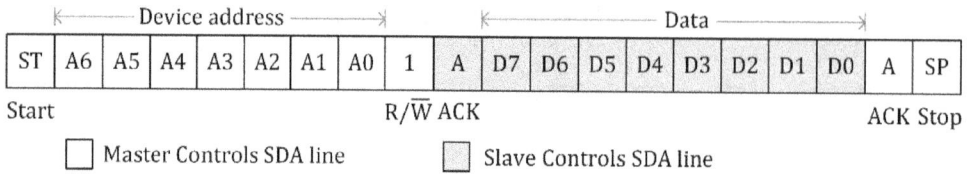

| ST | A6 | A5 | A4 | A3 | A2 | A1 | A0 | 1 | A | D7 | D6 | D5 | D4 | D3 | D2 | D1 | D0 | A | SP |

Start — R/$\overline{W}$ ACK — ACK Stop

☐ Master Controls SDA line   ☐ Slave Controls SDA line

Figure 19.8. I²C read transaction example.

I²C read and write operations can be performed by a combined transaction as shown in Figure 19.9. First, it performs an I²C write operation. However, it does not send a stop condition signal. Instead, it sends a repeated start signal, and it performs an I²C read operation. Instead of ACK, the master device sends NACK signal. Next, it sends a stop condition signal. This transaction sends a byte to the slave device first, and it receives one byte from the slave device.

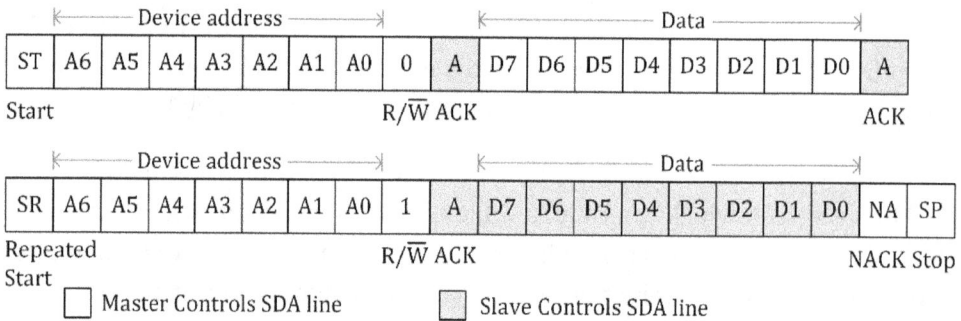

| ST | A6 | A5 | A4 | A3 | A2 | A1 | A0 | 0 | A | D7 | D6 | D5 | D4 | D3 | D2 | D1 | D0 | A |

Start — R/$\overline{W}$ ACK — ACK

| SR | A6 | A5 | A4 | A3 | A2 | A1 | A0 | 1 | A | D7 | D6 | D5 | D4 | D3 | D2 | D1 | D0 | NA | SP |

Repeated Start — R/$\overline{W}$ ACK — NACK Stop

☐ Master Controls SDA line   ☐ Slave Controls SDA line

Figure 19.9. Combined I²C write and read transaction example.

eUSCI – I²C Mode

An MSP430FR5994 MCU has a hardware module that can be used to configure I²C buses. The eUSCI_B module supports I²C mode, and it can provide an interface to communicate with I²C devices. A simplified block diagram of eUSCI_B2 – I²C mode is shown in Figure 19.10.

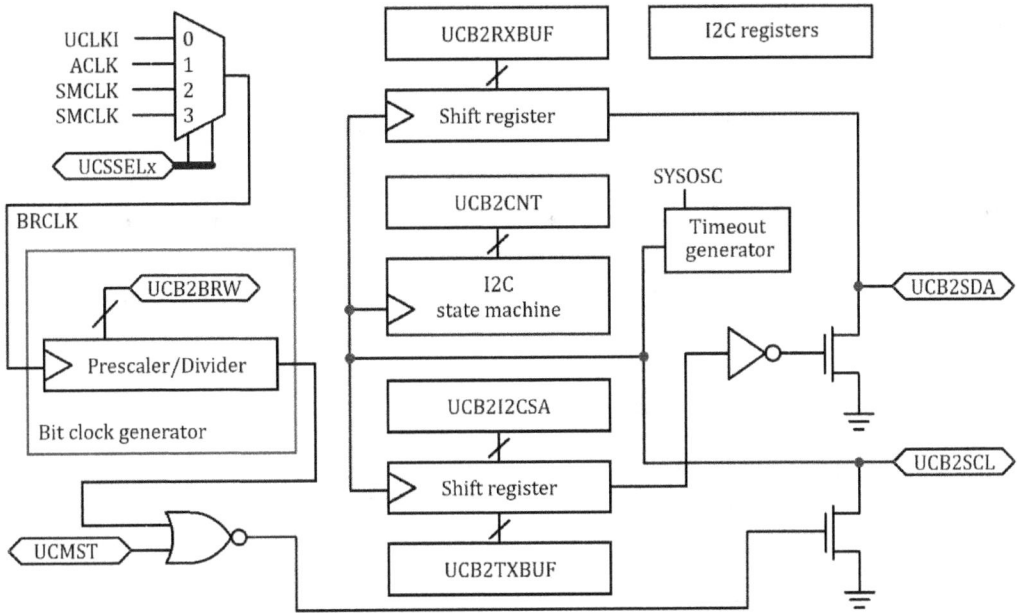

Figure 19.10. Simplified block diagram of eUSCI_B2 – I²C mode [9].

In this block diagram, open drain transistors were used, and they are connected to the *UCB2SDA* and *UCB2SCL* lines. The *UCB2SCL* line is associated with the clock circuit block. The *UCB2SDA* line is associated with transmitting and receiving data blocks. The I²C state machine block controls the operations of the I²C module.

For clarification, this block diagram is simply a conceptual functional diagram to describe the behavior of the module. This simplified block diagram does not necessarily represent the actual circuit implementation of this module.

PCF8574 I²C Example

Some embedded system applications may require many GPIO pins. These cases include keyboard applications and LED matrix applications. In some cases, unfortunately, the number of the available GPIO pins in an MCU may not be enough. In these cases, developers may choose to use GPIO expanders. These GPIO expanders provide a method of adding extra I/Os. As an example, a GPIO expander with an I²C interface can be used to control a parallel interface LCD. In this case, the LCD can be controlled by the I²C interface, and it can free up some GPIO pins of an MCU.

A PCF8574 IC is an 8-bit GPIO expander via an I²C bus [28]. The operating voltage range is 2.5 V to 6 V. It works with a 3.3-V device such as an MSP430FR5994 MCU. The PCF8574 IC has 8-bit quasi-bidirectional I/O ports. Three address pins of the IC can be used to provide 8 slave addresses. The active low open drain interrupt output ($\overline{INT}$) can be used to indicate whether the input status of the IC has changed or not.

A connection diagram of a PCF8574 IC is shown in Figure 19.11. The selected functions for the P6.4 and P6.5 pins are associated with SDA and SCL lines, respectively. The pin of P4.7 is used to read an interrupt output from the IC. Pull-up resistors are connected to these lines. The address is selected by the three pins named A2 ~ A0. Two I/O ports are connected to two LEDs in the connection diagram.

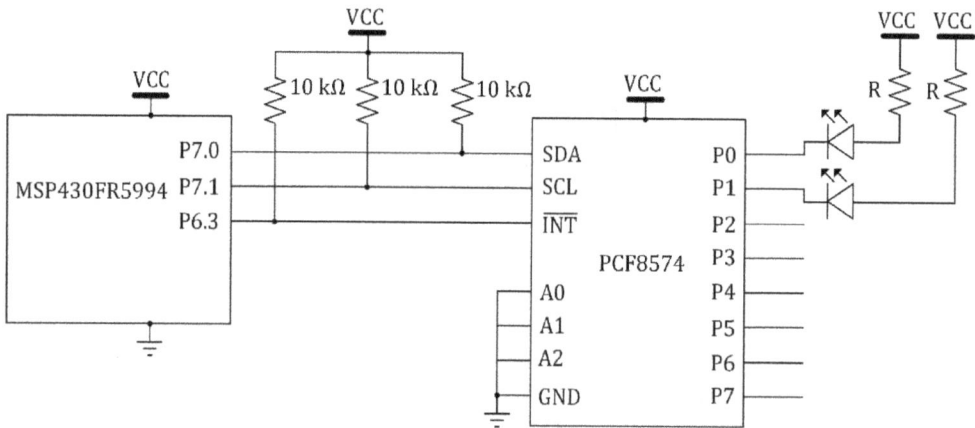

Figure 19.11. PCF8574 connection diagram.

The PCF8574 ICs are offered in many packaging types. They include a Dual In-line Package (DIP). This DIP IC can be mounted on a prototyping breadboard. Readers can perform the experiment using a prototyping breadboard. On a BH EDU board, the PCF8754 was placed, and users can access the IC pins through proper header pins.

Based on the connection shown in Figure 19.11, a programming example of the PCF8574 IC is written as shown in Program 19.1. In this program, the P7.0 and P7.1 pins are configured properly to provide the I²C functions. eUSCI B1 is configured to operate in I²C mode. The slave address is 0x20 in this setting. The *automatic stop generation function* is selected. It is configured to generate a stop condition after processing one byte.

```
#include <msp430.h>
unsigned char TXdata=0x01; // initialize variable
int main(void) {
    WDTCTL = WDTPW | WDTHOLD;  // hold the watchdog timer
    PM5CTL0 &= ~LOCKLPM5;  // clear LOCKLPM5 bit
    P6DIR |= ~BIT3;  // input direction (P6.3)
    P7SEL1 &= (BIT0 | BIT1);  // I2C function (P7.0, P7.1)
```

```
P7SEL0 |= BIT0 | BIT1;  // I2C function (P7.0, P7.1)
UCB2CTLW0 |= UCSWRST;  // eUSCI reset state
UCB2CTLW0 = UCSWRST | UCMODE_3 | UCMST | UCSYNC | UCSSEL_2;
                                // configure USCIB2 control register

UCB2BRW = 10;  // ~100kHz
UCB2I2CSA = 0x20;  // slave address
UCB2CTLW1 |= UCASTP_2;  // automatic stop generated after TBCNT is reached
UCB2TBCNT = 0x01;  // threshold (TBCNT)
UCB2CTLW0 &= ~UCSWRST;  // eUSCI operation state
_delay_cycles(2000);  // delay
while (1) {
    UCB2CTLW0 |= UCTR | UCTXSTT;  // I2C start, transmitter
    while ((UCB2IFG & UCTXIFG)==0);  // wait until UCB2TXIFG is set
    UCB2TXBUF = TXdata;  // store data in UB2TXBUF
    while (UCB2CTLW0 & UCTXSTP);  // ensure stop condition
    TXdata ^= 0x03;  // toggle two bits
    _delay_cycles(200000);  // delay
}
return 0;
}
```

Program 19.1. PCF8574 I²C example program.

In the while loop, the program generates the start condition in the master transmitter mode. Next, it waits until *UCTXIFG* is set. Then, the data will be stored in *UCB2TXBUF*. The next line is to ensure the stop condition. Now, the I²C transmit transaction is completed, and the LEDs connected to the I/O port are going to be turned ON or OFF according to the received data. *TXdata* variable was initialized as 0x01, and two bits are getting toggled in the loop. This will result in blinking two LEDs alternatively.

For some versions of BH EDU boards, a different version of PCF8574 such as PCF8754A may have been used instead. The difference is the device address. The relevant line of the code is as follows: "USCB2I2CSA = 0x20". For the PCF8754A IC, this line can be modified to change the device address to 0x38.

There are a wide range of ICs and modules with I²C interfaces. Particularly, many I²C-compatible sensor ICs can be found. For educational purposes, readers can choose their own I²C sensors for their experiments to study and expand their knowledge.

Chapter 20. Time Measurement

Some embedded system applications are based on relative time measurements between events. In an MSP430FR5994 MCU, the capture mode in a Timer_A module can be used in recording and processing timer events. We will learn about capture mode, ultrasonic distance sensor, and IR communication in this chapter.

Capture Mode in Timer_A

Timer events can be captured by several methods. An MSP430FR5994 MCU supports capturing timer events using Timer_Ax modules. A simplified block diagram of a Timer_A0 showing CCR1 block is presented in Figure 20.1. The CAPTURE MODE box was covered previously, in this figure, this CAPTURE MODE box is uncovered, and it is still enclosed with a thick dotted line.

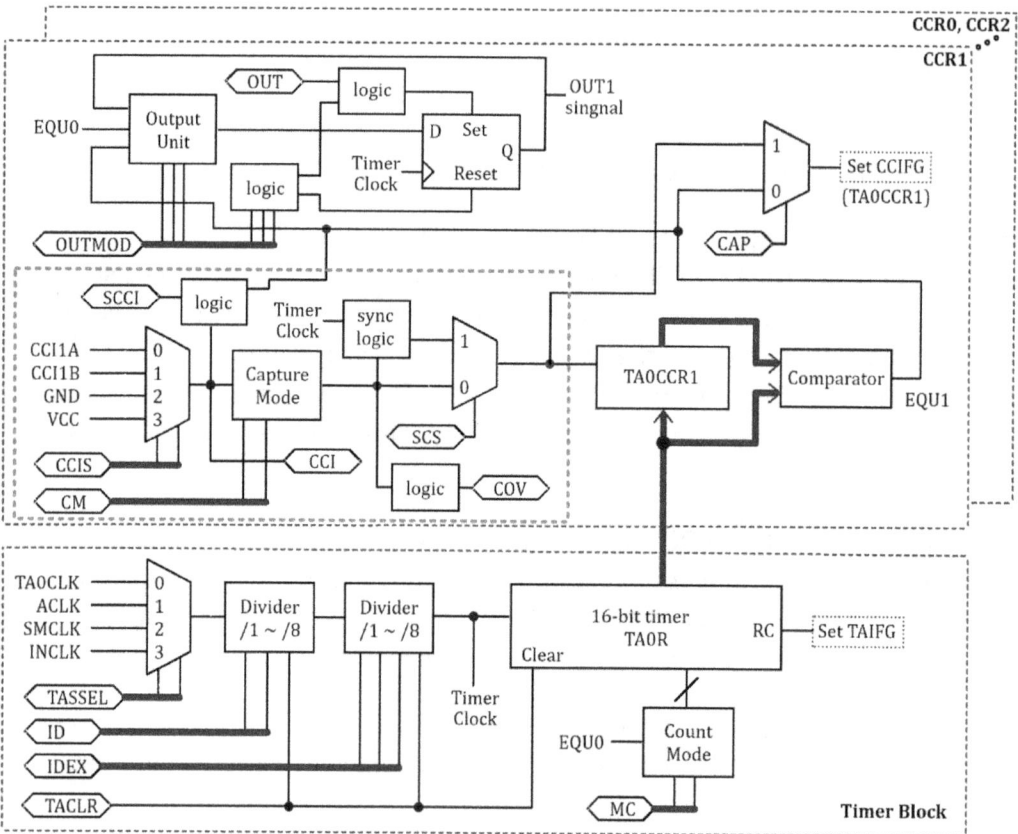

Figure 20.1. Simplified Timer_A0 block diagram showing CCR1 block [9].

The capture mode can be selected by setting *CAP* bit. The inputs relevant to the capture mode are *CCI1A* and *CCI1B*. They can be selected by the configuration of *CCIS* bits. The *CCIxA* and *CCIxB* can be connected to other components internally or externally through pins. The connection to the pins is device-specific information. In this case, *CCI1A* for Timer_A0 can be configured to receive input signals through the P1.0 pin.

The input signals can be captured on a rising or falling edge, or both edges. A capture mode can be configured by *CM* bits. In this setting, we use a *CCR1* block of Timer_A0. In this case, the captured timer value will be stored in the *TA0CCR1* register. The capture signal can be synchronized with the capture source by setting *SCS* bit.

A capture mode test program is shown in Program 20.1. This is a loopback test program. One jumper wire is needed to connect the pins of P1.0 and P6.3. The P6.3 pin will be used to generate test signals, and the P1.0 pin will be used to capture the edges of the digital signals.

```c
#include <msp430.h>
volatile unsigned int tcap=0; // variable
int main(void) {
  WDTCTL = WDTPW | WDTHOLD;  // hold the watchdog timer
  PM5CTL0 &= ~LOCKLPM5; // clear LOCKLPM5 bit
  P6DIR |= BIT3; // output direction (P6.3)
  P1DIR &= ~BIT0; // input direction (P1.0)
  P1SEL1 &= ~BIT0; // alternate function (TA0.1)
  P1SEL0 |= BIT0; // alternate function (TA0.1)
  TA0CTL = TASSEL_2 | MC_2 | TACLR; // TA0CTL setup
  TA0CCTL1 = CM_2 | CCIS_0 | CCIE | CAP | SCS; // TA0CCTL1 setup
  _enable_interrupt(); // enable general interrupt
  while (1) {
    // begin: capture test code
    P6OUT &= ~BIT3; // clear (P6.3)
    _delay_cycles(2000); // delay
    TA0CTL |= TACLR; // clear TA0R
    _delay_cycles(1000); // delay
    P6OUT |= BIT3; // set (P6.3)
    _delay_cycles(1000); // delay
    P6OUT &= ~BIT3; // clear (P6.3)
    _delay_cycles(1000); // delay
    // end: capture test code
    while(1) {
      _delay_cycles(1000); // delay
    }
  }
  return 0;
}

#pragma vector = TIMER0_A1_VECTOR
_interrupt void Timer0_A1_ISR(void) {
  if((TA0CCTL1 & CCIFG)!=0) { // check CCIFG
    tcap = TA0CCR1; // store TA2CCR0 in tcap
    TA0CCTL1 &= ~CCIFG; // clear CCIFG flag
```

```
    }
}
```

Program 20.1. Capture mode test program.

In order to access the P1.0. The jumper J7 may need to be temporarily removed for the example programs in this chapter. Regarding this access of the P1.0 pin, the detailed instructions were described at the end of Chapter 15.

In the test program in Program 20.1, the direction of the P6.3 is configured as output. The direction of the P1.0 is configured as input. *P1SEL1* and *P1SEL0* are configured to be operated in capture mode.

Previously, timers were configured to be operated in *Up mode*. In order to increase the range of the upper limit of the counter, we will configure the timer to be operated in *Continuous mode* for the example programs in this chapter. This can be configured by *MC* bits. This *continuous mode* was selected by selecting *MC_2* in the program. Given this configuration, the Timer_A0 can be operated to count up to 0xFFFF. The timer rolls off to zero when it reaches 0xFFFF. This is a pattern of counting operation, and it will keep repeating.

TA0CCR1 register is configured to enable the capture mode as well as to capture the signals on falling edges by choosing *CM_2*. The interrupt is configured and the *Timer0_A1_ISR* subroutine is the relevant ISR. In this ISR, it checks whether CCIFG is set or not. Then, the value of the TA0CCR1 register is going to be stored in the *tcap* variable.

In the while loop, a capture test code block can be found. This is simply a test code block to examine the behaviors for educational purposes. In this test code block, the logical values of P6.3 are controlled to generate a test signal through P6.3. This signal is going to be the input signal for P1.0 since the P6.3 and P1.0 pins are connected through a jumper cable.

In this test setup, the input signal can be captured, and a proper signal edge can trigger the ISR to store the counter value to *tcap* variable. In this given capture test behavior, the value of *tcap* can be about 2000 plus additional small values, when the program passes the test code and reaches the infinite loop with only a delay operation code line. After the TA0R is cleared, there was one falling edge in the capture test code block, and this final *tcap* value is related to the cycles needed for the _*delay cycle(2000)* subroutine calls. Besides, there were small additional cycles that were needed to process this internally including interrupt service routines.

This loop back program can be used to help users to understand the behavior of the capture mode. Moreover, this program can be modified for other applications. In the following section, we will learn about an ultrasonic sensor module and a program example.

Ultrasonic Sensor

Ultrasound technology uses sound waves that are higher than the upper limit of human hearing. Ultrasonic waves can be generated by a transducer. An ultrasonic device can be used as a ranging sensor. As an example, a low-cost ultrasonic ranging sensor module, HC-SR04, is selected. The measurement range of this ultrasonic sensor module is 2 cm to 400 cm. The frequency of the waves is about 40 kHz.

A timing diagram of an HC-SR04 ultrasonic sensor module is shown in Figure 20.2. This ultrasonic sensor module can receive a 10-µs pulse through a *trig* pin. Then, the sensor transmits the signals of 8-cycle sonic burst. These signals are going to travel, and some of them could be returned to the sensor if they were bounced back properly by an obstacle. The ultrasonic sensor module can respond to the returned signals to generate a corresponding digital output signal. The travel distance is related to the time measurement from transmitting the signals until receiving the returned signals. The distance can be converted from the time measurement using the speed of sound. The speed of sound in air is about $340\ m/s$. In order to obtain the distance, the travel time can be divided by roughly 2.

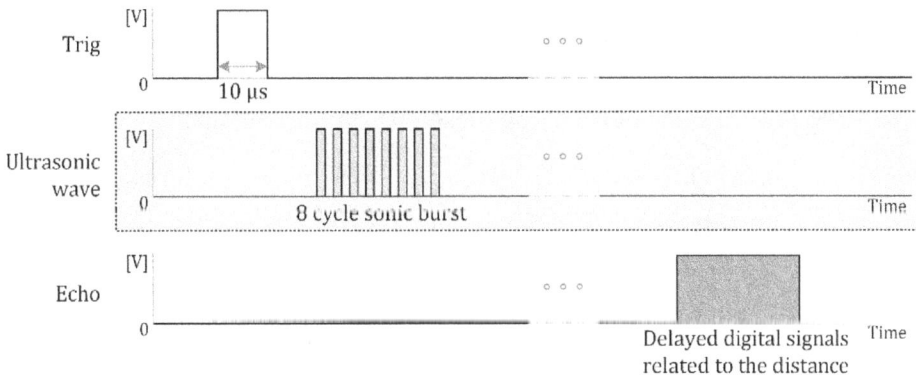

Figure 20.2. Timing diagram of an HC-SR04 ultrasonic sensor.

The HC-SR04 sensor module can be connected to an MSP430FR5994 MCU, and the connection diagram is as shown in Figure 20.3. The operating voltage of an HC-SR04 sensor module is +5 V. In order to interface with an MSP430FR5994 MCU safely, a bi-directional logic level converter can be used as we have studied in the previous chapter. There are several bi-directional logic level converters available. One of them is a Sparkfun® bi-directional logic level converter module [29]. In the connection diagram, the P6.3 and P1.0 pins are safely connected to *trig* and *echo* pins of the ultrasonic sensor module using a bi-directional logic level converter module. A BH EDU board includes bi-directional logic level converter circuits; therefore, users do not need an additional logic level converter module.

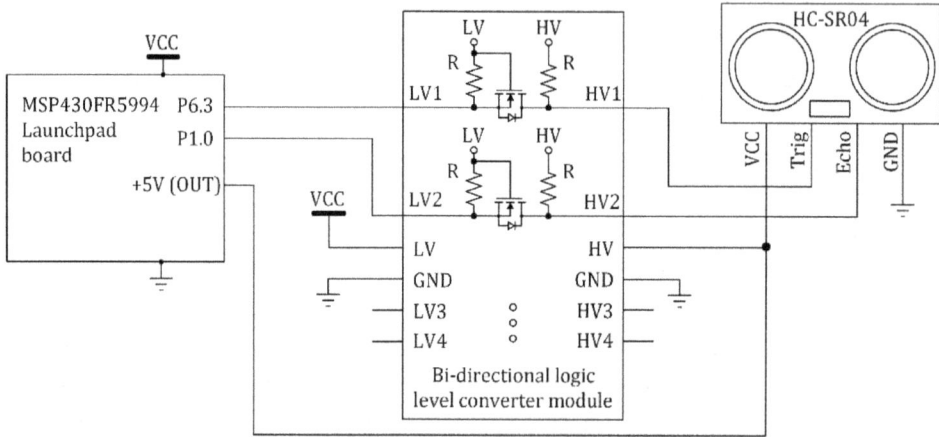

Figure 20.3. Connection diagram of an HC-SR04 ultrasonic sensor.

Let us examine +5V pins on an MSP430FR5994 Launchpad. These 5V pins are directly from the microUSB port on the Launchpad board. Since the operating current of the ultrasonic sensor is about 15 mA, it may be reasonable to use the +5V power from the Launchpad. It is worth mentioning that it is not a good idea to supply a device that can consume high power from these pins. For instance, you may not want to attempt to drive a motor using these +5V pins on the Launchpad.

An HC-SR04 example program is shown in Program 20.2. This is a modified program from the *capture mode test program* in the previous section. The initialization process in the code is similar. However, additionally, the *TAIE* interrupt is enabled, and the relevant *TAIFG* flag is going to be processed in an ISR.

```
#include <msp430.h>
#include <stdio.h>
volatile unsigned int tcap=0, tcap_flag=0, tcap_cov=0; // variables
int main(void) {
  WDTCTL = WDTPW | WDTHOLD;  // hold the watchdog timer
  PM5CTL0 &= ~LOCKLPM5; // clear LOCKLPM5 bit
  P1DIR |= BIT1; // output direction (P1.1)
  P6DIR |= BIT3; // output direction (P6.3)
  P1DIR &= ~BIT0; // input direction (P1.0)
  P1SEL1 &= ~BIT0; // alternate function (TA0.1)
  P1SEL0 |= BIT0; // alternate function (TA0.1)
  TA0CTL = TASSEL_2 | MC_2 | TACLR; // TA0CTL setup
  TA0CCTL1 = CM_2 | CCIS_0 | CCIE | CAP | SCS;  // TA0CCTL1 setup
  TA0CTL |= TAIE; // enable TAIE
  _enable_interrupt(); // enable general interrupt
```

```
  while (1) {
    tcap_flag=0;  // clear variable
    tcap_cov=0;  // clear variable
    TA0CTL |= TACLR;  // clear TA0R
    P6OUT |= BIT3;  // set P6.3
    _delay_cycles(10);  // delay for trigger signal
    P6OUT &= ~BIT3;  // clear P6.3
    _delay_cycles(30);  // delay
    while (tcap_flag==0);  // wait until tcap_flag is set
    if (tcap_cov==0) {
      if (tcap<2000) P1OUT |= BIT1;  // check the value of tcap
      else P1OUT &= ~BIT1;
    }
    _delay_cycles(20000);  // delay
  }
  return 0;
}

#pragma vector = TIMER0_A1_VECTOR
_interrupt void Timer0_A1_ISR(void) {
  if((TA0CTL & TAIFG)!=0) {  // check TAIFG flag
    tcap_cov=1;  // set tcap overflow flag
    tcap_flag=1;  // set tcap flag
    TA0CTL &= ~TAIFG;  // clear TAIFG flag
  }
  if((TA0CCTL1 & CCIFG)!=0) {  // check CCIFG flag
    tcap=TA0CCR1;  // store TA0CCR1 in tcap
    tcap_flag=1;  // set tcap flag
    TA0CCTL1 &= ~CCIFG;  // clear CCIFG flag
  }
}
```

Program 20.2. HC-SR04 example program.

If the returned signal is captured before the counter reaches the maximum, the value of the counter will be stored in the *tcap* variable. If the returned signal is captured after the timer rolls off to zero, this overflow condition can be processed in a custom overflow process, and the value of the *tcap* variable may remain as is.

In the while loop, P6.3 is set or cleared with a certain time delay. This is for the generation of the trigger pulse. Thus, the program repeatedly sends and receives ultrasonic signals to measure the distances, and the captured timer values will be checked in the loop. When an object is detected within a few inches, a green LED will be turned on. When the object is removed, the green LED will be turned off.

This ultrasonic test program is simply one of the examples written for educational purposes. This test program is not optimized. It also does not guarantee the good performance or good functionality of the ultrasonic sensor module. Readers can modify and write their own code to improve the behavior and the quality of the ultrasonic distance measurement.

IR Communication

Infrared (IR) communication is an inexpensive wireless communication technology that has been used in many electronic systems such as IR remote control devices. The wavelengths of the infrared light are longer than the ones of the visible light. For this reason, IR signals are generally invisibly to human eyes.

There are many applications using IR signals. One of the applications is a short-range wireless communication. A simplified IR communication block diagram is shown in Figure 20.4.

On the left side of the figure, a transmitter circuit block can be found. This transmitter circuit block includes transistor and IR LED components. This block can control the IR LED to turn ON or OFF. An amplitude shift keying (ASK) modulation is to send two different frequencies depending on whether the logic level is 0 or 1. For instance, it can generate a signal pattern at a certain carrier frequency for logic 1. For IR communication, the carrier frequency can be found in the range between 30 kHz to 60 kHz.

On the right side of the figure, it shows the receiver circuit block. An IR photodiode can receive the transmitted signal. Next, the signal is amplified. A bandpass filter passes the frequencies of interest, and it can block the noise. After the demodulation, the digital output signals can be generated.

In order to configure a test system for IR communication, we can choose an IR receiver module. A TSOP38238 device is an IR receiver module that includes a PIN diode and a preamplifier [30]. On a BH EDU board, this IR receiver module was placed. A TSOP38238 device has three pins of Vs, GND, and OUT. That is similar configuration as it was shown in the figure.

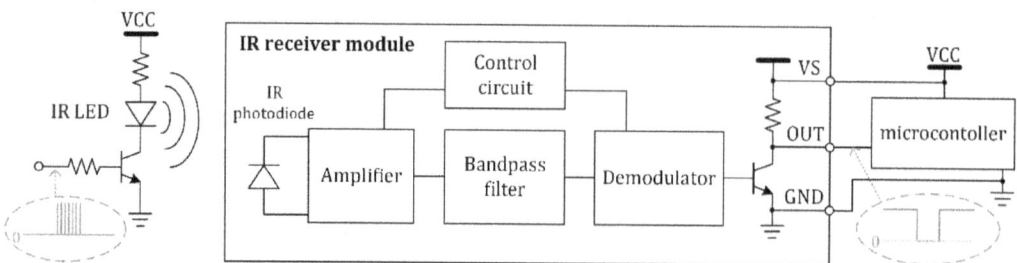

Figure 20.4. Simplified IR communication block diagram.

NEC IR Protocol

There are several IR communication protocols. One of them is a NEC® IR protocol that is commonly used in IR controlled devices. The carrier frequency is 38 kHz. The signals for logical low and high levels have the total transmit time of 1.125 ms and 2.25 ms, respectively. As you can see, there is a time difference between the signals for logic 0 and 1. This time difference can be detected by using a timer capture mode in an MSP430FR5994 MCU.

The NEC IR protocol can be summarized as follows:

(a) 9-ms leading pulse burst
(b) 4.5-ms space
(c) 8-bit address
(d) 8-bit logical inverse of the address
(e) 8-bit command
(f) 8-bit logical inverse of the command
(g) 562.5-μs pulse burst (end of message transmission)

The protocol begins with 9 ms leading pulse burst and 4.5 ms space signals. Next, the 8-bit address and its inverse can be sent. Then, the 8-bit command and its inverse can be sent. The transmission can be ended with the 562.5 μs pulse burst. An example of the NEC IR protocol is shown in Figure 20.5. In this example, the address code is 0 and the command code is 0x6A.

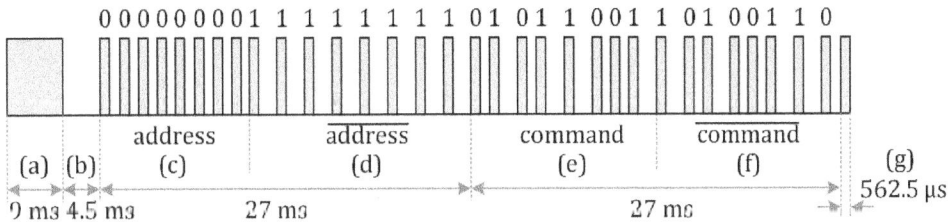

Figure 20.5. NEC® IR protocol example.

The address range can be chosen between 0 to 255. It is possible to increase the addresses range. There is an "Extended NEC IR protocol." A major difference is whether it uses a 16-bit address or an 8-bit address and the inversion of the address. A majority of modern IR remote devices based on an NEC IR protocol use an extended NEC IR protocol.

There are other IR protocols such as SONY®, RC5, and RC6. Many IR devices. For some of the IR devices, they choose not to follow a standard protocol. They may send raw data, or they send data using their own format.

There are several types of IR receiver modules. As mentioned, one of them is a TSOP38238 IR receiver. This IR receiver module can be easily connected to an MSP430FR5994 MCU. The receiver module has three pins. The "OUT" pin of the IR receiver can be connected to one of the pins of an MSP430FR5994 MCU. It can be the pin of P1.0 as studied in the previous examples.

An IR remote control device can transmit an IR signal pattern if a user push one of the buttons on the IR remote control device. The IR receiver can generate output signals. Using the capture mode through Timer_Ax in an MSP430FR5994, readers can write a program that can record the sequence of the captured timer values in an array. By analyzing this array, they can determine which button was pressed on the IR remote.

An IR remote control device is an example of simple wireless communication. An IR communication is only valid within a certain angle between the transmitter and receiver. This IR communication system can be used in a mobile application such as a mobile robot. However, the robot may not be controllable if it is out of a certain angle. If this is not desired, a 2.4-GHz wireless module can be used instead. We will learn about a wireless module in the next chapter.

Chapter 21. Wireless Modules

The choices of wireless connectivity for embedded systems have become more popular, and they could lead to innovative new electronic systems and products. For instance, Apple®'s AirPods® and Amazon® Echo® Buds provide an alternative way to access the main unit remotely. Moreover, a majority of the modern IoT (Internet of Things) devices have WiFi connectivity. In this chapter, we will learn about a simple 2.4-GHz module to provide a wireless link for an MSP430FR5994 MCU.

Wireless Embedded Systems

Wireless technologies in embedded systems can be applied to sensor network technologies. For instance, small sized sensor electronics devices may obtain data from multiple locations and send the data wirelessly. The wirelessly transmitted data can be received and processed by another electronics device. There are many wireless technologies and standards including WiFi, Zigbee, and Bluetooth® technologies.

WiFi is a family of wireless networking technologies based on IEEE 802.11 standards. They can be used in networking between devices, and they can provide internet access for an IoT system. However, typically, power consumption is an important factor and can be an important factor for battery-operated WiFi sensor devices. Optimizing WiFi energy consumption is the key. Moreover, another effort is to use appropriate batteries to extend the time of the use until the next battery replacement or recharge period.

ZigBee can be used for personal area networks. It is based on IEEE 802.15.4 standards. It has been used in many low power sensor devices. Digi XBEE® is a brand name. Some of the XBEE modules support the Zigbee protocol. It could be a suitable choice for low-power sensors. However, currently, the Zigbee protocol may not be available for widely used electronic systems such as smart phones and tablet PCs.

Bluetooth® is a wireless standard that can be used in exchanging data between fixed and mobile devices. The supported frequencies include the ISM (Industrial, scientific, and medical) 2.4 GHz frequency band. The Bluetooth 5.2 version is released in 2020. Bluetooth technology is widely accepted in many electronic systems including smart phones, tablet PCs, and laptops. Moreover, it is suitable for low power devices. However, the communication range of the Bluetooth devices may not be satisfactory depending on the applications. If longer distance communication is desired, a class-1 Bluetooth device can be considered. For instance, a class-1 Bluetooth could transmit the power of 100 mW, and the range can extend to about 100 meters (328 ft). In this chapter, we will use a simple

Bluetooth module for testing. An HC-05 module is chosen, and it is a class-2 Bluetooth module based on Bluetooth v2.0+EDR.

HC-05 Bluetooth Module

There are many Bluetooth modules. One of the low-cost Bluetooth modules is HC-05. The operating voltage of this Bluetooth module is 3.6 to 6 V. Typical supply voltage to this module is 5V. In order to connect safely with an MSP430FR5994 MCU, a bi-directional logic level converter can be used. The connection diagram of an HC-05 module is shown in Figure 21.1. On a BH EDU board, the logic level converter is already applied. Users do not need an additional converter module.

The RX and TX lines are connected through the bi-directional logic converter. As mentioned in the previous chapter, the 5-V power pins on an MSP430FR5994 Launchpad board are directly connected to the microUSB. Since the current consumption of the HC-05 module is reasonably small, in this example, we will use these 5-V pins to supply power to the HC-05 module.

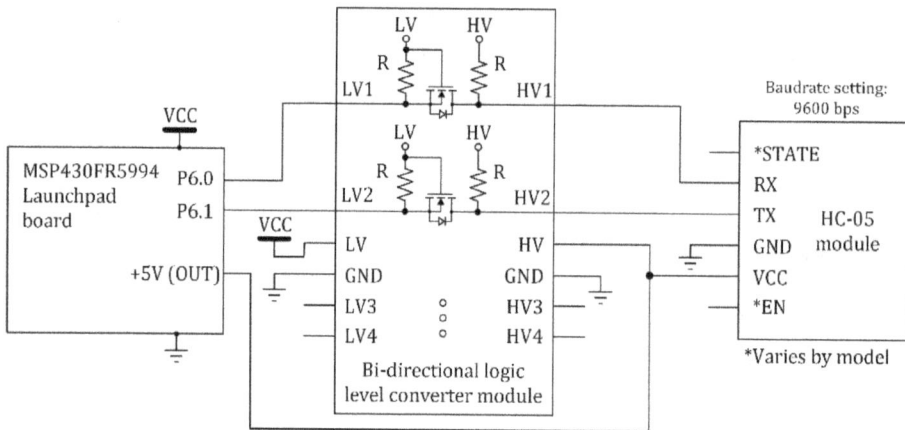

Figure 21.1. Connection diagram of an HC-05 module.

When the HC-05 module is powered, an LED on the HC-05 board may be flashing. it can be paired with a PC. If it asks to enter password, a user can try to enter the default password that is 1234 or 0000 depending on the HC-05 model.

For Windows O/S (Windows 10), after it is paired, you can find two virtual COM ports over the Bluetooth link as shown in Figure 21.2. You can select *More Bluetooth Settings*. Then, it will open a *Bluetooth Settings* window. It shows a COM port with the description of *Outgoing*. This is the COM port that will be used in opening a serial terminal for the Bluetooth test code in the following section. The Bluetooth connection status may become *paired* instead of *connected* when the Bluetooth communication channel is not used. This is an expected behavior. When data is sent over the Bluetooth link, it will be changed to *connected*.

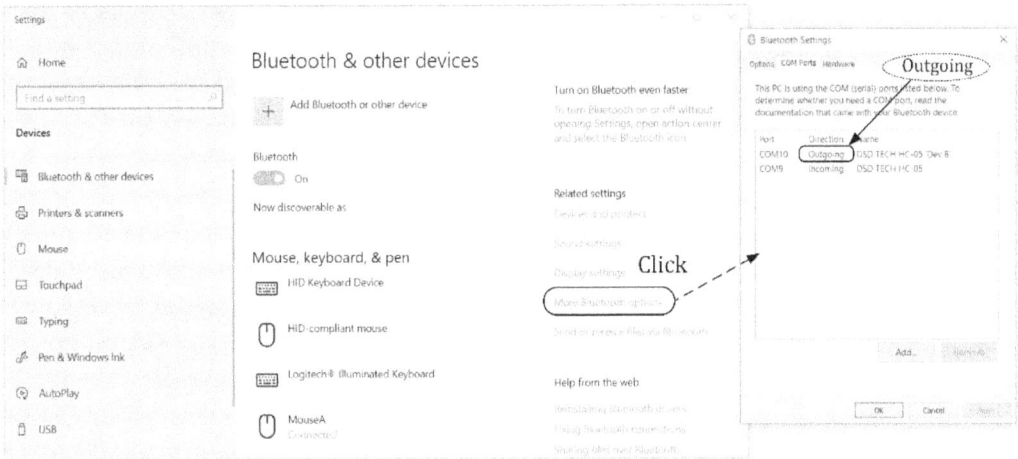

Figure 21.2. Bluetooth settings and Virtual COM port (Windows 10).

For Mac® users, they might experience some difficulties in using this HC-05 module. They can try a different Bluetooth module that supports an iOS®. Or they can refer to the following description that would make the HC-05 module functional for the Bluetooth Test Program in this Chapter.

Figure 21.3. Bluetooth configuration and terminal (MacOS).

For macOS (Monterey), the Bluetooth module can be paired as shown in Figure 21.3. During the pairing process, a password might be asked. It is 1234 or 0000 depending on the HC-05 model. After it is connected, users can see the serial devices, and it can even be accessed by a serial terminal program. However, the communication may not be successful. In order to resolve this problem, they can use *Terminal* on Mac to access the serial device. Specifically, they can type "Terminal" in a search box, and open *Terminal* as shown Figure 21.3. Next, they can type the following command:
*ls /dev/tty.**

Then, they can find the serial device name. For instance, the serial device name can be */dev/tty.DSDTECHHC-05*

In this case, the device name is DSDTECHHC-05. However, it would be different on readers' Mac. Next, they can type this command:

screen /dev/tty.DSDTECHHC-05 9600, cs8

Then, the terminal may work as a serial terminal for the Bluetooth link, and this method can be used for the test program in the following section.

For more information, the serial terminal needs to be closed properly. By pressing "Ctrl + A" and "Ctrl + \", it would be asked to exit the session completely. Or, "Ctrl + D" can be pressed. It would minimize the screen. In order to restore it, "screen -r" can be used.

Bluetooth Test Program

A Bluetooth test program for a HC-05 module is shown in Program 21.1. The RX and TX pins of the eUSCI_A3 in UART mode are P6.0 and P6.1. These pins are configured for the eUSCI A3 function. The baud rate generator is configured for 9600 bps as we have studied previously.

```c
#include <msp430.h>
volatile unsigned char ch; // temporary variable
int main(void) {
    WDTCTL = WDTPW | WDTHOLD;  // hold the watchdog timer
    PM5CTL0 &= ~LOCKLPM5; // clear LOCKLPM5 bit
    P1DIR |= 0x01; // output direction (P1.0)
    P6SEL1 &= ~(BIT0 | BIT1); // UART function (P1.2, P1.3)
    P6SEL0 |= BIT0 | BIT1; // UART function (P1.2, P1.3)
    UCA3CTLW0 = UCSWRST; // eUSCI reset state
    UCA3CTLW0 |= UCSSEL_2; // eUSCI clock source: SMCLK
    UCA3BRW = 6; // BRx
    UCA3MCTLW = UCOS16 | (8 << 4) | (32 << 8); // UCOS16, BRFx, BRSx
    UCA3CTLW0 &= ~UCSWRST; // eUSCI operation state
    UCA3IE |= UCRXIE; // set UCRXIE
    __delay_cycles(200); // delay
    __enable_interrupt(); // enable general interrupt
    while(1){
        if (ch=='1') {
            P1OUT ^= BIT0; // toggle (P1.0)
            UCA3IFG &= ~UCTXIFG; // clear UCTXIFG flag
            UCA3TXBUF=ch; // store data in UCA3TXBUF
            while ((UCA3IFG & UCTXIFG)==0); // wait until UCTXIFG is set
            ch=0; // clear the variable
        }
        __delay_cycles(200000); // delay
    }
    return 0;
}

#pragma vector=EUSCI_A3_VECTOR
```

```
_interrupt void USCI_A3_ISR(void) {
    if ((UCA3IFG & UCRXIFG)!=0) {  // check UCRXIFG flag
        ch=UCA3RXBUF;  // read the data from UCA3RXBUF
        UCA3IFG &= ~UCRXIFG;  // clear UCRXIFG flag
    }
}
```

Program 21.1. Bluetooth test program.

The *UCRXIE* interrupt is configured to be enabled. When the UART module receives a byte, it triggers to execute the interrupt service routine. In the ISR, the code line checks whether the *UCRXIFG* is set or not. Then, the byte data will be read and stored in the "ch" variable. Next, it clears the interrupt flag. Thus, when a user types a character in a terminal, it will be sent to the MSP430FR5994 MCU and it is going to be stored in the 'ch' variable. In the while loop, it reads the 'ch' variable. If it is '1', it can toggle the output of P1.0 that is connected to a red LED. And this received character will be sent back to the terminal. Therefore, when a user types '1' on the serial terminal, it can toggle a red LED to be ON or OFF. If the communication is successful, you can see the '1' printed on the serial terminal.

This is a simple test program. However, it can be modified to provide more complex functions. In the next chapter, we study an educational robot application. This wireless control method can be found useful in mobile robot applications.

Bluetooth ICs and Modules

Many Bluetooth modules are commercially available. Designers and programmers can search and find the best one that meets the functional requirements of the given project. There are also MCUs that support Bluetooth connectivity. For instance, Texas Instruments and Microchip® provide MCUs, ICs, and modules with Bluetooth connectivity. Readers can find the information related to Bluetooth connectivity from manufacturers' website.

As the complexity of the system is increasing, it is preferable to use high level driver library and Real-Time Operating Systems. Moreover, if a developer wants to create fast prototype devices, an open electronics development tool can be used. We will study briefly about the driver library, real-time operating system, and open electronics development platforms in Chapter 23, 24 and 25.

Chapter 22. Embedded System Integration

Embedded systems can be easily found in modern electronics products. They are used across a wide range of industries. It is typical to find these products are integrated systems with multiple sub-systems. We have studied various components and the programming techniques to control them using an MSP430FR5994 MCU. In this chapter, approaches and considerations in integrating systems are presented.

System Integration

Generally, in engineering, system integration is the process of putting sub-systems together to make one larger system. The discrete sub-systems function together as a system. A system integration typically focuses on increasing the value and functionality. Developers put all relevant things together in order to make the system work as a single integrated system. Developers work together as a team to meet given project milestones.

Top-down Approach

Developers may share a big goal or idea of the system to build. Next, they can communicate with each other to come up with a plan. The project can be processed as a top-down approach. Typically, this method could spare an extensive research and planning phase before the next execution phase of the project such as hardware assembly or software programming.

Top-down Approach in embedded systems development is a problem-solving strategy related to many areas including hardware, software, and mechanical. During the analysis and planning phase, the system can be divided into hardware, software, and mechanical tasks.

On the software development side, structured programming is relevant to this approach. It performs a top-down analysis. Next, the program has been broken down into sub-tasks to reduce the complexity of each sub-task.

Modular programming could be adopted, which is the software design technique to separate the functionality of a program into independent and interchangeable modules. Thus, sub-tasks can be divided into modules. These modules can be independently developed, and they are preferred to be reusable.

The top-down programming method is organized, and it is typically easier to maintain a program in the long run. However, it may be slow to start since it may take an extensive time in planning, and it is slow to obtain the first executable program. Moreover, as mentioned, the sub-tasks have to be specifically defined, and they could be developed separately. If the specification of the product happens to be changed after the planning phase, it might require an extended extra effort, if it would change the major structure.

This explanation is similar to the overall top-down approach. It can solve a complex problem by breaking it down into sub-tasks. It is suitable for a traditional structured approach. However, due to the needs of extensive planning and analysis, the top-down approach may be slow in delivering the first prototype, and it is less flexible in adapting to the change of product specifications.

Bottom-up Approach

Developers share a big goal or idea of the system. Next, they can communicate with each other to come up with a plan. This process is similar to the previous top-down approach. However, it can be processed as a bottom-up approach. This means, in planning, the goal and problems are outlined. However, in this approach, it does not spend an extensive effort in breaking down the tasks and identifying the problems. After the initial planning phase, they can move on to the execution phase to start building hardware assembly or writing a piece of software code.

On the software development side, bottom-up programming is also a relevant approach. It tends to be less organized than the top-down approach. The code tends to be difficult to maintain later. However, it allows getting it started fast and it may generate the first executable program fast. Moreover, bottom-up programming may provide a solution to a complex problem that is not clearly defined.

Traditionally, this bottom-up approach may not be highly encouraged, but a structured approach like the top-down approach is more emphasized in formal educational or training settings. One of the reasons is that it could generate a *spaghetti code*. This code refers to the source code negatively that is difficult to maintain. However, this bottom-up approach may be suitable for experienced developers who already hold a fair understanding of the technology and can maintain good communication with the team.

In order words, inexperienced developers who lack understanding of technology may eventually generate a functional code at some point by a trial-and-error approach. But, the code may not be well-written, and the developers may fail to communicate with their team members due to the code that cannot be understood easily by other developers. This may be one of the unfavorable scenarios for a majority of product design projects.

If it is well managed, the bottom-up approach may result in providing an innovative solution to a difficult problem that would not be solved easily in a traditional formal setting. Moreover, it is flexible and can be adaptable to the specification changes after the initial planning phase. This approach may be found suitable in a research project type rather than consumer electronics project types.

Blending Top-down and Bottom-up Approaches

Depending on the projects, the blended top-down and bottom-up approaches can be chosen. If it is a well-structured problem to solve, a top-down approach can be a good choice. However, if the specification needs to be changed in the middle of the execution of the project, it may not be an easy process for the top-down approach.

The bottom-up approach may be less structured to begin with. However, it can be flexible to adapt to the change. Moreover, the decision process in a top-down approach tends to be centralized by leaders, and the decision process in a bottom-up approach tends to be decentralized.

In software development, there is a waterfall methodology. It is a linear project management approach where the stakeholders and customers set up requirements at the early stage of the project. And, the rest of the project period is based on the execution of the project based on the requirements. Typical phases of the waterfall model are *requirements*, *design*, *implementation*, *verification*, and *maintenance*.

Agile Software Development

Waterfall project management in software development is a plan driven approach. There is another software development process. It is Agile software development. This is effective in a complex environment. Agile is based on the interactive process to receive and accept feedback and review from the customer during product development.

The process is streamlined. This means that it reduces unnecessarily long meetings and documentation but has quick meetings and less documentation to move the project fast. Agile is based on time-boxed events and iterations. A time-box is an agreed maximum period for a person or a team for a certain goal. For instance, when the time limit is reached, it evaluates the task.

The key to agile is collaboration. For instance, the specifications may be open to change according to the communication with the client even in the middle of the project execution. Agile approach may result in creating a better product, and it can improve the product continuously.

Design Project Management Consideration

A top-down approach is a typical choice for many companies. The changes in specifications are necessary due to the changes in the demand in the todays' electronics market. Bottom-up approach may respond to the change easier than the top-down approach. Also, the bottom-up approach can be used in tacking difficult problems or creating an innovative solution. However, the lack of organization can become a problem. Depending on the project, blended approach can be effectively used. In software development, instead of Waterfall project management, Agile software development can provide a continuously improving product.

BH EDU Robot Platform

In the previous chapters, we have studied various functions that can be applied to embedded systems. For learning purposes, readers can choose a goal of their own embedded system to design and build as a small educational project.

At the early stage of the development, a conceptual block diagram can be drawn, which shows the high-level description of the project. The conceptual block diagram (CBD) can serve as a roadmap for the project. Next, a functional block diagram (FBD) with more details including components, wiring and connections information can be created. As the system becomes more complicated, it will become challenging in making all the relevant components function properly. The FBD can be used to check to see whether there is any resource conflict or not.

Figure 22.1. BH EDU robot platform example [8].

As an example, a mobile robot can be built using a BH EDU board with an MSP430FR5994 Launchpad board as shown in Figure 22.1. The robot base kit is assembled with a BH EDU board. The robot base kit includes the DC motors and wheel sets, and a manipulator set with a servo motor. On the BH EDU board, it has a motor driver, an accelerometer, an ultrasonic sensor, an LCD module, buttons, and a

5V regulator. This robot can be controlled wirelessly through an IR receiver or a Bluetooth module.

For educational purposes, various robot missions can be given such as solving a maze and moving objects to specified locations. As there are many components to make them operate concurrently, programming can be challenging. It may need several iterative efforts of programming, debugging, and testing.

Readers can choose any other educational embedded system examples including calculators, alarm clocks, music players, fan control systems, robot arms, and remote controlled four-wheeled or tracked robots. They can choose their own robot chassis kits and DIY kits to implement their systems. However, the recommended supply voltage for many of these kits could be 5 V. Since the operating voltage that we used in this book for an MSP430FR5994 MCU is 3.3V, readers should check and provide proper and safe interfaces between the board and the components that they have chosen. It is recommended that the wiring and connections need to be carefully reviewed. If it involves any components that could use high current such as a motor driver, it should not use the power from the Launchpad. Instead, separate regulated power such as through external batteries can be used for the motor driver.

Chapter 23. Driver Library

Developers may find a low-level programming method difficult in describing complex tasks. In addition, they may want to write a program that is reusable on other platforms. For this reason, developers can choose high-level programming methods instead, and several high-level programming methods are available. One of them is based on the hardware abstraction layer (HAL) and application programming interfaces (APIs). A HAL creates abstract and high-level functions that can make the hardware do some tasks. APIs can provide high-level interfaces that can be used in creating an application.

For MSP430 MCUs, Texas Instruments provides an MSP430 Peripheral Diver Library. It supports a higher-level programming method. The MSP430 Driver Library is included in the MSP430Ware. The MSP430Ware is a collection of resources for MSP430 MCUs. The MSP430 Driver Library is an essential library to help developers create MSP430 applications. The code written using Driver Library in one MCU platform can be reusable on other MCU platforms. In addition, the code can be written without an in-depth understanding of the hardware. This is a middleware approach, and this is one of the recommended methods in writing a program for an MSP430FR5994 MCU.

Driver Library

TI MSP430 Driver Library (DriverLib) is a set of Application Programming Interfaces (APIs) [31]. It can be used to control MSP430 peripherals. DriverLib provides a higher level of programming compared to register-based C programming. The code written using this high-level software programming method can be reusable on other MCU platforms. In addition, it is more readable, intuitive, and easy to program. As an example, the code that configures P1.0 as an output port can be written using DriverLib as follows:

GPIO_setAsOutputPin(GPIO_PORT_P1, GPIO_PIN0);

The DriverLib package contains various examples. In order to access and use the DriverLib, a proper setup process such as setting up the path for the library folder is needed.

In order to access a Driver Library example project and set it up easily, you can use *Resource Explorer*. It can be found in *View* on your code composer studio and click *Resource Explorer*. Next, click *MSP430™ microcontrollers*. Next, click *MSP430Ware-3.xx.xx.xx*. Then, click the "install" icon to install *MSP430Ware* as shown in Figure 23.1. The installation process can be running in the background, and it may take some time to complete the installation of the software package.

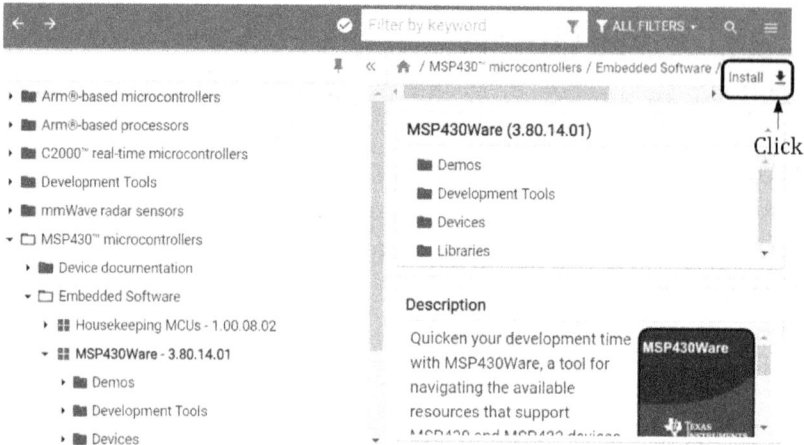

Figure 23.1. MSP430Ware installation.

After the installation of *MSP430Ware* is completed, you continue to use *Resource Explorer* to import an example project. You can go back to the MSP430Ware window by the selection as follows:

Resource Explorer → MSP430™ microcontroller → MSP430Ware-3.xx.xx.xx

Next, you can find the *empty* project through the sequence of selections as follows:

Development Tools → MSP-EXP430FR5994 → Peripheral Examples →

Driver Library → Example Projects → FRAMCTL_A → framctl_a_ex1_write

Then, you can find "*import*" icon as shown in Figure 23.2 and click the icon to import the project.

Figure 23.2. DriverLib example project on TI resource explorer.

Next, you can find the example project that was imported into the project list. As shown in Figure 23.3, you can rename the project, and you can use it as a template project. You can also rename the file name of "framctl_a_ex1_write.c" to "main.c". For the programming examples in this chapter, you can modify this *main.c* file to enter the code.

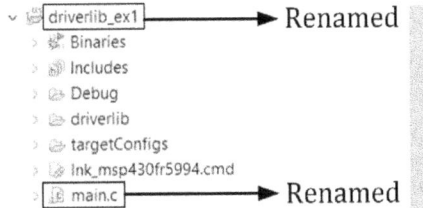

Figure 23.3. Renaming a project.

DriverLib GPIO

A set of functions provides the control of a GPIO module. Let us consider some of the selected functions in this section. They are introduced in the following paragraph, and they are self-explanatory from the names of the functions.

The GPIO pin can be configured as an input or output pin with *GPIO_setAsOutputPin*, *GPIO_setAsInputPin*, *GPIO_setAsInputPinWithPullDownResistor*, or *GPIO_setAsInputPinWithPullUpResistor*.

The GPIO pin can be configured to operate in the alternate function using *GPIO_setAsPeripheralModuleFunctionOutputPin* or *GPIO_setAsPeripheralModuleFunctionInputPin*.

The port interrupt on the selected pin can be configured using *GPIO_enableInterrupt*.

The interrupt flag on the selected pin can be cleared using *GPIO_clearInterruptFlag*.

The interrupt status of the selected pin can be obtained using *GPIO_getEnabledInterruptStatus*.

Some functions that can generate output on the selected pin are GPIO_setOutputHighOnPin, GPIO_setOutputLowOnPin, and *GPIO_toggleOutputOnPin*.

Using some of these GPIO functions, a DriverLib GPIO example is written as shown in Program 23.1. Some of these APIs have been used in this example. This program starts with the initiation process. In the main loop, it toggles the pin of P1.0, and the pin is connected to LED1 (Red LED). In the interrupt service routine, the interrupt status can be read, and the program can check whether the P5.6 pin is set or not. Then, it will toggle the P1.1 pin that is connected to LED2 (Green LED).

A port interrupt is configured for the P5.6 pin, and it is connected to the push button located on the left side. If successful, a red LED will keep flashing, and the other LED will be turned on or off as the button is pressed or released by a user.

```
#include <msp430.h>
#include "driverlib.h"
int main (void) {
  WDT_A_hold(WDT_A_BASE); // hold the watchdog timer
  PMM_unlockLPM5(); // clear LOCKLPM5 bit
  GPIO_setAsOutputPin(GPIO_PORT_P1, GPIO_PIN0); // output (P1.0)
  GPIO_setAsOutputPin(GPIO_PORT_P1, GPIO_PIN1); // output (P1.1)
  GPIO_setAsInputPinWithPullUpResistor(GPIO_PORT_P5, GPIO_PIN6);
                                      // input, pull-up resistor (P5.6)
  GPIO_clearInterrupt(GPIO_PORT_P5, GPIO_PIN6); // clear interrupt flag (P5.6)
  GPIO_enableInterrupt(GPIO_PORT_P5, GPIO_PIN6); // enable interrupt (P5.6)
  _enable_interrupt(); // enable general interrupt
  while (1) {
    GPIO_toggleOutputOnPin(GPIO_PORT_P1, GPIO_PIN0); // toggle (P1.0)
    _delay_cycles(250000); // delay
  }
  return 0;
}

#pragma vector=PORT5_VECTOR
_interrupt void Port5_ISR_handler(void) {
  uint32_t status;
  status = GPIO_getInterruptStatus(GPIO_PORT_P5, GPIO_PIN6);
                                      // read interrupt status (P5.6)
  if(status) { // check whether the PIN is set
    GPIO_toggleOutputOnPin(GPIO_PORT_P1, GPIO_PIN1); // toggle (P1.1)
  }
  GPIO_clearInterrupt(GPIO_PORT_P5, GPIO_PIN6); // clear port1 interrupt flag
}
```

Program 23.1. DriverLib GPIO example.

DriverLib UART

DriverLib package includes functions for a UART module. The data format for the UART configuration is defined as a *struct* data type, and the name is *EUSCI_A_UART_initParam*.

A UART module can be initialized using *EUSCI_A_UART_init*.

The UART block can be enabled by *EUSCI_A_UART_enable*.

The UART interrupt can be configured using *EUSCI_A_UART_enableInterrupt*.

The UART interrupt status can be obtained by *EUSCI_A_UART_getInterruptStatus*.

The data can be transmitted or received using
EUSCI_A_UART_transmitData or *EUSCI_A_UART_receiveData*.

A DriverLib UART example is written as shown in Program 23.2. Some of these
UART functions are used in this program. This is a UART echo program, and the
baud rate is selected as 9600 bps. "*uartConfig*" variable contains the UART
configuration data. The pins of P2.0 and P2.1 are configured to operate in UART
mode.

The RX UART interrupt is configured. When data is received, the interrupt service
routine is going to be executed. In the ISR, it can check whether the UART interrupt
flag is set or not. Then, it is going to read the data and send it back over UART
communication.

```c
#include <msp430.h>
#include "driverlib.h"
// UART config, 9600 baud rate
struct EUSCI_A_UART_initParam uartConfig = {
  EUSCI_A_UART_CLOCKSOURCE_SMCLK, // SMCLK
  6, // BRx
  8, // BRFx
  32, // BRSx
  EUSCI_A_UART_NO_PARITY, // no parity
  EUSCI_A_UART_LSB_FIRST, // LSB first
  EUSCI_A_UART_ONE_STOP_BIT, // one stop bit
  EUSCI_A_UART_MODE, // UART mode
  EUSCI_A_UART_OVERSAMPLING_BAUDRATE_GENERATION, // oversampling
};
int main (void) {
  WDT_A_hold(WDT_A_BASE); // hold the watchdog timer
  PMM_unlockLPM5(); // clear LOCKLPM5 bit
  GPIO_setAsOutputPin(GPIO_PORT_P1, GPIO_PIN0); // output (P1.0)
  GPIO_setAsPeripheralModuleFunctionInputPin(GPIO_PORT_P2, (GPIO_PIN0 |
GPIO_PIN1), GPIO_SECONDARY_MODULE_FUNCTION); // UART mode (P2.0, P2.1)
  EUSCI_A_UART_init(EUSCI_A0_BASE, &uartConfig);
                                    // configure UART module (ECUSCI_A0)
  EUSCI_A_UART_enable(EUSCI_A0_BASE); // enable UART module
  EUSCI_A_UART_enableInterrupt(EUSCI_A0_BASE,
EUSCI_A_UART_RECEIVE_INTERRUPT); // enable ISR (RX)
  _enable_interrupt(); // enable general interrupt
  while(1) {
    GPIO_toggleOutputOnPin(GPIO_PORT_P1, GPIO_PIN0); // toggle (P1.0)
    _delay_cycles(250000); // delay
  }
  return 0;
}
```

```
#pragma vector=EUSCI_A0_VECTOR
_interrupt void USCI_A0_ISR(void) {
  uint8_t status;
  status = EUSCI_A_UART_getInterruptStatus(EUSCI_A0_BASE,
EUSCI_A_UART_RECEIVE_INTERRUPT_FLAG);  // read eUSCI_A0 interrupt status
  if(status) {  // check whether the UART RX flag is set
    EUSCI_A_UART_transmitData(EUSCI_A0_BASE,
EUSCI_A_UART_receiveData(EUSCI_A0_BASE));  // read the data and send it back
  }
}
```

Program 23.2. DriveLib UART echo example.

Similar to other echo program examples shown previously, users can modify this code to provide the functions for their project. For more information about the Driver Library, TI provides a Peripheral Driver Library User's Guide [31]. Further details can be found in the user's guide.

Chapter 24. Introduction to TI-RTOS

Developers can choose to use TI Driver Library to describe functions as a high-level programming method. It is a middleware approach. Another high-level approach is to use a Real-Time Operating System. There are several RTOSs for MSP430 MCUs. In this chapter, we will learn about TI-RTOS. TI-RTOS can accelerate development because it can eliminate the need to create basic software functions. TI-RTOS provides a real-time kernel.

TI-RTOS

TI-RTOS is a real-time operating system. It is an embedded system development package with source files and pre-compiled libraries. TI-RTOS contains these components. Let me briefly introduce a few key components.

SYS/BIOS is a scalable real-time kernel, and it supports real-time scheduling and synchronization [32]. SYS/BIOS provides preemptive multithreading and hardware abstraction as well as real-time analysis and configuration tools. SYS/BIOS is used as the TI-RTOS kernel component in TI-RTOS.

SYS/BIOS provides a deterministic performance, and it enables applications to meet real-time deadlines. SYS/BIOS also provides various thread types, and it supports *hardware interrupts (Hwi)*, *software interrupts (Swi)*, *tasks*, and *idle* functions. Moreover, SYS/BIOS supports synchronization between threads including *semaphores*, *mailboxes*, *events*, *gates*, and *messaging*.

TI-RTOS includes board support and drivers for peripherals. These drivers are written to be thread-safe for use with the TI-RTOS Kernel. Moreover, there is an XDCtools component. It is a core component that provides tools to configure and build SYS/BIOS and other components.

GPIO Driver

TI-RTOS includes various software libraries and drivers. GPIO driver is one of them [33]. It is an API set to manage GPIO pins and ports. TI GPIO Driver provides GPIO APIs that are easy to use; however, they may not be the same APIs in TI Driver Library. However, there is a similarity between TI-RTOS GPIO APIs and TI Driver Library APIs.

In order to use the GPIO module in TI-RTOS, the proper GPIO header needs to be included as follows: #include <ti/drivers/GPIO.h>

Moreover, the proper API names need to be used. Selected GPIO APIs and their description will be followed.

GPIO pins can be initialized as it is pre-defined using *GPIO_init()*.

The specified GPIO pin can be configured using *GPIO_setConfig()*.

The status of the specified GPIO input pin can be read using *GPIO_read()*.

The state of the specified GPIO output pin can be set or cleared using *GPIO_write()*.

The state of the specified GPIO output pin can be toggled using *GPIO_toggle()*.

A call-back function to the specified GPIO pin can be configured using *GPIO_setCallback()*.

An interrupt on the specified GPIO pin can be enabled or disabled using *GPIO_enableInt()* or *GPIO_disableInt()*.

The interrupt flag for the specified GPIO pin can be cleared using *GPIO_clearInt()*.

For instance, an LED defined as "Board_LED0" can be turned ON, OFF, or toggled using code lines as follows:
GPIO_write(Board_LED0, CONFIG_GPIO_LED_ON),
GPIO_write(Board_LED0, CONFIG_GPIO_LED_OFF), or
GPIO_toggle(Board_LED0).

TI-RTOS configuration for an MSP430FR5994 MCU

In order to access and use TI-RTOS, proper software packages need to be installed and configured. This setup process would be complex and difficult if it has to be done manually from scratch. However, this setup process can be relatively easily completed by importing a project template in Code Compose Studio. In this section, the setup process is described.

First, it is recommended to install *MSP430Ware* as described in the previous chapter. For TI-RTOS, a *TI-RTOS product for MSP430* needs to be installed. The *TI-RTOS product for MSP430* could be accessed and installed using *Resource Explorer*. You can try to locate it through the selections of *View → Resource Explorer*.

However, if the *TI-RTOS product for MSP430* is not available or there is any difficulty in accessing it through *Resource Explorer*, developers can choose to install the *TI-RTOS product for MSP430* manually and import project examples at their own risk and discretion. If this is the developers' choice, they can visit the following web address:

http://downloads.ti.com/dsps/dsps_public_sw/sdo_sb/targetcontent/tirtos/index.html

Then, developers can find the list of the released TI-RTOS products. The *TI-RTOS product for MSP430* can be located and downloaded via accessing the webpage as shown in Figure 24.1. After the download is completed, developers can install the downloaded TI-RTOS software package.

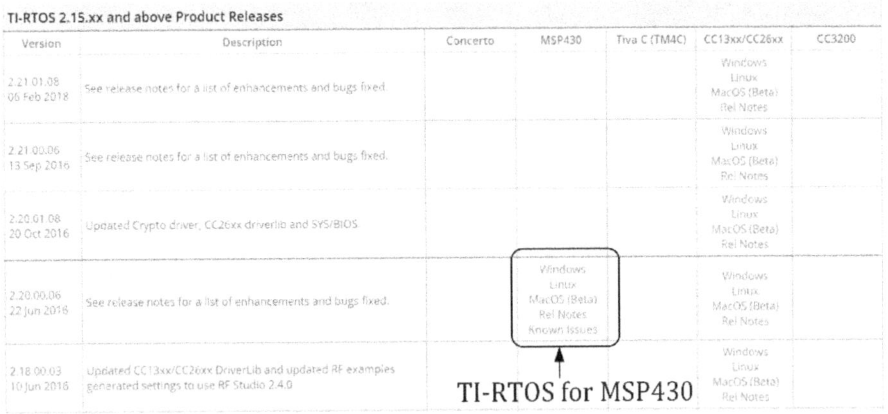

TI-RTOS 2.15.xx and above Product Releases

Version	Description	Concerto	MSP430	Tiva C (TM4C)	CC13xx/CC26xx	CC3200
2.21.01.08 06 Feb 2018	See release notes for a list of enhancements and bugs fixed.				Windows Linux MacOS (Beta) Rel Notes	
2.21.00.06 13 Sep 2016	See release notes for a list of enhancements and bugs fixed.				Windows Linux MacOS (Beta) Rel Notes	
2.20.01.08 20 Oct 2016	Updated Crypto driver, CC26xx driverlib and SYS/BIOS				Windows Linux MacOS (Beta) Rel Notes	
2.20.00.06 22 Jun 2016	See release notes for a list of enhancements and bugs fixed.		Windows Linux MacOS (Beta) Rel Notes Known Issues		Windows Linux MacOS (Beta) Rel Notes	
2.18.00.03 10 Jun 2016	Updated CC13xx/CC26xx DriverLib and updated RF examples generated settings to use RF Studio 2.4.0				Windows Linux MacOS (Beta) Rel Notes	

TI-RTOS for MSP430

Figure 24.1. TI-RTOS product for MSP430.

For the version of the *TI-RTOS product for MSP430* in Figure 24.1 is 2.20.00.06. In addition, a proper version of a TI compiler that works with this version of this specific TI-RTOS version may need to be installed. This TI compiler version is 16.12.0.STS, and the installation file can be found and downloaded via the following web address:

https://www.ti.com/tool/download/MSP-CGT/16.12.0.STS

Once the download is finished, developers can install the TI compiler. During the installation of this TI compiler, it can be prompted to enter the destination directory. A proper folder name should be entered, and the proper folder name is dependent on the chosen default TI folder. For instance, if the default TI folder is "C:\ti", the destination directory can be "C:\ti\ti-cgt-msp430_16.12.0.STS".

After the successful installation of the proper *TI RTOS product for MSP430* and the TI compiler. Next, developers need to run the Code Composer Studio and choose the following selections:

Windows → Preferences → Code Composer Studio → Products

Then, developers can see the window shown in Figure 24.2. On this window, developers can click "refresh" on the right, and these manually installed products can be discovered, and the message window can be prompt to install. Then, after choosing to install, it will be processed. Next, it may ask to reboot the Code Composer Studio.

The installation can be easily completed as the developers clock the "refresh" icon as described. In case they experience any difficulty, they can choose the "install" icon in Figure 24.2 to install and configure these packages in Code Composer Studio manually to complete the process.

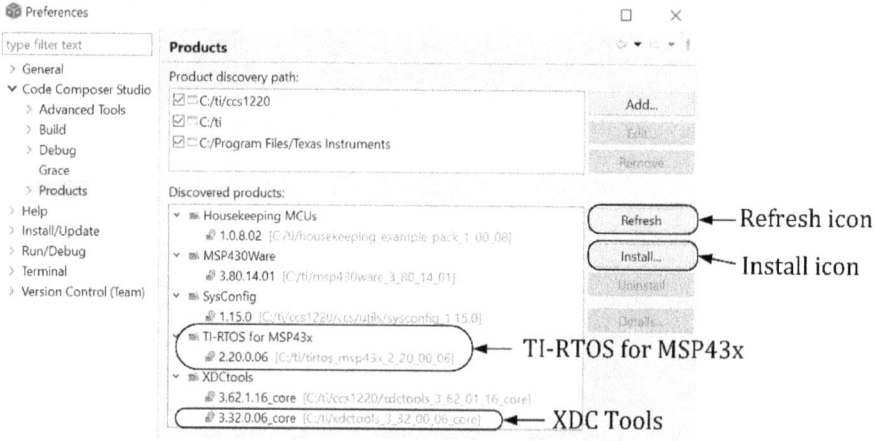

Figure 24.2. Preference-Products; Installed TI-RTOS for MSP43x and XDC Tools.

After the completion of this installation and configuration process, you can check whether these products are installed properly. Figure 24.2 shows the installed TI-RTOS for MSP43x and the XDC Tools in Code Composer Studio.

Moreover, developers can check whether the proper TI compiler is installed and configured in Code Composer Studio by choosing the following selections:

$$Windows \rightarrow Preferences \rightarrow Code\ Composer\ Studio \rightarrow Build \rightarrow Compilers$$

Then, developers can see the windows as shown in Figure 24.3, and they can check the proper version of the TI compiler is stalled.

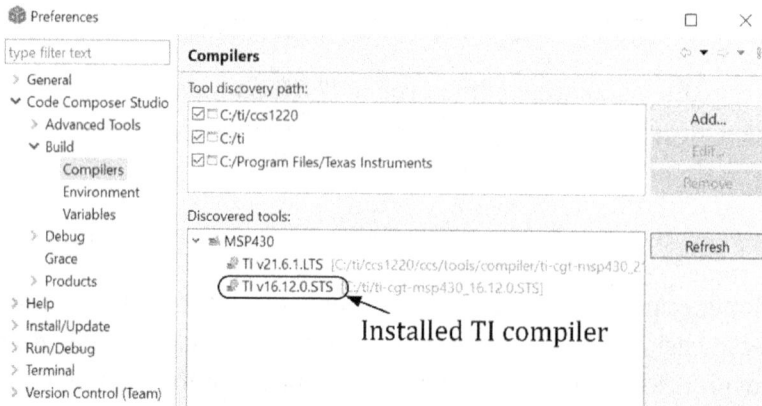

Figure 24.3. Preference–Compilers; Installed TI compiler.

After the verification of the installation of the proper TI-RTOS for MSP430, XDC Tools, and TI compiler is finished, developers can import a TI-RTOS project template by choosing following sections:

New → Import → Code Composer Studio -> CCS Projects

Next, the *import CCS Projects* window can be accessed as shown in Figure 24.4. In this window, click the *browse* icon to choose a proper folder for *Select search-directory*. Assuming the TI-RTOS product is installed in the default TI folder (C:\ti), an example project can be accessed by selecting a proper folder as follows:

C:\ti\tirtos_msp43x_2_20_00_06\resources\msp_exp430FR5994Launchpad\driverExamples

Once the search of the projects in the example project folder is successfully completed, the *empty* project template can be found in the *discovered projects* as shown in Figure 24.4. This *empty* project can be selected and click the "Finish" icon.

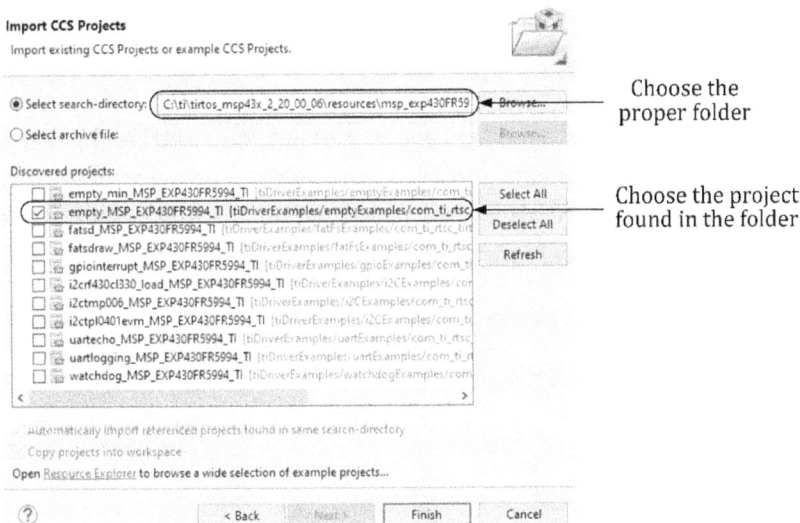

Figure 24.4. Search directory selection and the discovered project (*empty* project).

Next, developers can see the "New CCS Project" window as shown in Figure 24.5. In this window, the proper version of the installed TI compiler needs to be selected. The selection of the proper TI compiler is as shown in Figure 24.5.

Next, a new project can be created, and it contains library, header, source, and configuration files. There is an "empty.c", and the main() routine can be found in this source file. We will continue to learn how to set up the project properly in the *GPIO program example* section after the following *Task execution states* section.

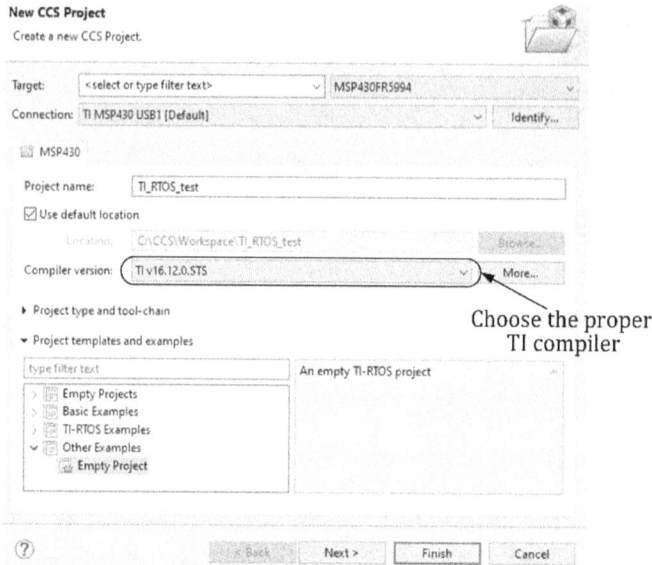

Figure 24.5. Selection of the TI compiler version.

Task Execution States

Tasks objects are threads managed by Task module. It schedules and preempts tasks based on their priority levels and execution states. The priority level can be assigned up to 31. The priority level of 0 is reserved for the idle loop. Tasks can be created by calling *Task_create()* functions.

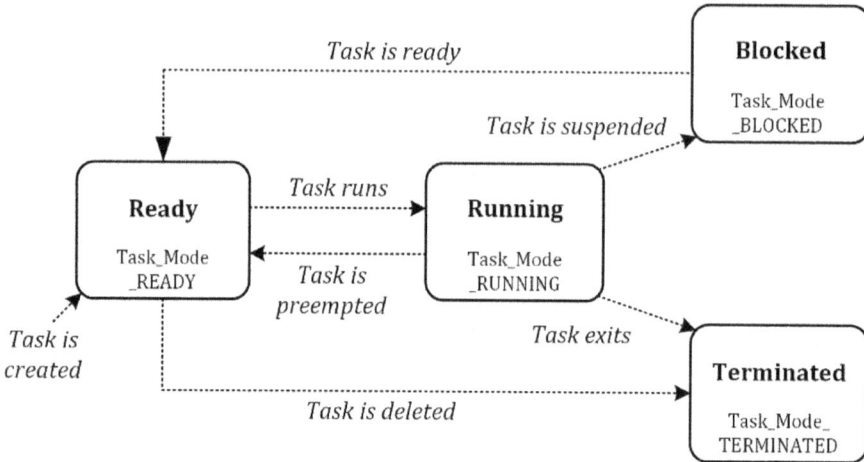

Figure 24.6. Task Execution States [32].

A task object is one of four states of execution. They are **running**, **ready**, **blocked**, and **terminated**. Task execution states are shown in Figure 24.6. They are named *Task_Mode_RUNNING*, *Task_Mode_READY*, *Task_Mode_BLOCKED*, and *Task_Mode_TERMINATED*, respectively.

The running state is the one that is actually executing using the processor time. The ready state is the one scheduled to be executed depending on the availability of the processor. The blocked state is the one that cannot be executed until a particular event. The terminated state is the one that is not executed anymore.

Tasks are scheduled to be executed according to assigned priority levels. There is one task that can be in the running state. In this case, let us suppose that a higher priority task is ready to run. Then, this task preempts, and the lower priority task that was in the running state is going to be in the ready state.

A task that is in a running state can be in a blocked state if the current task is suspended. Then, the task waits for a resource or a signal. For instance, the blocked state can be caused by *Task_sleep()* or *Semaphore_pend()*. A task can be terminated by calling *Task_exit()*, or automatically called when a task returns from its top-level function.

TI-RTOS GPIO Example

As it was described, you can import an *empty* project example. After it is imported, you can rename the project as shown in Figure 24.4. It is renamed to "TI_RTOS_test". However, you can choose any project name. Next, you can find the "empty.c" file, and you can rename this file to "main.c". Next, you can find the "empty.cfg" file, and you can rename this file to "main.cfg". The screenshot after this setup process is shown in Figure 24.7 for reference. This setup process will be used for the TI-RTOS examples in this chapter.

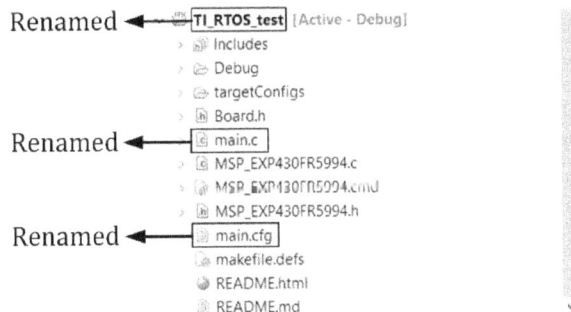

Figure 24.7. TI-RTOS example project set-up.

You can double-click "main.cfg" file, and you can see a text-based cfg file. Or, you move your mouse over the "main.cfg" file and click the right mouse button. Then, you can see "Open With", and choose "XGCONF". In this way, you can open the file using XGCONF configuration tool. Using this XGCONF configuration tool, you can easily change the configuration of the TI-RTOS project.

There are some of the parameters defined in "board. h" for an MSP430FR5994 Launchpad. For instance, there are two LEDs and two Buttons, and the relevant information is shown in Table 24.1. The names that were pre-defined for the LEDs and buttons will be used in the TI-RTOS example program in this chapter.

Parameters	LED1	LED2	Button (S1)	Button (S2)
Name	Board_LED0	Board_LED1	Board_BUTTON0	Board_BUTTON1
Hardware	Launchpad LED1 (Red)	Launchpad LED2 (Green)	Launchpad Button S1 (Left)	Launchpad Button S2 (Right)
Mode	Output	Output	Input	Input

Table 24.1. Parameters; LEDs and Buttons.

Next, you can type your code in "main.c". You can use the example code shown in Program 24.1. You can run this example project. If successful, you can see that two LEDs on your Launchpad board can blink simultaneously. There are two tasks defined in this code. They can be found in the subroutines named "task1Fxn" and "task2Fxn." Each task is blinking LED1 or LED2.

```
#include <xdc/std.h> // XDCtools
#include <xdc/runtime/System.h> // XDCtools
#include <ti/sysbios/BIOS.h> // SYS/BIOS
#include <ti/sysbios/knl/Task.h> // task module
#include <ti/drivers/GPIO.h> // GPIO driver
#include "Board.h"
#define TASKSTACKSIZE  512
Task_Struct task1Struct, task2Struct; // task_Struct
Char task1Stack[TASKSTACKSIZE],task2Stack[TASKSTACKSIZE]; // task stack

Void task1Fxn(UArg arg0) {
   while (1) {
     GPIO_write(Board_LED0, Board_LED_ON); // LED0 (high)
     Task_sleep((UInt)arg0); // task sleep
     GPIO_write(Board_LED0, Board_LED_OFF); // LED0 (low)
     Task_sleep((UInt)arg0); // task sleep
   }
}

Void task2Fxn(UArg arg0) {
   while (1) {
     GPIO_write(Board_LED1, Board_LED_ON); // LED1 (high)
     Task_sleep((UInt)arg0); // task sleep
     GPIO_write(Board_LED1, Board_LED_OFF); // LED1 (low)
     Task_sleep((UInt)arg0); // task sleep
   }
}

int main(void) {
   Task_Params task1Params, task2Params;
   Board_initGeneral();
```

```
Board_initGPIO();
GPIO_write(Board_LED0, Board_LED_OFF);  // LED0 (low)
GPIO_write(Board_LED1, Board_LED_OFF);  // LED1 (low)
Task_Params_init(&task1Params);  // task1Params init.
task1Params.arg0 = 100;  // arg0, 100
task1Params.stackSize = TASKSTACKSIZE;
task1Params.stack = &task1Stack;
task1Params.priority = 1;  // priority, 1
Task_construct(&task1Struct, (Task_FuncPtr)task1Fxn, &task1Params, NULL);
                                                        // task1 creation

Task_Params_init(&task2Params);  // task2Params init.
task2Params.arg0 = 100;  // arg0, 100
task2Params.stackSize = TASKSTACKSIZE;
task2Params.stack = &task2Stack;
task2Params.priority = 1;  // priority, 1
Task_construct(&task2Struct, (Task_FuncPtr)task2Fxn, &task2Params, NULL);
                                                        // task2 creation

BIOS_start();  // start BIOS
return 0;
}
```

Program 24.1. TI-RTOS GPIO example.

In the *main* loop, it includes hardware initializations. Next, it has task definitions. The values of task1Params.arg0 and task2Params.arg0 are used in *Task_sleep* functions in each task. These arguments were passed to each task, and they determine the duration of a blink. For the priority, both tasks have the same priorities. Next, the BIOS_start() code line can be found, it will start the TI-RTOS. When the program is run successfully, two LEDs will be turned ON and OFF simultaneously.

Synchronization Modules

TI-RTOS supports several synchronization modules. They are *Semaphores, Event Module, Gates, Mailboxes,* and *Queues*. These modules can be used to coordinate access to shared resources. Multiple tasks can be run concurrently. If a resource is shared among the tasks. In order to avoid conflict, access to the shared resource can be controlled properly by the use of the synchronization modules.

Semaphores can be used for inter-task synchronization and communication. Semaphore objects in TI-RTOS can be either counting or binary semaphores. Counting semaphores keep a count of the number related to the availability of the corresponding resource. When the counter is greater than zero, it can be considered that the resource is available. Semaphores can be configured as either simple FIFO (First-In, First-Out) or priority-aware semaphores. The default setting for semaphores in TI-RTOS is the simple counting semaphore. On the other hand, binary semaphores can represent either available or unavailable. The value of the binary semaphore cannot exceed more than 1.

The semaphore objects can be created or deleted using *Semaphore_create()* and *Semaphore_delete()*. The semaphore count needs to be initialized properly when it is being created. Typically, it is initialized as the number of resources. The task waits for a semaphore at the function of *Semaphore_pend()*. It waits for the signal. If the number of the count is greater than zero, simply, the number of the count is decreased and returns. However, if the number of the count is zero, the semaphore keeps waiting for the signal. The signal can be generated by *Semaphore_post()* because it increments the number of counts and returns.

TI-RTOS Semaphore Example

You can repeat the same setup as in the previous TI-RTOS GPIO example. Or, simply you can reuse the project by updating your "main.c" file for the example program in this section.

The semaphore example program is shown in Program 24.2. In this example, a semaphore is used to synchronize two tasks. The task1 is to turn on a red LED and to turn off a green LED. The task2 is to turn off the red LED and turn on the green LED.

```
#include <xdc/std.h> // XDCtools
#include <xdc/runtime/System.h> // XDCtools
#include <ti/sysbios/BIOS.h> // SYS/BIOS
#include <ti/sysbios/knl/Task.h> // task module
#include <ti/sysbios/knl/Semaphore.h> // semaphore module
#include <ti/drivers/GPIO.h> // GPIO driver
#include "Board.h"
#define TASKSTACKSIZE  512
Task_Struct task1Struct, task2Struct; // task_Struct
Char task1Stack[TASKSTACKSIZE], task2Stack[TASKSTACKSIZE]; // task stack
Semaphore_Struct semStruct;
Semaphore_Handle semHandle;

Void task1Fxn(UArg arg0) { // task1
  while (1) {
    Semaphore_pend(semHandle, BIOS_WAIT_FOREVER); // pend on a semaphore
    GPIO_write(Board_LED0, Board_LED_ON); // LED0 (high)
    GPIO_write(Board_LED1, Board_LED_OFF); // LED1 (low)
    Task_sleep((UInt)arg0); // task sleep
    Semaphore_post(semHandle); //post a semaphore
  }
}

Void task2Fxn(UArg arg0) { // task2
  while (1) {
```

```
    Semaphore_pend(semHandle, BIOS_WAIT_FOREVER);  // pend on a semaphore
    GPIO_write(Board_LED0, Board_LED_OFF);  // LED0 (low)
    GPIO_write(Board_LED1, Board_LED_ON);  // LED1 (high)
    Task_sleep((UInt)arg0);  // task sleep
    Semaphore_post(semHandle);  // post a semaphore
  }
}

int main(void) {
  Task_Params task1Params, task2Params;  // Task_Parms
  Semaphore_Params semParams;  // semaphore_Parms
  Board_initGeneral();
  Board_initGPIO();
  GPIO_write(Board_LED0, Board_LED_OFF);  // LED0 (low)
  GPIO_write(Board_LED1, Board_LED_OFF);  // LED1 (low)
  Task_Params_init(&task1Params);  // task1Params init.
  task1Params.arg0 = 100;  // arg0, 100
  task1Params.stackSize = TASKSTACKSIZE;
  task1Params.stack = &task1Stack;
  task1Params.priority = 1;  // priority, 1
  Task_construct(&task1Struct, (Task_FuncPtr)task1Fxn, &task1Params, NULL);
                                                    // task1 creation

  Task_Params_init(&task2Params);  // task2Params init.
  task2Params.arg0 = 100;  // arg0, 100
  task2Params.stackSize = TASKSTACKSIZE;
  task2Params.stack = &task2Stack;
  task2Params.priority = 1;  // priority, 1
  Task_construct(&task2Struct, (Task_FuncPtr)task2Fxn, &task2Params, NULL);
                                                    // task2 creation

  Semaphore_Params_init(&semParams);  // semParams init.
  Semaphore_construct(&semStruct, 1, &semParams);
                                    // construct a semaphore, initial count 1
  semHandle = Semaphore_handle(&semStruct);  // instance handle
  BIOS_start();  // start BIOS
  return 0;
}
```

Program 24.2. TI-RTOS Semaphore example.

By using *semaphore_pend()*, task1 waits for a signal. When it is signaled, the red LED will be turned on; and the green LED will be turned off for a certain duration. During processing this code block controlling LEDs in task1, the other task, task2, cannot enter the code block controlling LEDs in task2, but it will wait for a signal at *semaphore_pend()*. Once the task1 sends a signal, the task2 can enter the code that will turn off the red LED; and turn on the green LED for a certain duration. Similarly, task1 cannot enter into the code block that controls the LEDs in task1, but it will wait for a signal. Once the code block that controls LEDs in task2 is processed, task2 will send a signal and the code block that controls LEDs in task1 can be executed.

This behavior of task1 and task2 keeps repeating. This results in blinking two LEDs alternatively.

This is a simple visual demonstration of how shared resources can be accessed one at a time. Both LEDs are shared between two tasks, and they are accessed properly using the semaphores. While one of the tasks is accessing the LEDs, the other task needs to wait for a signal. This concept can be applied and extended to other cases where the data or resources are shared in concurrent processing.

TI-RTOS UART and Semaphore example

For a demonstration purpose of serial communication, the DriverLib UART example in Chapter 23 is applied to the previous TI-RTOS Semaphore example. An example code using UART/Semaphore is shown in Program 24.3. TI-RTOS has its own UART driver APIs, but they are not used in this example. In Program 24.3, TI DriverLib APIs are used instead in this example.

For this project example, you can repeat the same set-up process as shown in the previous TI-RTOS semaphore example. Or simply you can reuse the semaphore example project by updating your "main.c" file.

```c
#include <xdc/std.h> // XDCtools
#include <xdc/runtime/System.h> // XDCtools
#include <ti/sysbios/BIOS.h> // SYS/BIOS
#include <ti/sysbios/knl/Task.h> // task module
#include <ti/sysbios/knl/Semaphore.h> // semaphore module
#include <ti/drivers/GPIO.h> // GPIO driver
#include "driverlib.h" // TI driverlib
#include "Board.h"
#define TASKSTACKSIZE   512
Task_Struct task1Struct, task2Struct; // task_Struct
Char task1Stack[TASKSTACKSIZE], task2Stack[TASKSTACKSIZE]; // task stack
Semaphore_Struct semStruct;
Semaphore_Handle semHandle;

Void task1Fxn(UArg arg0) { // task1
    while (1) {
        Semaphore_pend(semHandle, BIOS_WAIT_FOREVER); // pend on a semaphore
        GPIO_write(Board_LED0, Board_LED_ON); // LED0 (high)
        GPIO_write(Board_LED1, Board_LED_OFF); // LED1 (low)
        Task_sleep((UInt)arg0); // task sleep
        Semaphore_post(semHandle); //post a semaphore
    }
}

Void task2Fxn(UArg arg0) { // task2
    unsigned char ch, cnt; // variables
    struct EUSCI_A_UART_initParam uartConfig = {
        EUSCI_A_UART_CLOCKSOURCE_SMCLK, // SMCLK
```

```
    52, // BRx
    1, // BRFx
    37, // BRSx
    EUSCI_A_UART_NO_PARITY, // no parity
    EUSCI_A_UART_LSB_FIRST, // LSB first
    EUSCI_A_UART_ONE_STOP_BIT, // one stop bit
    EUSCI_A_UART_MODE, // UART mode
    EUSCI_A_UART_OVERSAMPLING_BAUDRATE_GENERATION, // oversampling
  }; // UART config, 9600 baud rate, 8 MHz
  EUSCI_A_UART_init(EUSCI_A0_BASE, &uartConfig); // configure UART Module
(ECUSCI_A0)
  EUSCI_A_UART_enable(EUSCI_A0_BASE); // enable UART module
  while (1) {
    Semaphore_pend(semHandle, BIOS_WAIT_FOREVER); // pend on a semaphore
    GPIO_write(Board_LED0, Board_LED_OFF); // LED0 (low)
    GPIO_write(Board_LED1, Board_LED_ON); // LED1 (high)
    ch='0'+cnt++; // count
    EUSCI_A_UART_transmitData(EUSCI_A0_BASE, ch);
    if (cnt>9) { // check the range
      cnt=0;
      EUSCI_A_UART_transmitData(EUSCI_A0_BASE, '\r');
      EUSCI_A_UART_transmitData(EUSCI_A0_BASE, '\n'); // newline
    }
    Task_sleep((UInt)arg0); // task sleep
    Semaphore_post(semHandle); // post a semaphore
  }
}

int main(void) {
  Task_Params task1Params, task2Params; // Task_Parms
  Semaphore_Params semParams; // Semaphore_Parms
  Board_initGeneral();
  Board_initGPIO();
  GPIO_setAsPeripheralModuleFunctionInputPin(GPIO_PORT_P2, (GPIO_PIN0 |
GPIO_PIN1), GPIO_SECONDARY_MODULE_FUNCTION); // UART mode (P2.0, P2.1)
  GPIO_write(Board_LED0, Board_LED_OFF); // LED0 (low)
  GPIO_write(Board_LED1, Board_LED_OFF); // LED1 (low)
  Task_Params_init(&task1Params); // task1Params init.
  task1Params.arg0 = 100; // arg0, 100
  task1Params.stackSize = TASKSTACKSIZE;
  task1Params.stack = &task1Stack;
  task1Params.priority = 1; // priority, 1
  Task_construct(&task1Struct, (Task_FuncPtr)task1Fxn, &task1Params, NULL);
                                                    // task1 creation

  Task_Params_init(&task2Params); // task2Params init.
  task2Params.arg0 = 100; // arg0, 100
  task2Params.stackSize = TASKSTACKSIZE;
  task2Params.stack = &task2Stack;
  task2Params.priority = 1; // priority, 1
  Task_construct(&task2Struct, (Task_FuncPtr)task2Fxn, &task2Params, NULL);
                                                    // task2 creation

  Semaphore_Params_init(&semParams); // semParams init.
```

```
    Semaphore_construct(&semStruct, 1, &semParams); // construct a semaphore, initial
    count 1
    semHandle = Semaphore_handle(&semStruct); // instance handle
    BIOS_start(); // start BIOS
    return 0;
}
```

Program 24.3. TI-RTOS UART and semaphore example.

In addition to the LEDs and buttons, you will use a UART module that was defined in the "board.h". In this program, task1 is the same as we have used in the previous semaphore example. However, task2 has additional functions of sending data over UART. When it is running successfully, certain code blocks in each task1 and task2 will be mutually executed. Two LEDs are going to flash but alternatively. In task2, data will be sent over UART. Users can see the numbers that will be displayed on a serial terminal, and the number will be incremented up to 9, then it will roll off to zero. This counting pattern and displaying on a serial terminal will keep repeating.

In this RTOS example case, it has only two tasks. However, developers can add more tasks as they need to add more functions. For instance, *task1* can process buttons. *task2* can read the ADC values from sensors. *task3* can process the control status of the device. *task4* can display the data on the device. *task5* can send the data over UART that is connected to a wireless module. This task configuration can be one of the implementations of simple wireless embedded systems, and this is also similar to the RTOS example that we have studied previously in Chapter 12.

TI provides a broad range of wireless connectivity such as Bluetooth, WiFi, Zigbee, and so forth. There are many options for developers to choose from these wireless technologies. One of the choices is to use MCUs that support TI-RTOS and the relevant wireless library. The development of the wireless protocol stack from scratch is not trivial. However, TI-RTOS provides a wireless protocol stack that is well-integrated with Code Composer Studio. Moreover, the code that is written in the TI-RTOS environment can be reusable on other TI MCUs.

Chapter 25. Open-Source Electronics Development Platform

Open-source hardware started in the late 1990s. It started much later than open-source software. Typically, hardware designs have not been shared outside of the company. This may be the case for many companies even these days. However, in some areas of electronic system development, hardware designs are not relativity complex, but common components and circuits such as basic functional microprocessor or microcontroller circuits can be reused. Given such a development platform with these common components, developers can add their own designs on top of it. Thus, it is capable of creating new prototype electronics in a short time. Besides, the designs can be shared via an internet community for further improvement. In this way, developers in the community may contribute to making it better. Or, some of the developers can even create new derivative prototype electronics. Currently, this model of open and fast-paced development operations has been widely accepted in many educational institutions and organizations.

One of these open-source electronics development platforms is Arduino®. An MSP430FR5994 MCUs can be programmed like Arduino using Energia. In this chapter, we will learn about open-source electronics development platform and Energia programming for an MSP430FR5994 MCU

Arduino

The Arduino project started in 2005. Arduino is an open-source computing platform with a simple I/O board and a simple development environment [25]. Arduino hardware design files are open and released under a Creative Commons Attribution Share-Alike license. This means it allows personal and commercial derivative works. However, the condition is to credit Arduino and to release their designs under the same license. Arduino software is also open and released under GPL (Java environment) and LGPL (C/C++ microcontroller libraries). This license allows manufacture and software distribution by anyone. Arduino has been widely used by open-source communities, hobbyists, and educators.

The programming language for Arduino boards is C/C++. Arduino provides an integrated development environment (IDE) that is easy to use. Many Arduino boards are based on Microchip/Atmel® 8-bit AVR® microcontroller models including ATmega328, ATmega8, ATmega168, ATmega1280, or ATmega2560. Arduino Due is based on Arm Cortex M3 (Microchip/Atmel SAM3X8E). Recent small Arduino boards are based on Arm Cortex M0+. In addition, there are many Arduino-compatible and Arduino-derived boards.

A *sketch* is a program that Arduino uses. It contains two functions which are setup() and loop(). The code in the "setup" function will be executed once, and the code in the "loop" function will be executed repeatedly.

Energia

Energia is an open-source electronics platform that started in 2012 [34]. It is a modified version of Arduino for selected TI Launchpads. It made it possible for the selected TI Launchpads to use the Energia sketch. Energia can be downloaded using the link as follows:

https://energia.nu

Energia IDE is similar to Arduino IDE. But, the color of the Energia IDE theme is red. In order to use an MSP430FR5994 Launchpad, the proper board package needs to be installed. "Boards Manager" can be selected using the sequence of selections as follows:

Tools → Board: "xxxx" → Boards Manager

Next, the *boards manager* window will be opened. In the search box, you can type, "MSP430" Then, you can see the narrowed choices. If needed, you can install the latest "Energia MSP430 boards".

You can connect the MSP430FR5994 launchpad board via USB, and upload programs to the MSP430FR5994 Launchpad board. In order to do so, as shown in Figure 25.1, you need to select the board and connect the port properly.

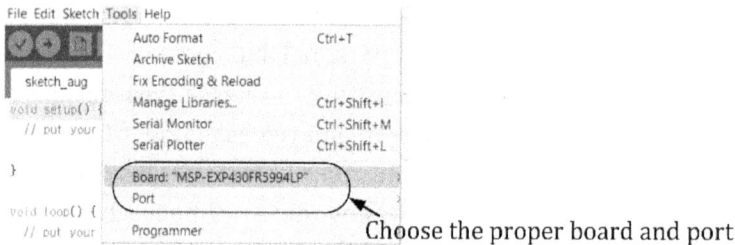

Figure 25.1. Selection of the board and port.

You can start learning Energia from example programs. The examples programs can be found in the Energia IDE by selecting "Examples" (Files -> Examples).

Eneriga GPIO and UART Example

An Energia GPIO and UART example is shown in Program 25.1. The buttons and LEDs are defined. In the *setup()* function, the pins are configured, and the UART is initialized. While the code in the *setup()* function is executed once, the code in the *loop()* function will be executed repeatedly. In the *loop()* function, it keeps checking the status of the two buttons. When button1 is pressed, the red LED will be turned on, and the green LED will be turned on when button2 is pressed. Moreover, a character array will be sent over UART depending on the press of the buttons.

```
const int button1 = PUSH1;  // push button (left)
const int button2 = PUSH2;  // push button (right)
const int led1 = RED_LED;  // LED1 (Red LED)
const int led2 = GREEN_LED;  // LED2 (Green LED)

void setup() {
  pinMode(led1, OUTPUT);  // output direction
  pinMode(led2, OUTPUT);  // output direction
  pinMode(button1, INPUT_PULLUP);  // input direction, pull-up resistor
  pinMode(button2, INPUT_PULLUP);  // input direction, pull-up resistor
  Serial.begin(9600);  // UART init.
  delay(100);  // delay
  Serial.println("Connected");  // send data over UART
}

void loop() {
  int buttonState;  // variable
  buttonState = digitalRead(button1);  // read button1
  if (buttonState == LOW) {  // check button state
    digitalWrite(led1, HIGH);  // turn on led1
    Serial.println("Button1 pressed");  // send data over UART
  } else digitalWrite(led1, LOW);  // turn off led1

  buttonState = digitalRead(button2);  // read button2
  if (buttonState == LOW) {  // check button state
    digitalWrite(led2, HIGH);  // turn on led2
    Serial.println("Button2 pressed");  // send data over UART
  } else digitalWrite(led2, LOW);  // turn off led2
  delay(100);  // delay
}
```

Program 25.1. Energia GPIO and UART example.

This Energia sketch is easier to understand, and the code can be written in a short time. Arduino or Energia can be effectively used in a rapid prototyping project or a quick verification of the functions. If a developer wants to create a commercial product using Energia, it is recommended to check the license information thoroughly and carefully, which can be found on the Energia and Arduino websites.

Chapter 26. Power Management Considerations

There are many battery-powered embedded systems. In these applications, energy consumption is an important factor. In order to increase the length of the operations, it may need various power management efforts. Even for applications that are not dependent on batteries, it is common to design electronics to consume low energy for green electronics. In this chapter, we will learn about the power management and lower power modes for an MSP430FR5994 MCU.

MSP430FR5994 Power management

There are various efforts and methods in power management. Typically, it is associated with reducing or minimizing overall energy consumption.

First, the supply voltage can be lowered to reduce power consumption. IC manufacturers provide the minimum and maximum supply voltage specifications in the datasheet. For instance, the supply voltage level of an MSP430FR5994 IC can be lowered to about 1.8 V. The lower voltage was determined by the voltage level to enable the supply voltage supervisor (SVS). For reference, the maximum supply voltage of an MSP430FR5994 IC is 3.6 V.

Second, the current consumption in a microcontroller system can be closely related to the operating frequency. The operating frequency can be lowered to reduce the power consumption of the system. The operating frequency of an MSP430FR5994 IC can be up to 16 MHz, and it can be lowered to a few hundred kHz. This would be effective in saving power for some embedded applications. However, in some real-time applications, there is a limitation in lowering the operating frequency because the CPU needs to be kept reasonably fast.

Third, in many embedded systems, the CPU resources are not constantly used, and a system may be in an idle or stand-by status for an extended period. This system can save power by entering a low-power state such as sleep mode instead. The effort of lowering the operating time in active mode but increasing the time in sleep mode can reduce power consumption.

Lastly, an embedded system may have dependencies in processing tasks on the both hardware and software sides. Some dependencies may have caused an increased time in active mode. There is a potential in reducing the time of active mode by managing the dependencies effectively. However, this task may not be necessarily straightforward depending on the degree of the interdependencies and the complexity of the system.

MSP430FR5994 Power Modes

An MSP430FR5994 MCU provides one active mode and seven software-selectable low-power modes. MSP430FR5994 power modes are shown in Figure 26.1. When the CPU is started up, the MSP430FR5994 MCU will be in active mode. As needed, the MCU can be operated in a lower power mode. And the MCU can be woken up by an event such as an interrupt event.

Let us examine Low power modes. The Low Power Mode (LPM0) can halt the CPU execution and the CPU can be in sleep mode. To reduce more power, there are other lower power modes such as Low Power Mode 3 (LPM3) and Low Power Mode 4 (LPM4). Moreover, the MSP430FR5994 IC provides more low-power modes such as Low Power Mode 3.5 (LPM3.5) and Low Power Mode 4.5 (LPM4.5).

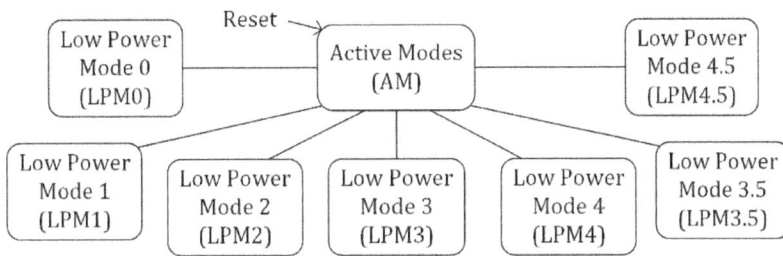

Figure 26.1. Simplified diagram of MSP430FR5994 power modes.

There are six lower power modes depending on several parameters including CPUOFF, OSCOFF, SCG1, SCG0, and other factors. Table 26.1 shows the description of the low power modes and the parameters.

Parameters	Power Mode	Description
Active Mode	AM	CPU/MCLK: active: modules: active (CPUOFF:0, OSCOFF:0, SCG1:0, SCG0:0)
Low Power Mode 0	LPM0	CPU/MCLK: off, FLL: on, ACLK: on, Vcore: on (CPUOFF:1, OSCOFF:0, SCG1:0, SCG0:0)
Low Power Mode 1	LPM1	CPU/MCLK: off, FLL: off, ACLK: on, Vcore: on (CPUOFF:1, OSCOFF:0, SCG1:0, SCG0:1)
Low Power Mode 2	LPM2	CPU/MCLK: off, FLL: off, ACLK: on, Vcore: on (CPUOFF:1, OSCOFF:0, SCG1:1, SCG0:0)
Low Power Mode 3	LPM3	CPU/MCLK: off, FLL: off, ACLK: on, Vcore: on (CPUOFF:1, OSCOFF:0, SCG1:1, SCG0:0)
Low Power Mode 4	LPM4	CPU/MCLK: off, FLL: off, ACLK: off, Vcore: on (CPUOFF:1, OSCOFF:1, SCG1:1, SCG0:1)
Low Power Mode 3.5	LPM3.5	Vcore: off, modules off, optional RTC, No memory retention (CPUOFF:1, OSCOFF:1, SCG1:1, SCG0:1)
Low Power Mode 4.5	LPM4.5	Vcore: off, modules off, no RTC op., No memory retention (CPUOFF:1, OSCOFF:1, SCG1:1, SCG0:1)

Table 26.1. Summary of MSP430FR5994 power modes.

Low Power Mode Example

The low power mode example in register C/C++ programming is shown in Program 26.1. This is a simple program that can turn on or off an LED for a certain amount of time when a button is pressed. The MSP430FR5994 MCU can enter a low power mode 3, while it waits for a button press. The code line that can put the MSP430FR5994 MCU to sleep is _low_power_mode_3(). This is an intrinsic function. When this code line is executed, the system goes into LPM3 sleep mode.

```
#include <msp430.h>
int main(void) {
  WDTCTL = WDTPW | WDTHOLD;  // hold the watchdog timer
  PM5CTL0 &= ~LOCKLPM5;  // clear LOCKLPM5 bit
  P1DIR |= BIT0;  // output direction (P1.0)
  P5DIR &= ~BIT6;  // Input direction (P5.6)
  P5REN |= BIT6;  // enable internal resistor
  P5OUT |= BIT6;  // pull-up resistor
  P5IES |= BIT6;  // interrupt on high-to-low transition
  P5IFG &= ~BIT6;  // clear interrupt flag
  P5IE |= BIT6;  // enable interrupt (P5.6)
  _enable_interrupt();  // enable general interrupt

  while(1) {
    _delay_cycles(250000); // delay
    P1OUT &= ~BIT0; // turn off LED1
    _low_power_mode_3(); // enter low power mode (LPM3)
  }
  return 0;
}

#pragma vector=PORT5_VECTOR
_interrupt void Port5_ISR_handler(void) {
  if(P5IFG & BIT6) {
    P1OUT |= BIT0;  // turn on LED1
    _low_power_mode_off_on_exit();  // low power mode off on exit
  }
  P5IFG &= ~BIT6;  // clear interrupt flag
}
```

Program 26.1. Low power mode example.

The Port 1 interrupt is configured. The system can wake up when Port 1 interrupt is triggered. In the Port 1 ISR, it checks whether the button is pressed or not. If pressed, the LED1 is going to be turned on. Developers can control the CPU to go into sleep mode or stay active as the program exits the ISR. In this example, The CPU stays active as the program exits the ISR. This behavior was described using the code line, "_low_power_mode_off_on_exit();" in the ISR. Therefore, when the button is pressed, the MSP430FR5994 MCU will wake up and operate in active mode, and it will turn the LED on. On exiting the ISR, the MCU will continue to operate, and it will execute the next instruction in the while loop. Next, it delays the program for a certain period, and it will turn the LED off. Next, the MSP430FR5994 MCU will enter sleep mode again. This pattern keeps repeating as the button gets pressed.

DriverLib - Low Power Mode Example

The low power mode example using TI driver library is shown in Program 26.2. The function of the program is similar to the previous low-power mode example program.

```
#include <msp430.h>
#include "driverlib.h"
int main (void) {
  WDT_A_hold(WDT_A_BASE); // hold the watchdog timer
  PMM_unlockLPM5(); // clear LOCKLPM5 bit
  GPIO_setAsOutputPin(GPIO_PORT_P1, GPIO_PIN0); // output (P1.0)
  GPIO_setAsOutputPin(GPIO_PORT_P1, GPIO_PIN1); // output (P1.1)
  GPIO_setAsInputPinWithPullUpResistor(GPIO_PORT_P5, GPIO_PIN6);
                                    // input, pull-up resistor (P5.6)
  GPIO_clearInterrupt(GPIO_PORT_P5, GPIO_PIN6); // clear interrupt flag (P5.6)
  GPIO_enableInterrupt(GPIO_PORT_P5, GPIO_PIN6); // enable interrupt (P5.6)
  _enable_interrupt(); // enable general interrupt
  while (1) {
    _delay_cycles(500000); // delay
    GPIO_setOutputLowOnPin (GPIO_PORT_P1, GPIO_PIN0); // clear (P1.0)
    _low_power_mode_3(); // enter low power mode (LPM3)
  }
  return 0;
}

#pragma vector=PORT5_VECTOR
_interrupt void Port5_ISR_handler(void) {
  uint32_t status;
  status = GPIO_getInterruptStatus(GPIO_PORT_P5, GPIO_PIN6);
                                    // read interrupt status (P5.6)
  if(status & GPIO_PIN6) { // check whether the PIN6 is set
    GPIO_setOutputHighOnPin(GPIO_PORT_P1, GPIO_PIN0); // set (P1.0)
    _low_power_mode_off_on_exit(); // low power mode off on exit
  }
  GPIO_clearInterrupt(GPIO_PORT_P5, status); // clear port1 interrupt flag
}
```

Program 26.2. DriverLib low power mode example.

The code line that can enter the low-power mode is _low_power_mode_3(). In Port 1 ISR, the code line of _low_power_mode_off_on_exit() is used. Therefore, as the button is pressed, it will turn on a red LED. While the LED is turned on, the MSP430FR5994 MCU is in active mode. While the LED is turned off, the MSP430FR5994 MCU is in sleep mode. This program has a code line to delay the time. This is an example pattern of the execution as an embedded system to perform necessary functions for a short amount of time and to enter sleep mode.

Users may need test equipment to measure the power consumption of the device for development. However, the MSP430FR5994 Launchpad board supports the EnergyTrace™ Technology. EnergyTrace Technology is useful in performing analysis of energy consumption. Code Composer Studio supports the EnergyTrace mode and provides an EnergyTrace Window. The energy measurement can be performed, and the data can be viewed using the EnergyTrace Window.

Chapter 27. Embedded System Security

The Internet of things (IoTs) are related to the systems and devices that are connected to the internet. Many of these devices and systems are commonly found in modern embedded systems. For devices and systems that were not traditionally connected to the internet, newer models of these devices and systems come with functionality to be connected to the internet. At the same time, embedded system security becomes more important as there are more IoT devices in our everyday lives. There are many aspects in the embedded system security. However, in this chapter, we will consider one specific hardware component that may cause security issues in embedded systems.

JTAG/Boundary Scan

A boundary scan technique provides a method of testing interconnections of sub-blocks inside ICs. It can test multiple cells inside of ICs or PCBs. Those multiple test cells can be internally connected to each other. To access the test cells, an external interface or external pins are needed. Boundary scan can be used as a test method for the components inside of an integrated circuit, and it is also widely used in debugging, analyzing, and monitoring circuit states, voltages, and memory devices inside ICs.

The Joint Test Action Group (JTAG) was formed in 1985, and the boundary scan architecture was approved in 1990 as IEEE Std. 1149.1. There have been enhancements, and the latest update was done in 2013. This technology has been widely adopted by electronic device companies. JTAG is an industry standard that can be used in verifying designs and testing after the fabrication. JTAG is named after the Joint Test Action Group. In some settings, the boundary scan can be called simply JTAG. This technology is relevant because it has been used for debugging, programming, and testing for most of the modern microprocessors and microcontrollers.

An MSP430FR5994 MCU supports four-wire and two-wire JTAG interfaces. Readers may already have used the two-wire JTAG that is Spy-Bi-Wire in loading programs on their MSP430FR5994 Launchpad boards. They have seen their MCU could be interrupted, and various internal registers could be read and displayed in Code Composer Studio. This JTAG interface can be used in providing a very effective and useful method for programmers to develop and debug embedded systems.

Typical four-wire JTAG uses several pins. For instance, "TDI" is used for *Test Data In*. "TDO" is for *Test Data Out*. "TCK" is for *Test Clock*. "TMS" is used for *Test Mode Select*. These TDI, TDO, TCK, TMS pins are typically used for the JTAG connection. Optionally, "TRST" pin is used for *Test Reset*.

The two-wire JTAG interface, Spy-Bi-Wire, uses pins including SBWTDIO and SBWTCK. On an MSP430FR5994 Launchpad board, these pins can be found on the header block that is located between the eZ-FET debug probe and the MSP430FR5994 IC.

As discussed, the MSP430FR5994 Launchpad board has an on-board debugger. This setting of the attachment of the JTAG may not be found suitable as a product. However, as an educational purpose, it is useful and effective as a development tool because users do not need to purchase a separate JTAG tool.

JTAG Security

JTAG is very useful and important. On the other hand, it can be a potential target for unwanted attacks. This vulnerability is supposed to be well known to the developers. In case a reader is not aware of this risk yet, it is worth understanding this security vulnerability. For instance, let us suppose a company developed a voice-activated alarm clock that can be connected to the WiFi network. If an unethical hacker could access JTAG connection of this device, then, the hacker could put their modified firmware that could hijack the data packet or to access the internet. In this case, this IoT alarm clock could be compromised, and it could be used in the wrong way by the hacker. A bigger problem may arise if the hacker could access bigger critical systems such as industrial robots, plants, or traffic control systems. It could jeopardize someone's physical safety due to the malfunction caused by the hacker. Although JTAG is very useful and important in embedded system development, if not properly handled, it could open a back door in a hardware level, and it could allow unwanted person to access the firmware, data, and the operating system. In the worst case, it could serve as a hidden gateway that opens unwanted access to a supposedly safe and secure system.

There are several efforts in securing JTAG. In some cases, JTAG header pins are not populated on the PCB board, and markings on the board are hidden purposefully from the users. However, even in this case, JTAG may be still accessible by populating the JTAG header pins back or soldering wires. It is a matter of simply figuring out the connection of the hidden pins. This would be one of the counter examples of open design projects. It could be a valid reason for keeping designs confidential as a product. Surprisingly, some electronics projects' JTAG can be accessible relatively easily after some moderate effort in modifications.

For production parts, a system can be deployed to end users with disabled JTAG access. This is an IC level protection. This can be achieved by blowing off the JTAG fuse. In this case, users cannot access the JTAG of the systems. Also, development and debugging tools provided by the manufacturer cannot access the JTAG. This means that it is hard to diagnose the problems for the devices in the field if the systems are not functioning as they are supposed to be. In addition, although this may seem an effective method, it is not the perfectly secured solution because there is a chance that the blown-out JTAG fuses could be restored by highly advanced hackers.

In addition, an MSP430FR5994 MCU supports more security features. An MSP430FR5994 MCU supports AES encryption. Moreover, it supports software IP protection (IPP). Furthermore, it supports a crypto-bootloader that is firmware update mechanism with authentication and encryption of a firmware image.

Developers may need to consider using the security features, as the embedded system in development is getting close to being a product and getting deployed. If necessary, additional security features might need to be applied depending on the security requirements of their embedded systems.

Chapter 28. Educational Embedded Linux System Platforms

MSP430FR59xx microcontrollers (MCUs) are based on 16-bit RISC cores. These MCUs can be used in various applications. However, in some embedded systems, more complex functions are required, and they may need higher performance computing systems. In this case, systems can be designed and built using Embedded Linux Operating Systems.

Examples of these Embedded Linux Operating systems are Android/Linux based smart phones and tablet PCs. In these applications, high-performance and low-power microprocessors are suitable. Arm Cortex-A processors are suitable for performance-intensive embedded systems, and some of the Linux distributions are available depending on the models. There are several platforms, and boards using Arm Cortex-A processors. Some of them are suitable for embedded Linux system education, and they include *Raspberry Pi®* and *BeagleBone®*.

In this chapter, educational Embedded Linux System platforms is going to be briefly covered in order to provide a perspective on embedded systems that can be used in processing complex tasks. Moreover, a great benefit of using educational embedded Linux systems is about rich educational resources that are shared through a large community. Furthermore, readers can gain and access development resources and information including programming examples through developers, manufacturers, and suppliers.

Raspberry Pi

Raspberry Pi series boards are small single-board computers [35]. The Raspberry Pi was developed in the United Kingdom by the Raspberry Pi Foundation. Initially, it was created for the use in teaching basic computer science in schools and in developing countries.

Raspberry Pi 1 Model B was released in 2012. In 2015, Raspberry Pi 2 Model B was released. In 2017, Raspberry Pi Zero was released. Raspberry Pi 3 Model B was released in 2016. Raspberry Pi 3 Model B+ was released in 2018.

Moreover, Raspberry Pi 4 Model B was released in 2019. The pictures of the Raspberry Pi 3 Model B+ and Raspberry Pi 4 Model B are shown in Figure 28.1. Raspberry Pi 4 Model B is faster than Raspberry Pi 3 Model B+. However, there are other factors including power consumption to consider in choosing a platform for your application.

These devices are based on Broadcom processors with Arm Cortex-A series cores. They are small-scale general-purpose computers; however, the performance is not as good as typical general-purpose computers like desktops or laptops. There are several Linux distributions that can run on these Raspberry Pi boards. One of them is a Raspberry Pi O/S, and this is based on Debian Linux and customized Linux distribution for Raspberry PI boards [35][36].

Figure 28.1. Raspberry Pi 3 Model B+ and Raspberry Pi 4 Model B.

Using Linux operating systems, developers can create their own customized applications fast and easy for their IoT projects or Robot projects. Developers can choose their preferred language for the development as many programming languages are available. One of the popular choices is Python [37].

Python programming language is generally easy to learn. Python is a script language, and python programs are generally slower than complied programs based on C/C++. Python programs are not necessarily simple. Python Language can be used in creating highly complex systems that need complex mathematical operations.

Raspberry Pi has a large size community. There are many shared sample projects and programs. It can be found that programming examples shared through the community are based on Python programming language. Readers can increase their knowledge by studying various shared projects and programming examples.

BeagleBone
Some of the BeagleBoard® series boards are single-board computers based on Texas Instruments processors with Arm Cortex-A series cores [38]. They were designed for hobbyists as educational tools.

BeagleBoard was released in 2008. It was based on a TI OMAP3530 processor. BeagleBone using a TI AM3358 processor was released in 2011. BeagleBone Black was released in 2013. PocketBeagle was released in 2017.

Moreover, BeagleBone AI was released in 2019. The pictures of the BeagleBone Black and BeagleBone AI are shown in Figure 28.2. The BeagleBone AI is faster than the BeagleBone Black. However, as mentioned, there are other factors including power consumption to consider in choosing a proper platform for your application.

Figure 28.2. BeagleBone Black and BeagleBone AI.

These devices are based TI Sitara™ processors with Arm Cortex-A series cores. *Node.js* is a JavaScript runtime environment. The BeagleBone.org foundation supports BoneScript that is based on a Node.js library. Moreover, users can install a Python package and use Python Programming Language.

Educational Embedded Linux Platforms

Educational embedded Linux system platforms can provide rich resources, examples, and friendly environment for students, hobbyists, and engineers. Readers can learn about embedded Linux systems rapidly. These educational embedded Linux systems have impacted a wide range of students in science and engineering fields.

Embedded Linux systems can be considered easy to learn. This would be partially because there are many approaches that are focused on high-level programming. An embedded system can be rapidly developed without the need for an in-depth understanding of hardware. Moreover, the development environment is rich, and it is similar to the one that we use in a desktop or laptop computer. Therefore, for the developers' side, they could view it as simply a slow computer.

These platforms can be used as an effective learning tool. It is great for developers to create a system rapidly using high level libraries obtained from the Internet. However, at the same time, it can be controversial because, in fact, embedded Linux systems are fairly complicated, and it might need a long-term training and learning about many aspects of hardware and software to become an experienced embedded Linux system developer. Moreover, the pace of the development in embedded Linux systems is very fast. If an embedded Linux system is no longer supported, this system without technical support could potentially cause significant damages such as by the accidental creation of security hole causing data privacy and data security issues. However, for entry level developers and hobbyists, it seems that these important concerns are easily overlooked. In some experimental development or educational environments, it seems that some of the security and privacy concerns may not be in their interests. However, for developers, it is important to understand the requirements of their systems and the security aspects of the systems, and they need to choose proper hardware and software platforms as well as to manage the systems properly.

In summary, embedded Linux system is a desirable solution in many applications these days. It has gained more attention as the computing requirements have been increasing. This is partially due to the increased popularity of machine learning, image processing, and IoT systems.

As an example of an IoT system, it can form a network with an MSP430FR5994 MCU and an embedded Linux system. An MSP430FR5994 MCU can work as a sensor device, and it can communicate with an embedded Linux system as a host or an IoT gateway.

What's next
We have studied various aspects of embedded systems using an MSP430FR5994 MCU and Composer Studio. We have studied low to high level programming as well as hardware concepts.

An embedded system is typically an integrated system that involves a wide range of knowledge. For embedded system developers, it is encouraged to have a good understanding of microcontrollers, modules, sensors, and mechanical systems that are used in their system.

Readers can create their own embedded systems. Examples of embedded systems can be found everywhere such as Game consoles, Mobile phone, Digital cameras, Vending Machines, Washing machines, Cooking machines, Toys, Printers, Scanners,

Televisions, and Electronic instruments. The list will go on as we will see more new and innovative embedded systems.

Lastly, we have studied embedded systems based on a specific MCU model for educational purposes. However, it would be desirable for readers to continue to learn about other microcontrollers and microprocessors and to expand their knowledge in embedded systems.

Appendix A. Basic Digital Logic Circuits

Firmware programmers may need to understand hardware components to a certain extent. In this Appendix A, basic digital logic circuits are presented. However, this is a simply brief introduction to the basic digital logic circuits. For readers who are not already familiar with basic logic circuits, it would be suggested to take other introductory level digital logic lessons.

Basic Digital Logic Gates

In digital circuits, a logic level is one of the finite number of states. Typically, we use a 2-level logic, which is a binary logic. The two levels are logical high and logical low, which are related to the binary number 1 and 0, respectively. In addition, there is another state to be considered, and it is a high impedance state. In this state, the signal is not clearly driven high nor low. This is similar to a floating state or an open circuit.

Some of the basic logic gates are shown in Figure A.1. An **AND** gate generates a logical high signal when both input signals are logical high. Otherwise, the output is a logical low signal. A **NAND** gate generates the inverted output of the **AND** gate.

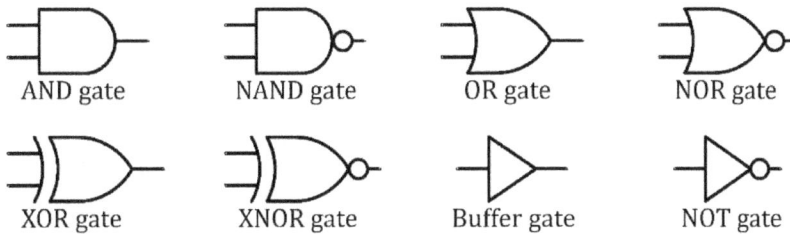

| AND gate | NAND gate | OR gate | NOR gate |

| XOR gate | XNOR gate | Buffer gate | NOT gate |

Figure A.1. Basic logic gates.

A **buffer** gate generates the same logical output signal as the logical input signal. On the other hand, a **NOT** gate or **inverter** gate generates an inverted logical output signal from the logical input signal.

An **OR** gate generates a logical low signal when both input signals are logical low. If any of the input signals is a logical high signal, the output of the **OR** gate is logical high. A **NOR** gate generates an inverted output of the **OR** gate.

A **XOR** gate generates a logical low signal when two input logic signals are the same. If two input logic signals are not the same, it generates a logical high signal. An **XNOR** gate generates an inverted output of the **XOR** gate.

Digital Logic Gates with Negated Inputs

It is common to use an **inversion bubble** in a circuit diagram. This is also simply called a **bubble**. This bubble inverts the logic signal. It is similar to an inverter gate. The **bubbles** can be used at input or output of a gate. Some of the examples are shown in Figure A.2.

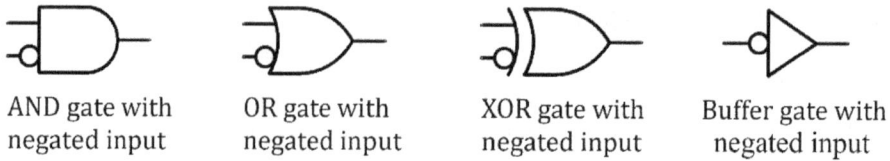

| AND gate with negated input | OR gate with negated input | XOR gate with negated input | Buffer gate with negated input |

Figure A.2. Gates with bubbles.

One of the input signals of an **AND** gate is negated. One of the input signals of an **OR** gate is negated. In addition, one of the input signals of an **XOR** gate is negated. Moreover, a **bubble** can be used in a **buffer** gate. In this case, the function is simply the same as an **NOT** gate or inverter gate.

The truth table for the **AND** gate with a negated input is shown in Table A.1. As it can be seen, the output behavior is different than a typical **AND** gate. The truth table for the **OR** gate with a negated input is shown on the right side. As it was shown, the output behavior is not same as a typical **OR** gate.

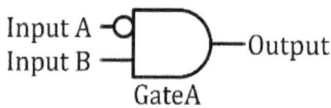

Input A	Input B	Output
Low	Low	Low
Low	High	High
High	Low	Low
High	High	Low

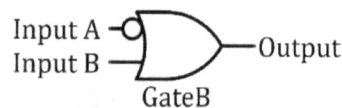

Input A	Input B	Output
Low	Low	High
Low	High	High
High	Low	Low
High	High	High

Table A.1. Gate with negated input.

Active Low Pin

In digital circuits, a logical low signal at a pin of an integrated circuit (IC) or digital circuits can enable an intended function. An example was shown in Figure A.3. The block of the digital circuits has a physical pin, and this pin is defined as active low input pin in the block diagram. When a logical low signal is provided at the pin, an intended function of the block of the digital circuits can be enabled.

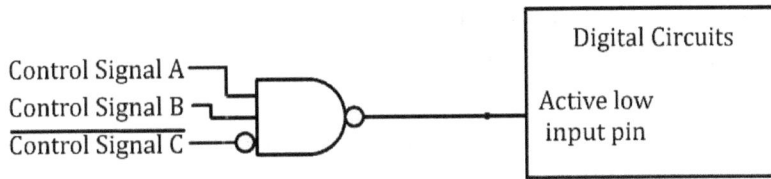

Figure A.3. Active low signal.

In this figure, there are three control signals, Control Signal A, Control Signal B, and Control Signal C. Due to the active low pin, a bubble is added to the output of the three input **AND** gate. Thus, it is a **NAND** gate with three input signals of Control Signal A, B, and C. Since the control signal C is active low, it was matched with a **bubble** at the one of the **NAND** input pins.

Therefore, an intended function of the block of the digital circuits can be activated when both logical levels of the control signals of A and B are high, and the logical level of the control signal of C is low.

Open Collector/Drain Circuits

Some pins of ICs are pre-defined as open collector type outputs. The **open collector** type output may have left a collector of a BJT (Bipolar Junction Transistor) open. In this case, this open collector output pin needs to be connected to a resistor tied to VCC. This is related to a pull-up resistor. Figure A.4 shows the case where it needs a pull-up resistor. One of the pins of an IC is an active low output, and it is connected to the block of digital circuits.

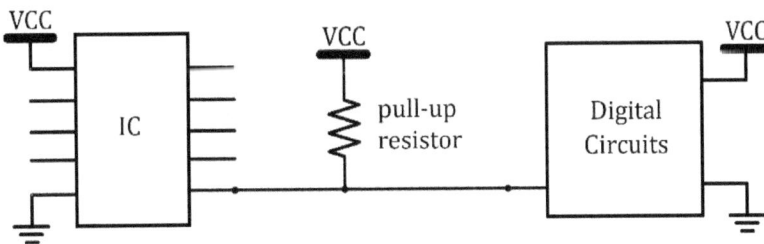

Figure A.4. Open collector type connection.

Some pins of ICs can be **open drain** type outputs. This open drain type output can be relevant to a FET (Field Effect Transistor). For this open drain type output pin, it also needs a pull-up resistor.

Tri-state Logic

A tri-state logic allows a high impedance state output. If the logical level of *"select"* control signal is high, the logical level of the output signal will follow the logical level of the input signal. If the logical level of "*select*" control signal is low, the output is considered to be in a high impedance state.

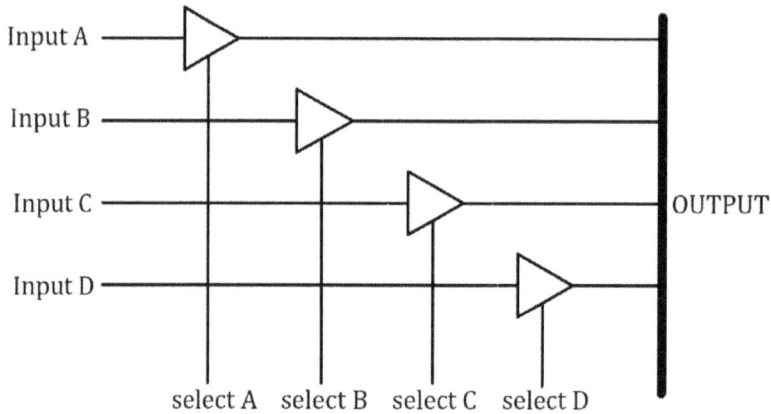

Figure A.5. Tri-state logic and multiplexing.

A multiplexing circuit is shown in Figure A.5. In this circuit, the output will follow the input signals of A, B, C, or D, as one of them is activated. You can see the output line that is drawn as a thick line. You can see that this output line can be a bus line for a single bit, and you can imagine multiple lines for a multiple bit data bus such as 16-bit or 32-bit data bus.

Propagation Delay Consideration
A propagation delay is the transition time for a digital signal to travel from a source to a destination. Propagation delays need to be considered for the practical implementation of logic gates.

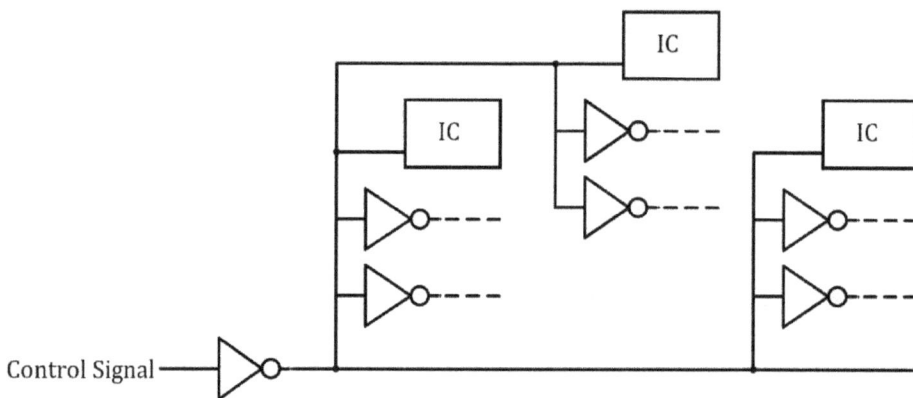

Figure A.6. Circuit with loading.

The propagation delay can also be affected by load capacitance. Figure A.6 shows a control signal, and it is connected to many circuit components. It can be understood as a large equivalent load capacitor for an inverter gate to drive. In this case, the propagation delay for the inverter gate may suffer and it may cause a slow response.

A prorogation delay can be improved by using a **buffer** gate as shown in Figure A.7. Using this **buffer** gate might be seen as adding more delay. However, if it is handled properly, the load capacitance can be divided properly by using this additional buffer gate. Assuming the buffer gate is reasonably well designed, it may result in improving the signal response.

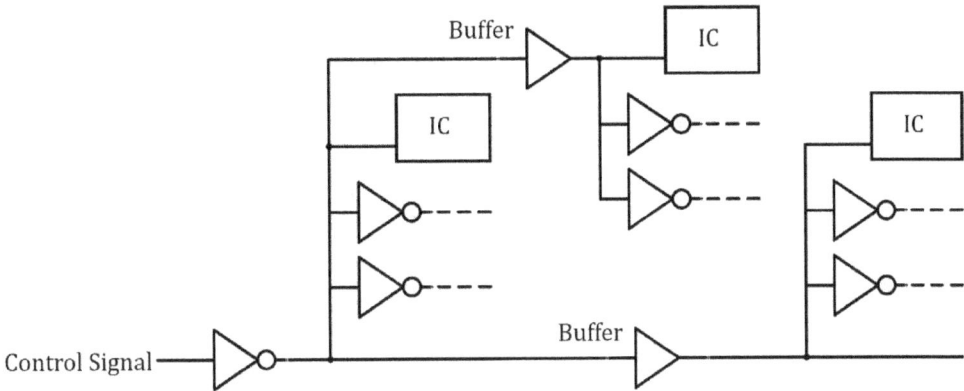

Figure A.7. Improved propagation delay.

It is worth mentioning that a buffer gate needs to be designed with the consideration of many aspects. You can image this can be one line for multiple bus lines, and many components may share these bus lines. Then, for a single line, an optimally designed buffer gate or multiple inverters in series called an inverter chain may improve the performance.

Decoupling Capacitors

It is common to find circuit schematics with many capacitors merged as shown in the upper portion of Figure A.8. Because the capacitors are connected in parallel. Theoretically, this can be seen as equivalent to one big capacitor. However, this would not be the actual implementation.

Practically, these capacitors can be distributed across a printed circuit board (PCB) as shown in the lower portion of Figure A. 8. Moreover, most likely, capacitors would be placed close to ICs. These capacitors are used as decoupling capacitors, and these capacitors may reduce the noise across VCC and ground.

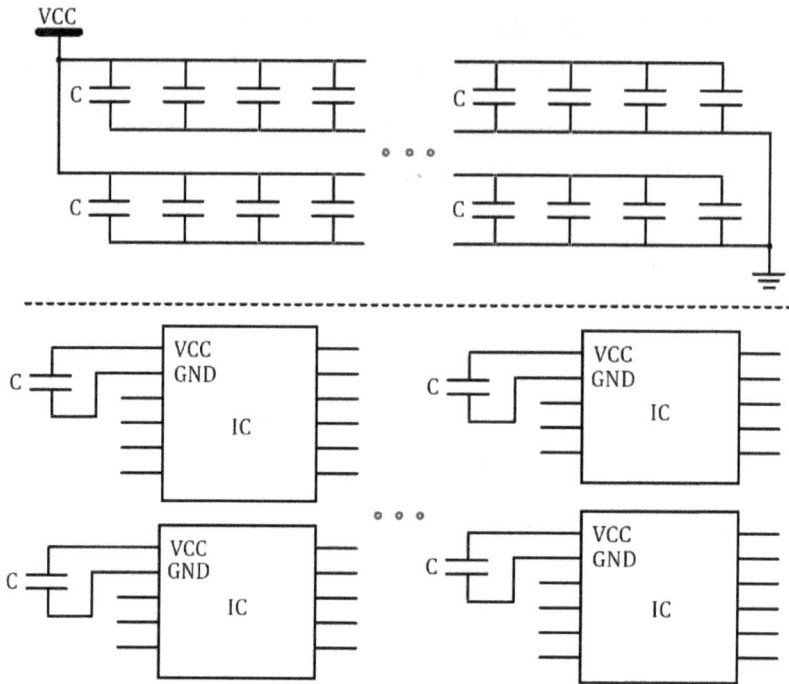

Figure A.8. Decoupling capacitors.

While decoupling capacitors are essential and effective, in this book, most of decoupling capacitors were purposefully not placed, or they were not drawn just to simplify block diagrams. It is up to readers to place additional decoupling capacitors as they are needed.

Memory Types

Memory is one of the essential components in microcontrollers. There is a type of memory called ROM which means Read Only Memory. For instance, certain lines of program code are not supposed to be modified, while in operation. And some of the numbers such as constants do not need to change while the program is running. ROM can be the memory that can contain these read only code blocks or constants.

There is another type of memory called RAM which means Random Access Memory. This is a memory space that can be read or written. RAM can be used to store some of the data that may need to be updated frequently. One of the examples is a stack memory. This is the memory space that can store temporary variables. As the program gets running, it could generate several arrays of data. They can be stored in the stack memory area.

There is a non-volatile memory. This is a type of memory that can hold the data even when the system would be turned off. Generally, ROM is a type of non-volatile memory.

EEPROM (Electrically erasable programmable read-only memory) is a non-volatile memory. Another example is Flash memory. It keeps the data when the power is turned off. Ferroelectric RAM (FRAM) is also non-volatile memory.

On the other hand, there is volatile memory. This is a type of memory that loses the data when the power goes off. Generally, RAM is a type of volatile memory. Particularly, static RAM (SRAM) and Dynamic RAM (DRAM) would be examples of volatile memory. Regarding SRAM and DRAM, internal SRAM is typically faster than DRAM in applications of microcontrollers or microprocessor-based systems.

An SRAM IC Example

In Figure A.9, an example of a SRAM IC is shown. This SRAM IC has 17 address lines and 16 data lines. The memory size of this chip is $(2^{17} - 1) \times 16$ bits. Therefore, the memory size is 128k $\times$ 16 bits.

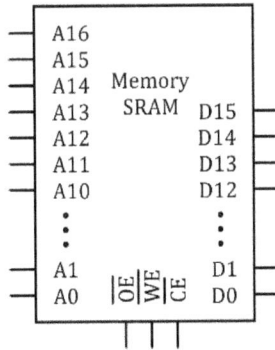

Figure A.9. A typical SRAM IC.

This IC has an *output enable pin* ($\overline{OE}$), a *write enable pin* ($\overline{WE}$), and a *chip enable pin* ($\overline{CE}$), and they are active low pins.

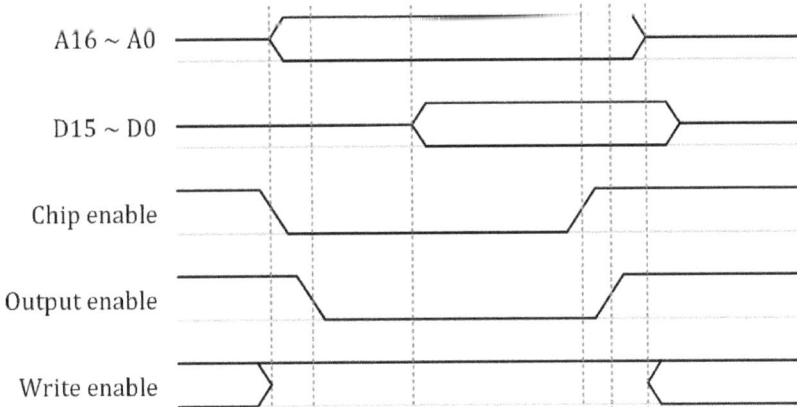

Figure A.10. Timing Diagram of an SRAM IC.

An example waveform is shown in Figure A.10. The address signals can be read when the logical level of the *chip enable* signal is low. During this operation, it is assumed that the logical level of the *write enable* signal kept high properly. Then, the IC can generate the output data signals when the logical level of the *output enable* signal is low. Both address and data lines become high impedance states when the logical level of the *chip enable* signal is high. Later, in Appendix C, we will use this SRAM IC as a component in simple embedded system examples.

Appendix B. Basic Verilog Hardware Description Language

A hardware description language (HDL) has been used in describing the structure and behavior of electronic circuit models. An HDL can be used for text-based expressions of the electronic systems and their behaviors. The first hardware description languages were introduced in the late 1960s. Programmable logic devices (PLDs) became popular in the late 1970s.

Types of Hardware Description Language

Verilog HDL was introduced by Gateway Design Automation in 1985, and Cadence Design Systems later acquired the rights. Later, Cadence Design Systems transferred it into the public domain under the Open Verilog International (OVI) organization. In 1987, VHDL (Very High speed integrated circuits Hardware Description Language) was developed by the request from the U.S. Department of Defense. There are other HDLs. However, these two HDLs, Verilog HDL and VHDL, are supported by IEEE, and they are the dominant HDLs in the industry.

Verilog HDL

In this book, we will use Verilog HDL. There are many FPGA boards that support Verilog HDL. As of 2023, one of the FPGA suppliers is Intel®. For those who are familiar with Altera®, Intel acquired Altea in 2015. Moreover, Xilinx® is also one of the FPGA suppliers. As an example of low-cost educational FGPA boards, Intel provides Terasic® DE 10-Lite boards, and Xilinx provides Basys 3 boards.

Verilog HDL uses pre-defined keywords, and it is a case-sensitive language. Examples of keywords are **module**, **endmodule**, **input**, **output**, **wire**, **and**, **or**, **not**, and etc.,

Verilog modules are like functions in other programming languages. Verilog modules are defined using the **module** keyword, and the modules end with the **endmoudle** keyword.

In order to leave comments, two slashes (//) can be used.

HDL Modeling

HDL has several abstraction levels, and HDL modeling can be described in one or any combination of these abstraction levels.

Gate-level modeling is a low-level abstraction approach. It describes the circuit through primitive gates and user-defined modules, and it describes how they are connected.

Data flow level modeling is a higher level of abstraction approach than gate level modeling. It describes the circuit through its functions and continuous assignments.

Behavioral modeling is a higher level of abstraction approach than data flow level modeling. It describes the circuit through procedural assignment statements.

Gate Level Description

Verilog HDL has primitive gates and instances. For instance, it supports **and, nand, or, nor, xor, xnor**, and **not** gates. A circuit can be described using these gates. Figure B.1 shows a simple logic circuit example.

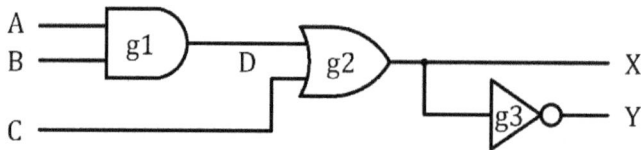

Figure B.1. Simple logic circuit example.

This circuit has three input nodes and two output nodes, and the circuit has three digital logic gates. This circuit can be described in a gate-level abstraction. This circuit is described in Program B.1. In order to describe this circuit, the **wire** keyword was used. The **wire** is a scalar net description. In this case, one wire net of D was used.

```
module LogicA(A, B, C, X, Y);
   input A, B, C;
   output X, Y;
   wire D;
   and  g1(D, A, B);
   or  g2(X, D, C);
   not  g3(Y, X);
endmodule
```

Program B.1. Gate level modeling for a simple logic circuit example.

Dataflow Modeling

Dataflow modeling can describe the circuit through its functions. Verilog HDL supports several operator types as shown in Table B.1. Also, dataflow modeling uses continuous assignments. Typically, it uses the **assign** keyword. A continuous assignment is associated with assigning a value to a net.

Symbol	Operation
&	bit-wise AND
|	bit-wise OR
^	bit-wise XOR
~	bit-wise NOT
+	addition
-	subtraction
==	equality
>	greater than
<	less than

Table B.1. Selected Verilog HDL operator types.

The dataflow-modeling example is shown in Program B.2. This is a description of the simple logic circuit example shown in Figure B.1. There are two **assign** statements used in this example. Output nodes of X and Y were described.

```
module LogicB(A, B, C, X, Y);
    input A, B, C;
    output X, Y;
    assign X=(A & B) | C;
    assign Y=~X;
endmodule
```

Program B.2. Dataflow Modeling for a simple logic circuit example

A 2-to-1 multiplexer circuit diagram is shown in Figure B.2. When the logic level of the select signal is low, the output will follow the input signal of "B". However, when the logic level of the select signal is high, the output will follow the input signal of "A". This circuit has two **AND** gates, one **OR** gate, and one **NOT** gate.

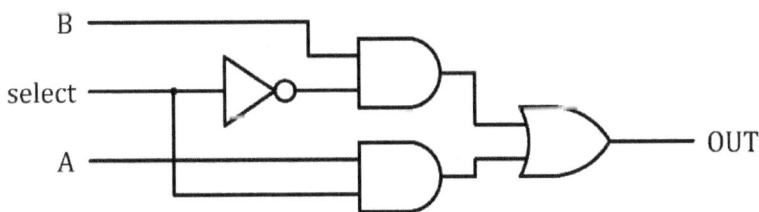

Figure B.2. 2-to-1 multiplexer circuit diagram.

The dataflow modeling of this circuit was implemented, and the description is shown in Program B.3. In this case, one **assign** keyword is used to describe this circuit.

```verilog
module mux2to1A(A, B, select, OUT);
   input A, B, select;
   output OUT;
   assign OUT=((A & select) | (B & ~select));
endmodule
```

Program B.3 Dataflow modeling for a 2-to-1 multiplexer

Behavioral Modeling

Behavioral modeling can describe the circuit at a functional and algorithmic level. It can describe sequential circuits and combinational circuits. Behavioral modeling uses **always** keywords with the procedural assignment statements. The output of the procedural assignment statement is **reg** data type. The **reg** is one of the data types. It represents the variable that can store data. Figure B.3 shows a 2-to-1 multiplexer symbol, and Program B.4 shows its behavior modeling.

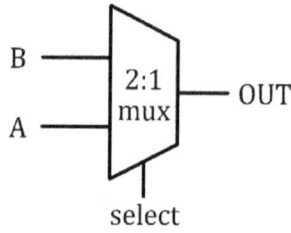

Figure B.3. 2-to-1 multiplexer symbol.

The procedural assignment statement in this example was described using an **always** block. If there is a change in any of the variables of "*Select*", A, or B, it will execute the "if else" block. And, if the logic level of "*Select*" is high, the logic level of the output will be the same as "A". Otherwise, the logic level of the output will be the same as "B".

```verilog
module mux2to1B (A, B, select, OUT);
   input A, B, select;
   output OUT;
   reg OUT;
   always @(select or A or B) begin
      if (select==1) OUT=A;
      else OUT=B;
   end
endmodule
```

Program B.4. Behavior modeling for a 2-to-1 multiplexer.

Tri-state Gates

As it was previously mentioned in Appendix A, tri-sate gates are useful in describing many circuit components including multiplexers and bus lines. In Verilog HDL, several types of tri-state gates are available. These symbols and the types are shown in Figure B.4.

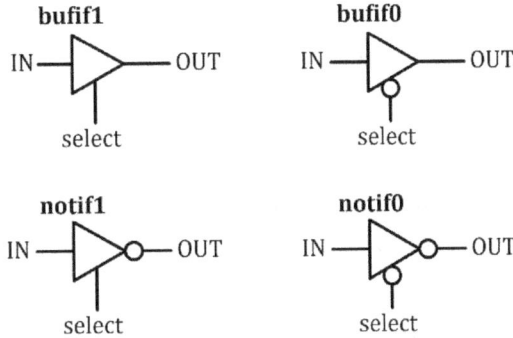

Figure B.4. Types of tri-state gates.

Tri- state gates have an input node and an output node with a control input node. The **bufif1** gate is a typical tri-state gate. And it behaves like a normal buffer when the logic level of the control input is high. The output becomes a high-impedance state when the logic level of the control input is low. **bufif0** gate has a bubble at the control input side. It will invert the control input. The **notif1** gate has a bubble at the output, which will invert the output signal. The **notif0** gate will invert both the control input signal and the output.

The output nodes of tri-state gates can be connected to each other to form a common output line. To define this type of connection, the keyword **tri** needs to be used to indicate that the output has multiple drivers. Figure B.4 and Program B.5 show a 2-to-1 multiplexer symbol and the Verilog HDL description example using tri-state gates.

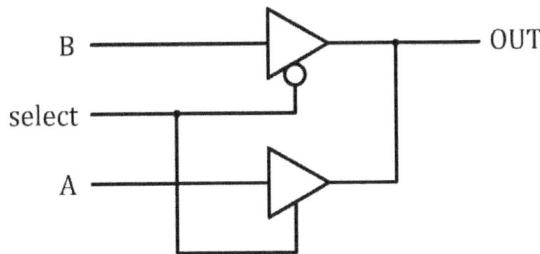

Figure B.4. Circuit diagram of a 2-to-1 multiplexer using tri-sate gates.

```
module mux2to1C (A, B, select, OUT);
  input A, B, select;
  output OUT;
  tri OUT;
  bufif1 (OUT, A, select);
  bufif0 (OUT, B, select);
endmodule
```

Program B.5. Verilog HDL modeling for a 2-to-1 multiplexer.

Net Data Types

Verilog HDL net data types are summarized in Table B.2. We have used **wire** and **tri** previously. There are more net data types such as wired OR and wired AND connections. In addition, **supply0** and **supply1** can be used to describe logical low or logical high signals.

Symbol	Operation
wire, **tri**	Interconnection wire
wand, **triand**	Wired AND connection
wor, **trior**	Wired OR connection
supply0, **supply1**	Logic 0, Logic 1

Table B.2. Selected Verilog HDL net data types.

Appendix C. Memory-Mapped I/O

CPU (Central Processing Unit) can perform logical and arithmetic operations. Typically, a memory-mapped I/O technique has been used in exchanging data between the CPU and peripheral devices. The CPU can read and write the data by accessing memory spaces. For the memory-mapped I/O, a certain address of the memory area can be related to physical hardware components and peripherals. Let us examine the memory-mapped I/O technique for a microcontroller or microprocessor-based system.

For educational purposes, we will study a case of a simplified 16-bit CPU and its system to explain this memory-mapped I/O further. It is worth mentioning that the simplified 16-bit CPU in Appendix C is not a representation of an MSP430 MCU. The purpose is to study the memory-mapped I/O behavior using a theoretical representation of a CPU.

Simplified 16-bit CPU model

A simplified 16-bit CPU model is shown in Figure C.1. This CPU has sixteen data signal pins (D0 ~ D15), twenty address line pins (A0 ~ A19), one *read control* ($\overline{RD}$) pin, one *write control* pin ($\overline{WR}$), and one clock pin.

In this simplified 16-bit CPU model, memory devices were not included. We will add memory devices as well as other devices later. In this CPU, data lines are bidirectional, and they form a 16-bit data bus. The CPU has a 20-bit address bus. The *read control* pin ($\overline{RD}$) is an active low output pin. This *read control* signal indicates that the CPU needs to read data from the specified address. The write control pin ($\overline{WR}$) is an active low output pin. This *write control* signal indicates that the CPU needs to store data at the specified address.

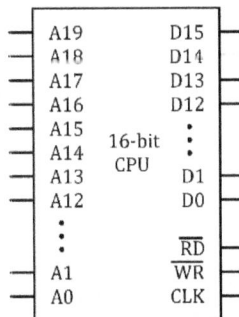

Figure C.1. A simplified 16-bit CPU [18].

16-bit CPU with memory ICs

The connections of the 16-bit CPU and memory ICs are shown in Figure C.2. A non-volatile memory IC is used for a program section. Examples of non-volatile memory

ICs are Flash memory and EEPROM ICs. An SRAM memory IC is used for a data section. A memory IC has three control pins of $\overline{OE}$, $\overline{WE}$, and $\overline{CE}$. And, they are *Output Enable* pin, *Write Enable* pin, and *Chip Enable* pin, respectively. These pins are active low input pins.

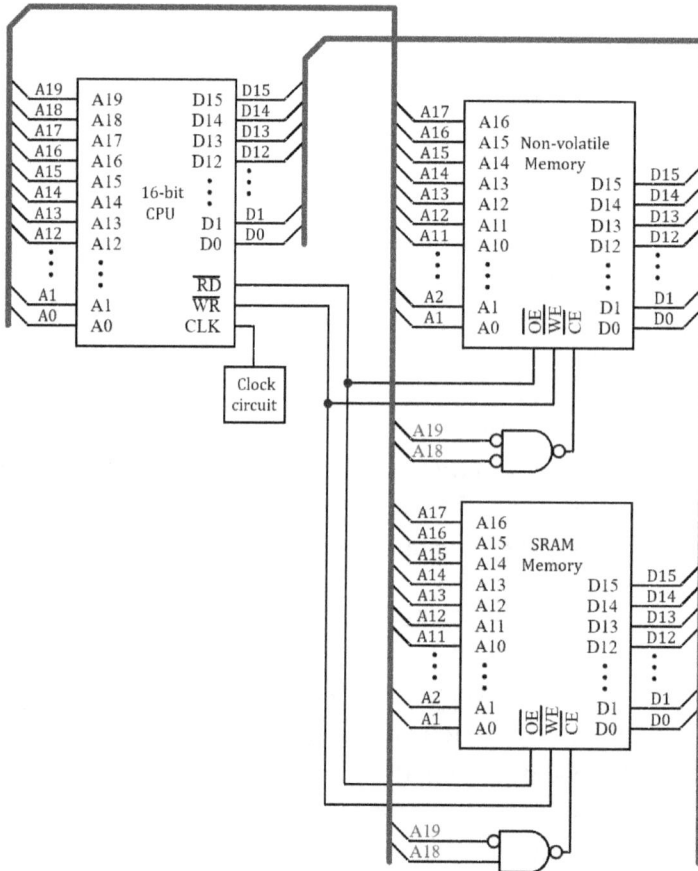

Figure C.2. 16-bit CPU and memory ICs.

The two address lines (A19 and A18) are connected to the chip enable pins, and they control the memory ICs, which can make the ICs accessible through certain address ranges. Based on this configuration in Figure C.2, the low and high addresses can be defined as shown in Table C.1.

	Low address	High address
Non-volatile Memory	0x00000	0x3FFFF
SRAM memory	0x40000	0x7FFFF

Table C.1. Address space (Memory ICs).

Let's say this is a basic configuration as a 16-bit system. The non-volatile memory IC may include the program routines such boot firmware, and the SRAM memory IC may be used to store temporary variables that are needed to execute a program.

Adding more devices

More devices can be added to this basic system studied in the previous section. Now, two devices of Device A and Device B are added, and their connections are shown in Figure C.3.

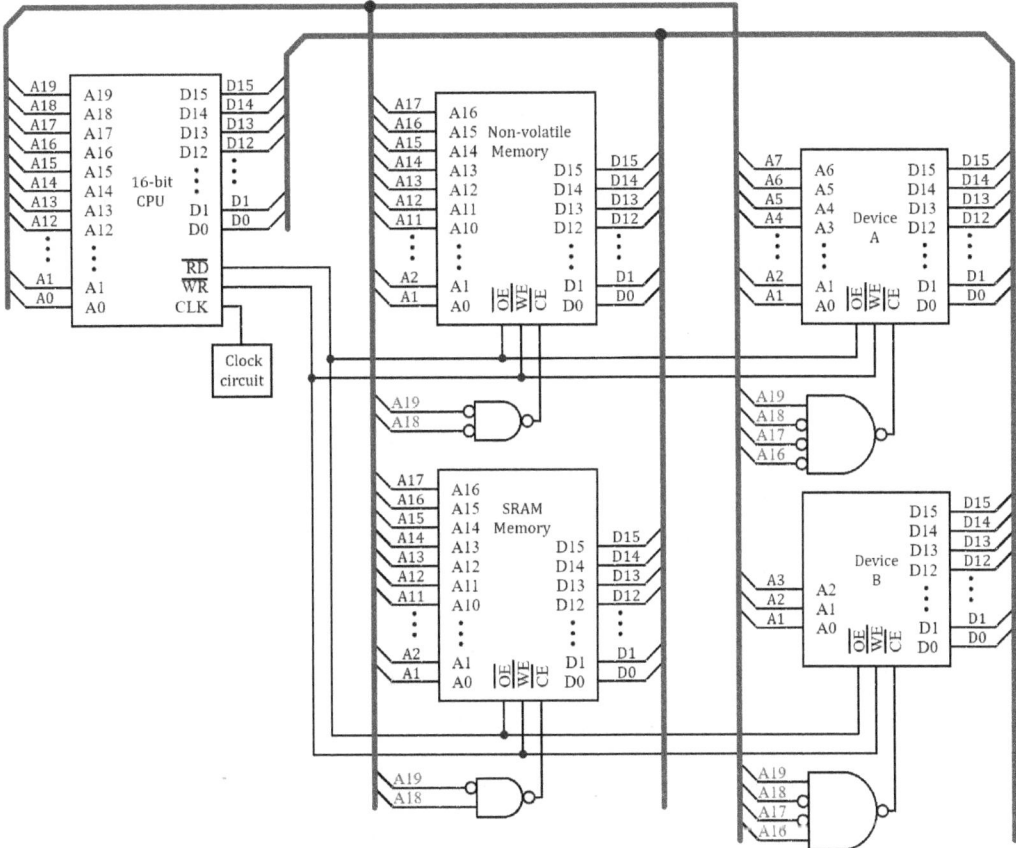

Figure C.3. 16-bit CPU, memory ICs, and two devices.

Device A has 8-bit address lines. Device B has 4-bit address lines. Regarding a method of control, these devices can perform read or write operations. Moreover, the four address lines (A19, A18, A17, and A16) can control the *chip enable* pins, and the devices can be accessed through certain address ranges. Given this configuration, the low and high addresses with these additional two devices are shown in Table C.2.

	Low address	High address
Non-volatile memory	0x00000	0x3FFFF
SRAM memory	0x40000	0x7FFFF
Device A	0x80000	0x800FF
Reserved	0x80100	0x8FFFF
Device B	0x90000	0x9000F
Reserved	0x90010	0x9FFFF

Table C.2. Address space (Memory ICs and Devices).

Let us examine this address space allocation. If the CPU performs read or write operations, for the address space of Flash or SRAM ICs, the CPU can read data from the memory, or write data to the memory. This is a typical memory operation. However, if the CPU performs read or write operations for the address space allocated to Device A or B, this is not a typical memory operation. But, it is accessing peripheral devices. It was generalized as Device A and Device B in Figure C.3. These devices can be specific modules. For instance, Device A can be a general-purpose I/O, and Device B can be a timer.

This is a simplified explanation of how the memory-mapped I/O works and the connection scheme for these devices to the CPU. In a modern microprocessor system, interconnections are much more complex, as they have more address lines and more peripheral devices.

Moreover, in order to make the CPU more efficient, some of the peripheral devices are controlled by a direct memory access (DMA) unit that allows accessing memory from certain external devices without the intervention of the CPU.

FPGA implementation for the control logic

The control circuit components were implemented using simple digital logic gates in the previous examples. However, these control circuits can be implemented using an FPGA IC instead. For instance, a developer can design their control digital logic using Verilog HDL, and the control logic can provide proper control signals. Figure C.4 shows an FPGA implementation example.

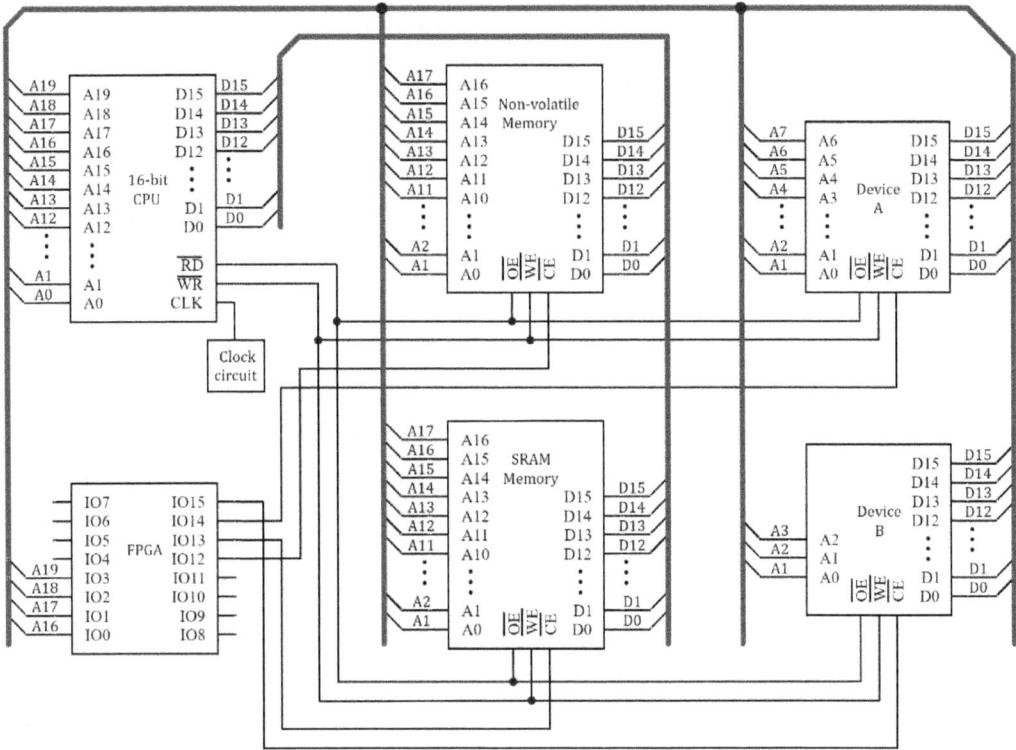

Figure C.4. An example of an FPGA implementation for the control logic.

The FPGA IC shown in the figure is a simplified version, and it has 16 IO pins (IO0 ~ IO15). IO0 ~ IO3 pins are connected to A16 ~ A19, respectively. IO12 ~ IO15 pins are connected to the *chip enable* pins of memory ICs and devices. To implement the equivalent functions previously shown in Figure C.3, the logical expressions for the control signals can be derived as follows:

$$IO12 = \overline{\overline{IO3} \cdot \overline{IO2}}$$

$$IO13 = \overline{\overline{IO3} \cdot IO2}$$

$$IO14 = \overline{IO3 \cdot \overline{IO2} \cdot \overline{IO1} \cdot \overline{IO0}}$$

$$IO15 = \overline{IO3 \cdot \overline{IO2} \cdot \overline{IO1} \cdot IO0}$$

These logical expressions can be implemented using Verilog HDL. An example of the Verilog HDL code is shown in Program C.1.

```
module GCA(IO3, IO2, IO1, IO0, IO15, IO14, IO13, IO12);
    input IO3, IO2, IO1, IO0;
    output IO15, IO14, IO13, IO12;
    assign IO12=~(~IO3 & ~IO2);
    assign IO13=~(~IO3 & IO2);
    assign IO14=~(IO3 & ~IO2 & ~IO1 & ~IO0);
    assign IO15=~(IO3 & ~IO2 & ~IO1 & IO0);
endmodule
```

Program C.1. Verilog HDL code for control signals.

An FPGA implementation of the control signals may have an advantage in resolving complex hardware issues that might occur after production. Many issues can be resolved at a software level; however, sometimes, hardware modifications can be effective and needed to tackle complex problems such as critical timing or resource conflict issues.

Appendix D. C/C++ Data Types

Table D.1 lists the sizes and ranges of the selected data types for an MSP430FR5994 MCU [39].

Type	Size	Minimum	Maximum
signed char	8 bits	−128	127
unsigned char	8 bits	0	255
signed short	16 bits	−32,768	32,767
unsigned short	16 bits	0	65,535
signed int	16 bits	−32,768	32,767
unsigned int	16 bits	0	65,535
signed long	32 bits	$\sim -2.147 \times 10^9$	$\sim 2.147 \times 10^9$
unsigned long	32 bits	0	$\sim 4.295 \times 10^9$
float	32 bits	$*\sim 1.175 \times 10^{-38}$	$\sim 3.403 \times 10^{38}$
Double	64bits	$*\sim 2.225 \times 10^{-308}$	$\sim 1.798 \times 10^{308}$

Table D.1. Selected C/C++ data types for an MSP430FR5994 MCU (*Excluded negative cases) [39].

For a developer, it is important to understand data types and the range of data. For instance, a program to test the data range for an MSP430FR5994 was written, and it is shown in Program D.1.

```
#include <msp430.h>
int main(void) {
    WDTCTL = WDTPW | WDTHOLD;  // hold the watchdog timer
    PM5CTL0 &= ~LOCKLPM5;  // clear LOCKLPM5 bit
    P1DIR |= 0x03;  // output direction
    P1OUT = 0x01;  // turn on a LED1
    unsigned char kp;  // data type definition
    for (kp=0; kp<255; kp++) {
        _no_operation();
    }
    P1OUT = 0x02;  // turn on LED2
    whilc(1);
    return 0;
}
```

Program D.1. Data range test.

In this code, a variable *kp* was defined as *unsigned char*. During the initialization, this program will turn on a Red LED. Next, there is a *for-loop*. When this *for-loop* block is running, the value of the variable *kp* gets changed. After proper interactions, the program will exit the *for-loop*, and it will turn on a Green LED.

For an experiment, let us modify this code by changing 255 to 256 in the *for-loop*. Then, this program will not exit the *for-loop* as it keeps repeating the *for-loop*. This is because the value of the variable *kp* is unable to become 256. Instead, the value of *kp* becomes zero, and this would cause an infinite loop. The program cannot execute the line that can turn on the green LED. Therefore, it will turn on the red LED only. This is just an example, but it demonstrates a case where developers may need to understand the minimum and maximum numbers of the variable types that they use in their programs.

References

[1]   B. Hur, "Learning Embedded Systems with MSP432 Microcontrollers: MSP432P401R with Code Composer Studio," Fourth edition, 2022.

[2]   Texas Instruments, "MSP430FR599x, MSP430FR596x Mixed-Signal Microcontrollers datasheet," Revision D, 2021.

[3]   Texas Instruments, "MSP430F552x, MSP430F551x Mixed-Signal Microcontrollers datasheet," Revision P, 2020.

[4]   Texas Instruments, "MSP430FR2311 LaunchPad Development Kit (MSP-EXP430FR2311) User's Guide," Revised, 2017.

[5]   Texas Instruments, "MSP430FR2355 LaunchPad Development Kit (MSP-EXP430FR235) User's Guide," 2018.

[6]   Texas Instruments, "MSP430FR5969 LaunchPad Development Kit (MSP-EXP430FR5969) User's Guide," Revised, 2015.

[7]   Texas Instruments, "MSP430FR5994 LaunchPad Development Kit (MSP-EXP430FR5994) User's Guide," Revised, 2019.

[8]   B. Hur, "TI BH EDU Board Kit," DOI: 10.5281/zenodo.2538993, [Online]. Available: https://github.com/bh-projects/TI-BH-EDU-board-kit

[9]   Texas Instruments, "MSP430FR58xx, MSP430FR59xx, and MSP430FR6xx Family User's Guide," Revised, 2020.

[10]   Texas Instruments, "MSP430 Assembly Language Tools," v18.1.0.LTS, 2018.

[11]   Velleman, "Keyboard 16 Keys - Matrix Output".

[12]   TDK Corporation, "Piezoelectric Buzzer," Model: PS1740P02E.

[13]   Newhaven Display, "NHD-0216HZ-FSW-FBW-33V3C product specification".

[14]   Sitronix , "ST7066U datasheet," 2006.

[15]   H. Nyquist, "Certain topics in telegraph transmission theory," IEEE Trans., vol. 47, pp. 617-644, 1928.

[16]   Analog Devices, "ADXL335 Datasheet," Rev. B,

[17]   Sparkfun, "SparkFun Triple Axis Accelerometer Breakout - ADXL335,".

[18]   D. E. Simon, "An embedded software primer," Vol. 1. Addison-Wesley Professional, 1999.

[19]   Texas Instruments, "DRV8833 Dual H-Bridge Motor Driver Datasheet," Rev. E, 2015.

[20]   Adafruit, "Adafruit DRV8833 DC/Stepper Motor Driver Breakout Board".

[21]   Maxim Integrated, "MAX220–MAX249 datasheet," Rev. 18, 2019.

[22]   Maxim Integrated, "MAX3222/MAX3232/MAX3237/MAX3241 datasheet," Rev. 10, 2019.

[23]   Maxim Integrated, "MAX485 datasheet," Rev. 10, 2014.

[24]   Maxim Integrated, "MAX3485 datasheet," Rev. 1, 2019.

[25]   "Arduino," [Online]. Available: https://arduino.cc

[26]   Microchip Technology, "MCP3004/3008 datasheet," 2008.

[27] Moelands et al., "Two-wire bus-system comprising a clock wire and a data wire for interconnecting a number of stations," US4689740A, Aug. 1987.

[28] NXP Semiconductors, "PCF8574; PCF8574A datasheet," Rev. 5, 2013.

[29] Sparkfun, "Sparkfun Logic Level Converter - Bi-Directional".

[30] Vishay Semiconductors, "TSOP38238 datasheet," Rev. 1.7, 2018.

[31] Texas Instruments, "MSP430 DriverLib for MSP430FR5xx_6xx Devices, Users' guide", 2020.

[32] Texas Instruments, "TI-RTOS Kernel (SYS/BIOS) User's Guide," 2018.

[33] Texas Instruments, "TI-RTOS 2.20 User's Guide", 2016.

[34] "Energia," [Online]. Available: https://energia.nu

[35] "Raspberry Pi," [Online]. Available: https://www.raspberrypi.org

[36] "Debian", [Online]. Available: https://www.debian.org

[37] "Python", [Online]. Available: https://www.python.org

[38] "BeagleBone," [Online]. Available: https://beagleboard.org

[39] Texas Instruments, "MSP430 Optimizing C/C++ Compiler," SLAU132R, 2018.

www.ingramcontent.com/pod-product-compliance
Lightning Source LLC
Chambersburg PA
CBHW081809200326
41597CB00023B/4202